Abortion Politics

ABORTION POLITICS
THE HAWAII EXPERIENCE

Patricia G. Steinhoff
Milton Diamond

THE UNIVERSITY PRESS OF HAWAII
Honolulu

Manufactured in the United States of America

Library of Congress Cataloging in Publication Data

Steinhoff, Patricia G 1941–
Abortion politics.

Includes bibliographical references and index.
1. Abortion. 2. Political participation—Hawaii. 3. Abortion—Law and legislation—Hawaii. I. Diamond, Milton, 1934– joint author. II. Title.
HQ767.5.U5S75 301 77-3655
ISBN 0-8248-0550-X
ISBN 0-8248-0498-8 pbk.

Contents

Preface

THIS STUDY is both a history of the repeal of Hawaii's criminal abortion law and an analysis of the processes by which the repeal came about. Hawaii's action was part of a much broader movement for abortion law reform throughout the United States. It was also an independent decision, generated by a unique constellation of personalities, circumstances, and events.

There are many ways to change a criminal law in the United States: through court decision, administrative action, legislative action, or popular referendum. In the six years from 1967 to 1973, all of these methods were used in the abortion law reform movement to eliminate restrictive laws. The changes began when state legislatures in Colorado and several other states cautiously broadened the permissible conditions for abortion in the late 1960s, and culminated in the United States Supreme Court decisions of January 22, 1973 *(Roe* v. *Wade* and *Doe* v. *Bolton),* which declared restrictive abortion laws to be unconstitutional. In the intervening years, anti-abortion laws were repealed by the state legislatures in Hawaii, New York, and Alaska; a popular referendum to repeal the anti-abortion law succeeded in Washington (but failed in Michigan); lower courts struck down anti-abortion laws in Washington, D.C. and California; and administrative action considerably loosened abortion restrictions in California and Maryland. The repeal of Hawaii's law against abortion in March, 1970 marked a major turning point in this movement. It was the first time that virtually all prohibitions on abortion had been removed by a legislative body responsible—and responsive—to an electorate.

Both in philosophy and in practice, the new Hawaii law and its successors in New York, Washington, and Alaska were radically different from the liberalized or reform laws adopted by Colorado and several other states in the late 1960s. Under the restrictive abortion laws which were found in all states until that time, abortion was defined as a criminal act which could be exempt from penalties under certain extraordinary circumstances, such as to preserve the life of the mother. The reform laws enacted in Colorado and elsewhere maintained the position that abortion was a criminal act, but broadened the definition of the extraordinary circumstances under which it could be justified. By contrast, the new repeal laws in Hawaii, New York, Washington, and Alaska assumed that abortion was a private, noncriminal act. This position was subsequently taken by the U.S. Supreme Court when it struck down the reform laws along with the restrictive ones in January, 1973.

In Hawaii, as elsewhere, the major impetus for reversal of the century-old criminal abortion statute was a dramatic change in public consciousness and attitudes regarding abortion. In comparison with other social movements of similar magnitude, the movement to end restrictive abortion laws is remarkable for the speed with which public interest in the issue was aroused, and the effectiveness with which that public concern was translated into genuine institutional changes. Hawaii was the first place in the United States where the new public concern about abortion actually brought about a fundamental change in the law, not simply a minor modification.

In telling the story of abortion law repeal in Hawaii, we have focused on community involvement in the legislative process. Like most political activity, the campaign for abortion law repeal in Hawaii had its share of private caucuses, logrolling for extra votes, and delicate compromise. Our account touches on these matters but does not emphasize them heavily. We have chosen to stress the public campaign and the forces that seem to have shaped the legislative interplay. This is because we feel the public campaign was the more critical force and also because it has greater relevance to the general study of social change than traditional political maneuvers. Moreover, much in the story of the private legislative and lobbying campaign can only be told by those who were personally involved behind the scenes.

Political events are not only composed of issues, but are also constructed of names, personalities, and connections. We have tried to capture the flavor of the Hawaii campaign by describing the key figures involved and tracing their impact on events and the impact of events on them. We have tried equally hard to resist the temptation to describe the campaign solely as a product of dynamic personalities. In analyzing this momentous social change, we have focused on a broad range of social and political factors affecting both Hawaii and the United States as a whole. We have concentrated on the process as a means of understanding the past and of helping to guide future social action.

A variety of materials and techniques were employed in the research. Both authors were present during the abortion law repeal campaign as observers and participants. At the state Senate hearing in February, 1970, we both presented testimony supporting repeal of the abortion law. Though we are partisans in the cause of abortion law repeal, we have tried to be objective as analysts of the repeal campaign. Wherever possible, we have relied on documents and sources other than our own recollections.

Chapter 1, which traces the history of Hawaii's former restrictive abortion law, is based primarily on legal records and committee reports of the state legislature. Chapter 2, which presents the major personalities of the abortion law repeal movement in Hawaii, was developed from personal interviews with the participants. Chapters 3 and 4 describe and analyze the tactics used by both sides in the repeal campaign. The major documentation for these tactics is provided by newspaper files. The analysis of the effectiveness of various tactics is based on a questionnaire distributed to state legislators shortly after the abortion bill was passed.

Chapters 5, 6, and 7, outlining the issues raised by both sides in the repeal campaign, are documented by the written and oral records of the state Senate committee hearings on the bill. The assessment of the impact of the various arguments is substantiated by the questionnaire responses of legislators. Chapters 8 and 9, with the aid of legislative records and personal interviews, trace the passage of the repeal bill into law.

Chapter 10, which provides a brief overview of the immediate impact of the law, is based primarily on the research reports of the Hawaii Pregnancy, Birth Control and Abortion Study (which was conducted by the authors and our colleagues, Dr. Roy G. Smith, and James A. Palmore, Jr. with support from The Population Council and the National Institute of Child Health and Human Development and the Ford Foundation). The final chapter of the book presents our analysis of how and why the repeal came about, and what its significance may be.

The idea of writing this historical account developed naturally out of our participation in the abortion law repeal campaign. Shortly after the passage of the law, with the encouragement of Dr. Alan F. Guttmacher, we asked Dr. Bernard Berelson whether The Population Council would be interested in funding a study of the events and processes that led to the historic change in the law. The request was granted, and funds from The Population Council (D70.084C) were allocated. This support made the study possible.

A questionnaire was distributed to all Hawaii state legislators after the bill's passage to determine what tactics and issues had impressed the legislators and how they had participated in this issue. Peggy Bendet, Women's Editor of the *Honolulu Star-Bulletin,* kindly permitted us to use the newspaper's clipping file to document the events of the campaign. Senator Vincent Yano provided us with a full set of the written testimony presented to the Senate Committee; we had previously made our own tape of the hearings. Several of the key participants consented to personal interviews: Senator Vincent Yano, Representatives George Loo and Dorothy Devereux, Drs. George Goto and Frederick Dodge, Joan Hayes, Father Daniel Dever, and Robert Pearson. State personnel at both the Legislative Reference Bureau and the Public Archives were extremely helpful in providing legislative documents such as previous laws, bills, committee reports, minutes of hearings, and legislative debate. Dr. Roy Smith read the entire manuscript and made many helpful suggestions.

We wish to express our deepest thanks to all of these persons and institutions, without whom the study could not have been accomplished. Our thanks also go to Ben Janken, Joyce Chinen, and Hope Stevens, who performed countless tasks as research assistants, and to Joyce Ito and Lucille Maloney, who typed the manuscript.

We dedicate this volume to our spouses, Bill Steinhoff and Kit Diamond, and to our planned and very wanted children: Hinda, Irene, Sara, and Leah Diamond, and Laura Steinhoff.

CHAPTER 1

Setting the Stage

SMALL, remote Hawaii seems an unlikely state to have enacted the first fully permissive abortion law in the United States. The state did not even have a movement to repeal its existing restrictive abortion laws until six months before the landmark law was enacted. Nor, by some standards, did the state have an acute abortion problem. The public health and social consequences of illegal abortions, illegitimacy, and unwanted children were far more visible in the nation's major urban centers in New York and California than in isolated Hawaii. In those states, abortion law repeal advocates had been organized and active for years.

What Hawaii had to offer was a set of political and social conditions favorable for bringing about change. Building on these conditions, the leaders of the movement to repeal the restrictive abortion laws, themselves new converts to the cause, were able to educate and convince first the public and then the state legislature in a remarkably short period of time.

Hawaii's population and geography were important factors in the state's abortion politics. Hawaii is a geographically dispersed state consisting of seven major islands. More than three quarters of the population, however, lives on the island of Oahu, within fifty miles of the state capital in Honolulu. The government is thus physically accessible when people want to express their views. It is also socially accessible because the population is small and the scale of government is correspondingly reduced. Hawaii's state population was 769,000 in the 1970 census,[1] about the same size as the cities of Washington, D.C., Indianapolis, or Cleveland.

The twenty-five state senators and fifty-one state representatives are elected from small, multimember districts. They frequently campaign door-to-door. Ordinary citizens often know their legislators personally and call or write them concerning particular issues. Besides its usual function of maximizing the possibility of representation of special interest groups, the multimember district system in Hawaii also seems to increase the sense of personal contact between representatives and their constituencies. A resident may approach several different legislators and feel that they all represent him personally and need his vote.

Hawaii's residents also participate directly in political issues by testifying at public hearings. Ordinary citizens from all ethnic groups and all social classes appear at legislative hearings to present their views. Social agencies and voluntary associations frequently send representatives to speak at hearings. This public involvement is reciprocated by a relatively high degree of governmental responsiveness.

While much of this town hall democracy may be attributed to the state's small size, part of it is also due to the prevailing balance of political power. Almost immediately after Hawaii attained statehood in 1959, a Democratic coalition, supported by the leading labor unions and the large ethnic community of Americans of Japanese ancestry, wrested political control from the predominantly Caucasian and Republican elite which had traditionally dominated the economics and politics of the Territory of Hawaii.[2] A decade later, the coalition was still functioning smoothly. Its leader, second-term Governor John Burns, maintained close ties to the solid Democratic majority in both houses of the legislature. The composition of the legislature closely reflected the ethnic distribution and social origins of the state's population. Government was responsive partly because it was genuinely representative.

One further social condition in the state of Hawaii was probably significant for the success of abortion law repeal: the position of women. By the 1970 census, 41 percent of the State's civilian labor force was female. Half of the women in the state aged sixteen years and older were working, as were 48 percent of married women living with their husbands. A high 38 percent of married women living with their husbands and having children under the age of six were working.[3] Hawaii's high cost of living had already made the two-income family the norm rather than the exception. Although there was not a great deal of organized women's liberation activity in the state, women already held positions of social and economic responsibility both in the community and in the home.

These favorable factors loom large in retrospect, but potentially unfavorable factors were also present. The most important of these was the religious composition of the state. In addition to the sizeable (28 percent) Catholic population, there were large Buddhist and Mormon groups whose response to the issue of abortion law reform could not be easily predicted. In addition, the governor of the state was a devout Roman Catholic. Against this background of social and political conditions, the issue of a radical change in abortion law was raised.

THE OLD LAW

Hawaii's original abortion law was incorporated in the *Code of Laws of the Kingdom,* enacted by the King and the Legislative Assembly of the Hawaiian Islands in 1869. It provided that:

> Whoever maliciously, without lawful justification, administers, or causes or procures to be administered any poison or noxious thing to a woman when with child, in order to produce her miscarriage, or maliciously uses any instrument or other means with like intent, shall, if the woman is then quick with child, be fined not more than $1,000 and imprisoned at hard labor not more than five years; And if she is then not quick with child, shall be punished by a fine not exceeding $500 and imprisoned at hard labor not more than two years.
>
> Where means of causing abortion are used for the purpose of saving the life of the woman, the surgeon or other person using such means is lawfully justified.[4]

The law permitted abortion only to save the life of the woman, and it distinguished by severity of penalty between abortions before and after quickening (the point at which the woman feels the fetus move, usually between twelve and eighteen weeks of gestation). In a later legal ruling, the court established that only physicians could be protected by the law's second paragraph, for performing an abortion to save the life of the woman.[5]

In 1925, the following paragraph was added to the abortion law:

> If any woman conceals the death of an issue of her body, whether born alive or not, which if born alive would have been a bastard, so that it may not be known whether the issue was born alive or not, or whether it was murdered, she shall be punished by a fine of not more than $100 and imprisoned at hard labor not more than two years.[6]

The new paragraph appears to be directed at the infanticide of children born out of wedlock, but a narrow reading of the law would have required the reporting of all abortions, spontaneous and induced.

The revised law remained in the Hawaii statutes with minor changes through several revisions of the penal code and the transition to statehood in 1959. In 1935, the abortion law was catalogued under sex offenses; in 1945, the term "bastard" was changed to "illegitimate," and in 1955, following a court ruling, the footnote was added that a woman "is 'with child' although the fetus has lost its vitality."[7]

There is no complete tally of how many persons were prosecuted under the abortion statute during the hundred years the restrictive laws were in force. All felonies and misdemeanors regardless of type are filed together, consecutively by date, in the state's arrest and prosecution records. Even the annual statistics that are available for recent years follow the uniform crime reporting system and only list total numbers of felonies and misdemeanors.

During those hundred years, the Hawaii Supreme Court heard five appeals from persons who had been convicted in four separate cases of abortion.[8] The court rulings in two of these cases refer to previous abortion charges against the same defendants.[9] It is certain that more cases than these were tried. In two of the Supreme Court cases, the woman who received the abortion died as a result of the procedure. In the first case, a practicing physician was convicted of murder in the second degree in connection with the death of a woman on whom he had performed an abortion. In the second case, a midwife and a layman were convicted of manslaughter in connection with a woman's death following an abortion.[10]

These abortion cases provide only a glimpse into the operation of Hawaii's abortion law. The most recent case appealed to the higher court took place in the early 1950s. There have been rumors that a physician or two may have lost hospital privileges, or even had his license suspended, for performing abortions in the 1940s or 1950s. Such matters were apparently handled discreetly by the medical authorities involved. In the only documented case, a physician had his license quietly revoked in the late 1960s for performing an illegal abortion.[11]

The few known cases give little indication of the amount of activity in violation of the law. There are no statistics available that would permit a reliable estimate of the number of persons who performed illegal abortions, or the number of women who received illegal abortions before 1968, in the state of Hawaii.

In a poll of Hawaii physicians taken in 1969, 425 physicians (53 percent of all doctors in the state) reported a total of 1557 requests for abortions during the previous year. This figure represents a partial estimate of the demand for abortion. Although over 40 percent of these requests were referred somewhere for help, it is not known in what percentage of cases the demand was ultimately met, either within the state or elsewhere.[12] Data obtained in 1970–1972 from a statewide survey by the Hawaii Pregnancy, Birth Control and Abortion Study suggest that a substantial number of Hawaii women did obtain abortions before legalization. The study estimated that about eighteen in every thousand women in the state aged fifteen to forty-four obtained an abortion in 1969, compared to twenty-two per thousand after legalization in 1970.[13] It is not known where or how these abortions were performed. Some women undoubtedly went to Japan, where safe abortions were available legally.

It is certain that some illegal abortions were being performed in Hawaii. Informally, physicians and long-time residents report that abortions were readily available and were performed by competent persons. According to Honolulu obstetrician-gynecologist Dr. George Goto, septic abortions (those abortions followed by infection, usually indicative of a procedure done by an unskilled abortionist) most often involved military dependents or other newcomers in the postwar era. Dr. Goto suggested that such persons probably did not know where to obtain safer abortions.[14]

Because Hawaii public health statistics combine deaths from abortion with maternal deaths from all other causes, it is not possible to determine whether there were deaths from illegal abortion in addition to the two cases already noted. In such a small state, only two or three maternal mortalities occur each year from all causes, so that a death associated with abortion was a rare phenomenon.

Some abortions were also being performed as if they were legal. The Public Health Statistics Act of 1949, as amended in 1951, required that all abortions, spontaneous and induced, be reported to the Department of Health as fetal deaths.[15] Most Hawaii hospitals reported such cases routinely and completely, but abortions taking place outside of hospitals were rarely reported. A study of all induced abortions reported as fetal deaths from 1961–1970 disclosed that less than half of the induced abortions reported actually met the strict requirement of the abortion law.

> During the decade of 1961–1970, only 10.4 percent of all therapeutic abortions were performed because of medical indications which could have threatened the life of the mother. Another 29.2 percent were performed for psychiatric reasons which presumably were considered to threaten the life of the mother (i.e., she was suicidal). The largest number of therapeutic abortions (40.3 percent) were performed to prevent the birth of a defective child, despite the fact that Hawaii law did not permit this as a reason for abortion. Besides the 9.7 percent for which no reason was given, 10.4 percent were performed for medical reasons which neither threatened the life of the mother nor indicated the potential birth of a defective child.[16]

In 1964–1965, a German measles (rubella) epidemic in Hawaii prompted many obstetricians to perform abortions on pregnant women who had been exposed to or had contracted the disease. Because the disease affects the fetus but does not endanger the life of the mother, it did not technically constitute legal grounds for abortion. The medical societies did not officially sanction abortion in these circumstances, but hospitals did not prevent individual physicians from performing them. The required fetal death certificates were filed, and no further action was taken. Rubella was cited to justify 75 percent of all therapeutic abortions in 1965 and a smaller proportion of the cases over the next four years.

The rubella epidemic in Hawaii marked a general turning point in the willingness of physicians to perform therapeutic abortions in hospitals. The rate of therapeutic abortions for reasons other than rubella rose in 1965, and the overall rate never again fell to the 1964 level.[17]

The gradual liberalization of attitudes towards abortion during the 1960s in Hawaii paralleled the situation elsewhere. At the beginning of the decade, nearly every state in the United States prohibited abortion except to save the life of the woman. Laws in three states (Massachusetts, Pennsylvania, and New Jersey) prohibited unlawful or malicious abortion without specification. In Massachusetts, case law sanctioned abortion to preserve maternal life and protect maternal health. Statutes in Alabama and the District of Columbia permitted abortion to preserve the life or health of the woman.[18] A similar situation prevailed in all of Western Europe except for the Scandinavian countries of Denmark and Sweden, which had permitted abortion for medical and sociomedical reasons since the late 1930s. Japan had permitted abortion for loosely defined medical and socioeconomic conditions since 1948, while the USSR and Eastern Europe had generally permissive abortion laws.[19]

In Western Europe, public sympathy for abortion law reform was aroused by the appearance in 1961 of a large number of babies born with gross and distinctive congenital deformities caused by their mothers' use of the sedative thalidomide during early pregnancy. Although the United States had never licensed the drug for sale, a highly publicized situation in Arizona in 1962 directly linked the thalidomide tragedy to the issue of abortion law reform. A physicians' panel recommended that Mrs. Sherri Finkbine, who had taken thalidomide (purchased in England) during her early pregnancy, be permitted to undergo therapeutic abortion in order to prevent the anticipated birth of a deformed child. When the county medical society objected, Mrs. Finkbine filed suit in the local superior court seeking permission for the therapeutic abortion. The petition was denied, and Mrs. Finkbine subsequently applied for and obtained an abortion in Sweden.[20] Pathology reports found that the fetus was markedly defective. The widely publicized case aroused considerable public sympathy for Mrs. Finkbine and focused attention on restrictive abortion laws.

The nationwide rubella epidemic of the mid-Sixties affected medical thinking throughout the United States in much the same way it did in Hawaii. Many physicians considered rubella exposure a valid indication for therapeutic abortion because of the high risk of damage to the fetus, and many hospitals approved these cases for legal hospital abortion. When nine San Francisco physicians were charged with unprofessional conduct by the California Board of Medical Examiners in 1966 for performing rubella-linked abortions, two hundred of the nation's leading physicians, including many deans of medical schools, joined in their legal defense. The case resulted in disciplinary action by the Board against the nine defendants, but the penalties were subsequently nullified by court action.[21]

As these events were bringing the issue of therapeutic abortion to public attention in the United States, several voluntary organizations formed to promote abortion law reform,[22] and a small number of conferences were held to discuss the medical, philosophical, legal, and social aspects of abortion.[23]

In 1959, the American Law Institute (ALI) published the draft of its Model Penal Code, a major effort designed to help standardize the criminal law in all states. Included in the code was a model abortion law which still generally treated abortion as a crime, but provided for several specific exceptions: to preserve the physical or mental health of the woman, to prevent the birth of a deformed child, or for pregnancies resulting from rape or incest. The ALI model abortion law reflected the mainstream of the small but growing sentiment for liberalization of abortion laws in the early and mid-1960s', although some people had already begun to argue that the matter should be left completely to the judgment of the woman and her physician. Abortion law reform bills along ALI lines were introduced in the California state legislature in 1961, 1963, and 1965 without success. A similar bill introduced in the New York state legislature in 1966 also died in committee. In 1967, Colorado revised its laws to conform to the ALI code, becoming the first state to modify its laws in this direction. In the next two years, seven states made similar revisions in their abortion laws.

FIRST ATTEMPTS TO CHANGE THE LAW

The first attempts to ease Hawaii's abortion law came in 1967, when two bills were introduced in the state legislature.[24] Senator Nadao Yoshinaga introduced Senate Bill 619 on March 7, 1967. The bill proposed repeal of the existing abortion law (sections 309-3 to 309-5 of the *Revised Laws* of Hawaii, 1955) and substitution of the following paragraph:

> *Abortion.* Any person who is not a licensed physician in this State and who intentionally terminates the pregnancy of another

> otherwise than by live birth is guilty of abortion and shall be fined not more than $1,000 or imprisoned not more than five years, or both.[25]

Senator Yoshinaga introduced the bill as one of a series of population and ecology proposals which were intended to spark interest and provoke debate.

In a separate action in the House, Representative George Loo and seven other cosigners[26] introduced House Bill 76, patterned on the American Law Institute's model abortion legislation. It would have permitted abortions by licensed physicians in cases where

> there is substantial risk that continuance of the pregnancy would gravely impair the physical or mental health of the mother or that the child would be born with grave physical or mental defect, or that the pregnancy resulted from rape, incest, or other felonious intercourse. All illicit intercourse with a girl below the age of sixteen shall be deemed felonious . . . .[27]

Such abortions could only be performed in hospitals after certification by two physicians. Other sections of the bill prohibited self-abortion after twenty-six weeks of gestation, pretended abortion, and the distribution of abortifacients (drugs capable of inducing an abortion) through means other than professional medical channels. A qualifying paragraph exempted contraceptives from these prohibitions on abortifacients. "Pretended abortion" referred to the practice by illegal abortionists of falsely diagnosing a pregnancy, pretending to perform an abortion, and collecting a fee for the "service."

During the 1966 legislative session, Representative Loo had been asked by a woman acquaintance to submit an abortion reform bill. He was hesitant at first because of the controversial nature of the issue, but he studied the abortion problem and became convinced of the need for reform. In particular, he felt that abortion should be available to women who had been raped.[28] In January, 1967, Honolulu obstetrician George Goto, then chairman of the legislative committee of the Hawaii Medical Association, received an inquiry from the Legislative Reference Bureau asking whether the Medical Association would support a bill to liberalize the state's abortion law. Dr. Goto first took the matter to the Honolulu Obstetrical and Gynecological Society, where he introduced a resolution advocating liberalization in accord with the American Law Institute's 1962 model penal code. The Society adopted the resolution by an overwhelming majority. When Representative Loo introduced a reform bill the following month, the legislative committee of the Hawaii Medical Association voted to support it.[29]

The House bill was assigned to the Committee on Housing and Consumer Protection, which was chaired by Representative Loo. The committee held a hearing on the bill on March 20, 1967, at which time Dr. Arno Mundt, representing the Honolulu Obstetrical and Gynecological Society, and Dr. George Goto, representing the Hawaii Medical Association, testified in favor of the proposed reforms. Dr. Goto testified that physicians had already performed abortions in Hawaii hospitals for the reasons permitted in the bill, and urged that the legislature change the law to make the medical practice legal. Father Daniel Dever represented the Catholic Diocese of Honolulu in opposing the bill. Also testifying against the proposed reforms was Dr. Frederick Dodge, president of the Catholic Physicians' Guild. Two other Catholic physicians, Dr. William Bergin and Dr. Keith Kuhlman, and a retired Honolulu school teacher, Gerri Madden, testified as individuals against the bill.

The committee's report of March 31, 1967 supported the bill for medical and social reasons. It addressed itself to the Catholic Church's opposition with the following comment:

> The Catholic Church is opposed to any change in the abortion law for the reason that it is murder to perform an abortion. Your Committee respectfully believes that the Catholic Church or any other religious majority or minority should not restrict the practice of medicine by physicians who do not subscribe to the views of such religious majority or minority. Further, the present law is that it is not murder unless the infant can be said to have an independent existence.[30]

Eight of the committee's thirteen members concurred in the report, two signed with reservations, and three did not concur.[31] On the committee's recommendation, the bill was then sent to the House Judiciary Committee.

Both the Speaker of the House (Elmer Cravalho) and the Chairman of the Judiciary Committee (Hiroshi Kato) were opposed to the bill, but would have let it go to the floor if the provision concerning rape had been omitted. Since Representative Loo was personally committed to including the rape provision and felt that the bill had already served its purpose in opening discussion on the topic, he chose to let the bill die in the Judiciary Committee at the end of the session.[32]

The following year, a short form bill proposing reform of the abortion laws was introduced in the House by Majority Leader and Policy Committee Chairman Howard Miyake and three others, two of whom had been associated with the 1967 reform bill.[33] A short form bill states the need for legislation but does not contain the specific form of the proposed law. Representative Miyake introduced the bill to provide a vehicle for abortion reform legislation if there proved to be sufficient support for it during the session. Support was not forthcoming, and the bill died in committee. Representative Loo did not attempt to revive his bill because he felt the House leadership was still opposed. The Fourth Legislature closed in 1968 without taking any final action on the abortion issue.

All fifty-one state representatives were up for re-election in 1968, along with eleven of the twenty-five state senators. The sponsors of both of the first two bills, Senator Yoshinaga and Representative Loo, were Democrats, but the majority Democratic party had no official position on abortion law reform. In May, 1968, the State Republican Convention approved abortion law reform as a plank in its party platform. Although abortion was barely mentioned in the fall election campaign, the Republican legislators subsequently carried out the party platform promise by cosponsoring abortion law reform bills.

Inclusion of a pro-abortion reform plank in the 1968 Republican state platform was evidence of how respectable the issue had become. By the time the Fifth Legislature convened for the 1969 legislative session, abortion had been elevated from the private cause of individual lawmakers to the status of a substantial public issue worthy of consideration by the major political parties.

The national and international picture had also changed considerably during 1967 and 1968. Passage in 1967 of Colorado's abortion reform law along the lines of the ALI model abortion law was quickly followed by the passage of very similar legislation in California and North Carolina. The Colorado law permitted abortion to protect the physical or mental health of the woman, to prevent the birth of a deformed child, or in cases of forcible or statutory rape or incest. The California law covered the same conditions with the exception of the fetal deformity clause, which had been omitted at the insistence of Governor Ronald Reagan.[34] The North Carolina law was very similar. The physical and mental health of the woman were protected under the single term "health." Statutory rape was not included, but fetal deformity was. Similar legislation was passed by state legislatures in Maryland and Georgia in 1968. Variations of the ALI bill were also introduced in a number of other states.

In October, 1967, Great Britain passed the Abortion Act, which took effect early in 1968. The British law permitted abortion to prevent the birth of a defective or deformed child. It also permitted abortion if

> . . . the continuance of the pregnancy would involve risk to the life of the pregnant woman, or of injury to the physical or mental health of the pregnant woman or any existing children of her family, greater than if the pregnancy were terminated . . . .

A further clause provided that:

> In determining whether the continuance of a pregnancy would involve such risk of injury to health . . . account may be taken of the pregnant woman's actual or reasonably foreseeable environment.[35]

The reform laws passed in several U.S. states increased the number of legal abortions performed, although practice varied from state to state. For example, 5,030 abortions were reported in California in the first calendar year after the new law was passed, but by the end of 1969, 10,000 more abortions had been performed. Most abortions were performed on grounds of mental health, the medical category which could be given the broadest possible interpretation, but in general the conditions under which abortions were permitted remained very restrictive. However, the British law very quickly transformed the Anglo-American abortion scene. The number of abortions performed in British National Health Service hospitals more than doubled in one year from less than 10,000 in 1967 to 22,000 in the first full year of the new law. Another 15,000 abortions were performed in private practice during the first year of the act.[36] Some American women, along with many European women, also began traveling to Britain for abortions.

Abortion was rapidly becoming a socially acceptable topic of discussion. Newspapers and magazines carried many articles on the subject, and the British experience made it more and more apparent that great numbers of women sought abortion for reasons outside the scope of the ALI provisions. Interest in abortion also coincided with the growing worldwide concern with the ecological and social problems of pollution and population.

THE FIRST SUCCESS IN HAWAII

Against this background of social change, the new Fifth Hawaii Legislature began the 1969 session with a proliferation of abortion law reform bills. Four virtually identical bills were introduced in the House, signed by thirty-three legislators, some of whom signed more than one bill. This was already a majority of the fifty-one-seat House. House Bills 61, 104, and 107 were introduced on February 24, 1969. All followed the pattern of the American Law Institute model abortion law and had been drafted by the state's Legislative Reference Bureau.

House Bill 61 had been requested by the Democratic Policy Committee, which was composed of the key majority party members of the House. Although the Policy Committee had ordered legislation drafted at Representative Loo's suggestion, he was not certain that the committee would actually release the bill, so he introduced an identical bill, H.B. 104, on his own. Democratic floor leader Stuart Ho also introduced the same bill as H.B. 107.

Two days later, Representative Peter Iha introduced H.B. 204, a bill for complete repeal of the abortion law that was identical to a new Senate bill introduced by Senator Yoshinaga, S.B. 168. The following week, Iha introduced H.B. 497, which was the fourth copy of the American Law Institute model abortion law. There was no shortage of abortion legislation for House members to consider.

In the Senate, two very different bills were introduced. One was Senator Yoshinaga's second attempt to introduce a repeal bill. His bill, S.B. 168, proposed repeal of the existing abortion statute (sections 309-3, 309-4, and 309-5) and replaced them with a new section to read as follows:

> *Abortion; defense; penalty.* A person commits the offense of abortion if he intentionally causes the miscarriage of another. It is a defense to a prosecution under this section that the person was a physician authorized by law to practice medicine in this State and that he performed the abortion in a hospital licensed by this State.[37]

The intent of this bill was the same as that of Senator Yoshinaga's 1967 proposal: to permit physicians to perform abortions without legal restriction. Although the strategy and wording differed, the only substantive change in the new 1969 version was the additional requirement that abortions be performed in a hospital.

The second Senate bill, S.B. 521, was introduced by all eight Senate Republicans.[38] It contained many of the same qualifications as the American Law Institute model abortion law, but was worded much differently and included additional restrictions and qualifications. This bill required unanimous certification by a three-member hospital board before an abortion could be performed, rather than the "two physicians, one of whom may be the person performing the abortion" proposed in the House version. The physical and mental health conditions in the Republican senators' bill were also more conservative. Senate Bill 521 permitted abortion only when *permanent* impairment to the mother or child would result. Furthermore, exercise of the mental health clause explicitly required the written confirmation of a psychiatrist.

The Republican bill omitted the American Law Institute model abortion law's clause which classified all illicit intercourse with a girl below the age of sixteen as felonious. Maintaining such a clause would have made all resulting pregnancies automatically eligible for abortion. However, the senators added adultery to rape and incest as causes of pregnancies which were eligible for abortion. Two restrictions were added to these cases, however. First, the abortion could only be performed before sixteen weeks of gestation; and second, the abortion could not be performed unless

> . . . the county attorney of the county district in which the alleged rape, adultery or incest has occurred has informed the committee in writing under his signature, that there is probable cause to believe that the alleged violation did occur.[39]

In addition, two clauses specified that anyone causing the

death of a woman either through an abortion which was not medically justified (according to the conditions described above) or by "the intentional pretended ending of her real or apparent pregnancy" without medical justification is "guilty of murder and shall be punished accordingly." A final clause of the Republican bill guaranteed the right of any hospital, staff member, or employee not to participate in abortions.

In both Houses, the new abortion bills were assigned to committee review. The five House bills went to the Committee on Public Health, Youth and General Welfare. This committee was chaired by Representative George Loo, who had previously been chairman of the Housing and Consumer Protection Committee when that committee considered his 1967 abortion reform bill. Two other members of the Public Health, Youth and General Welfare Committee, Representatives Akira Sakima and Dorothy Devereux, had also been on the Housing and Consumer Protection Committee in 1967. All three had supported the reform bill at that time.

Upon accepting chairmanship of the Public Health, Youth and General Welfare Committee, Representative Loo anticipated resuming action on the abortion issue. He felt the general climate had changed along with House leadership and thought the bill had a good chance of passage. When committee assignments of bills were being made, he requested that if the new Speaker of the House, Tadao Beppu, supported the abortion reform bill, the bill should only be assigned to his committee in order to expedite its review. When bill assignments were announced, he saw that the abortion bills had been sent only to his committee and therefore knew that he had the Speaker's support.[40]

The Senate's two bills were sent to the Committee on Public Health, Welfare, and Housing, chaired by Senator Vincent Yano. One member of that committee, Senator Mamoru Yamasaki, had been a member of the House of Representatives and a member of the House Committee on Housing and Consumer Protection during the 1967 committee consideration of abortion law reform. At that time, Yamasaki had not concurred with the committee report favoring the bill.

Representative Loo's committee in the House, building on previous involvement in the issue, was the first to act. On March 10,

1969, the committee held an open hearing on the abortion reform bills. Fourteen persons testified at the hearing, eleven of them representing organizations.

Testifying in favor of reform were two representatives of the medical community: Dr. George Goto, then chairman of the legislative committee of the Hawaii Medical Association; and Charles Knobel of the Hawaii Public Health Association. Representatives of several Protestant religious groups spoke in favor of reform: Lois Goebel of the Public Affairs Council, First Unitarian Church of Honolulu; Florida Underwood, chairman of the Christian Social Concerns Committee of Ewa Beach United Methodist Church; Ray Elizabeth Herkner, secretary of the Episcopal Church Women of Hawaii; and Reverend Charles Crane, Rector of Holy Nativity Parish (Episcopal). Pro-reform testimony on behalf of community organizations was given by Marilyn Bornhorst of the Hawaii State Division of the American Association of University Women, Karen Tkach of the Hawaii Student Nurses' Association, and Cosette Mulder of Hawaii Planned Parenthood. Two public officials, Representative Stuart Ho of the State House of Representatives and Judge Samuel P. King of the Family Court, also offered their views favoring reform. Testifying in opposition to the proposed reforms were Father Daniel J. Dever of the Roman Catholic Diocese of Honolulu; Dr. Frederick A. Dodge, past president of the Hawaii Catholic Physicians' Guild; and Dr. W. N. Bergin, a Catholic physician.

Testimony at this hearing constituted the first formal public expression of community sentiment on the abortion issue. Although the public at large was not yet active, key persons and organizations were already committed to change. Some of these persons testified representing organizations which had already taken repeal positions at a national or local level, while others took the same position as private citizens. Laurel K. Kasaoka, a concerned citizen who did not testify at the hearing, was already beginning community activity on the abortion issue. She urged several of those testifying to make clear their preference for full repeal of all restrictions in order to raise the issue with the legislators.[41]

A full range of pro-repeal, pro-liberalization, and anti-reform views were voiced. Of the fourteen opinions expressed, only the Hawaii Public Health Association was solely for H.B. 204, the repeal bill, while four (Judge Samuel King, the Unitarian Church, Hawaii Planned Parenthood, and the American Association of University Women) favored the repeal bill but would accept any liberalization if H.B. 204 could not pass. Two other organization representatives, Florida Underwood of the United Methodist Church and Dr. George Goto of the Hawaii Medical Association, said they believed their organizations would support the repeal bill, but at the time of the hearing they were only authorized to testify in favor of the three liberalization bills. The three persons representing the Student Nurses' Association and the Episcopal Church testified in favor of the three liberalization bills but were silent on repeal. Representative Stuart Ho testifed in favor of the three liberalization bills but was explicitly opposed to "abortion on demand." The two Catholic physicians who testified were categorically opposed to all four bills. Father Daniel Dever, Superintendent of Hawaii Catholic schools, was opposed to all four, but said repeal was preferable to liberalization.[42] While this position might sound contradictory, Father Dever's preference for repeal was based on the ecclesiastical and civil law reasoning of Father Robert Drinan, then Dean of the Law School at Boston College. The Drinan argument, which preferred that the law remain mute on the abortion issue rather than sanction it, was to become important in the Hawaii debate. Later, however, Father Dever no longer publicly advocated it.[43]

Despite the fact that seven of the fourteen persons expressed support for full repeal of the abortion law (as embodied in H.B. 204), the committee report dealt with the issue as follows:

> It should be noted that your Committtee is not at this time going so far as to accept the proposition that no woman should be forced to bear a child against her will, but your Committee means to achieve a progressive step to at least measure the abortion law against today's time and tests . . . .[44]

Within the committee there was general support for the liberalization measure, and consequently the testimony was interpreted as widespread public acceptance of reform. Chairman Loo in particular favored liberalization but opposed repeal, a position which was echoed by Representative Stuart Ho's testimony at the hearing. The Chairman's opposition to the more radical repeal bill effectively killed it in the committee, but other political factors also contributed to its demise. Even those committee members who personally favored repeal, such as Representative Dorothy Devereux, felt that it would be years before such legislation could be passed.[45]

The aim of the committee members was to take a first step, and to do it with the bill most likely to pass. A combination of personal conviction and political sensitivity led the committee to ignore the strength of the pro-repeal sentiment and to report the liberalization bill out of committee without substantial amendment. Of the four identical copies of this bill, the Democratic Policy Committee's H.B. 61 was reported out because its sponsorship carried the most weight. The committee report was signed by Representatives George Loo, Stanley Roehrig, Clarence Akizaki, Pedro de la Cruz, Peter Iha, Robert Kimura, Jack Suwa, Dorothy Devereux, and Henry Meyer. Representative Tennyson Lum signed "with reservations," an indication that he disagreed with the committee report. Representatives Anthony Baptiste and Charles Ushijima were both excused and did not sign the report.

The House of Representatives considered second reading of H.B. 61 on April 3, 1969. Representative Bernaldo Bicoy offered an amendment to the bill requiring that the need for a therapeutic abortion be certified by two physicians. Where the reason for abortion was danger to the woman's mental health, one of the two physicians was reqired to be a psychiatrist. A second provision required that emergency therapeutic abortions performed outside of hospitals be reported within twenty-four hours. The amendment passed. After an hour of debate, the bill passed second reading with thirty-nine votes in favor and twelve opposed.[46] On April 7, after the mandatory waiting period, the bill passed third reading without incident.[47]

Hawaii had taken the first step toward abortion law reform. Passage of the liberalization bill in the House had been most uneventful, except for the slightly unusual procedure of a floor amendment after the bill had come out of committee. The bill had not aroused either great enthusiasm or great antagonism. The number of persons testifying at the committee hearings was average for a minor social welfare bill. There had been virtually no visible community interest in the issue and no attempt to mobilize public support or opposition. Although the legislators were divided, the issue had generated little public heat. It looked as though Hawaii would quietly and matter-of-factly join the growing ranks of those states with moderately liberalized abortion laws following the ALI model. The archaic law would be replaced by a more current version and little would change in practice.

CHAPTER 2

Personalities

EVEN AS THE HOUSE acted on the reform bill, community support for abortion law repeal (as opposed to abortion law reform) began to appear. Repeal bills had been introduced before by individual legislators, but they had been ignored by community, media, and legislature alike. A handful of community leaders were the first to stir, as the testimony at the House hearings shows. The media were still only mildly interested, legislators were ready for reform but not repeal, and the general public had not yet been aroused by the issue at all. As the scene shifted to the Senate, two key figures made their first entrance almost simultaneously: Senator Vincent Yano and Joan Hayes.

THE SENATE COMMITTEE

After its passage in the House, H.B. 61 was sent to the Senate Committee on Public Health, Welfare and Housing, chaired by Senator Vincent Yano. Senator Yano was Catholic, a lawyer, a Democrat, and the father of ten children. He had recently become involved in a broad range of social issues including liberal reforms within the Catholic Church and opposition to the Vietnam war. Four years earlier, he had left his home and the Church's formal institutions, yet he still considered himself a believing Catholic and was sensitive to the Church's position on abortion. Feeling the conflict between his religious commitments and his desire to evaluate the bill fairly, he began a serious study of the abortion law issue.[1]

He scheduled a Senate committee hearing on the bill for April 28 and 30, 1969. Since the motivation for the hearing was to receive testimony pertinent to H.B. 61, which had been passed by the House, this was the only bill considered. Both Senator Yoshinaga's repeal bill and the Republican reform bill were ignored and effectively eliminated from further consideration.

The Senate hearing was very similar to the House hearing one month earlier, with about half of the same participants. Ten persons testified in favor of the proposed abortion law reform. They included five organization representatives who had previously testified at the House hearings: Dr. George Goto, representing the Hawaii Medical Association; Charles Knobel, representing the Hawaii Public Health Association; Karen Tkach of the Student Nurses' Association; Florida Underwood of Ewa Beach United Methodist Church; and Reverend Charles Crane, Episcopal Rector of Holy Nativity Parish. New persons testifying in favor of the bill were Earlene Chambers, Director of Services at Palama Settlement (a local social agency); Dr. John Blaylock, Chief of the Mental Health Team for Courts and Corrections; Laurel K. Kasaoka, representing the Democratic Action Group (a reform Democratic group which developed out of the 1968 Presidential nomination campaign of Eugene McCarthy); Louise MacDonald, editor of *Pacific Health,* the University of Hawaii School of Public Health journal (testifying as a private citizen); and Joan Hayes, representing the American Association of University Women.

The only person present to testify in opposition was Dr. William Bergin, the Catholic physician who had also testified at the previous hearing. The U.S. Catholic Bishops' statement on abortion was submitted to the committee by Monsignor Francis A. Marzen, representing the Catholic Diocese of Honolulu.

These Senate hearings marked Joan Hayes' debut in the abortion controversy, although as a former Washington, D.C. lobbyist, she was far from being a political novice. Hayes had recently been elected legislative chairman of the Honolulu chapter of the American Association of University Women (AAUW). Under the leadership of its previous legislative chairman, Marilyn Bornhorst, the Honolulu AAUW had already expressed its support for repeal of abortion laws. When Joan Hayes first read the abortion reform bill in March, she reports,

> the House Bill, the so-called Model Law originally drafted by the American Law Institute, seemed to me adequate to cope with what I assumed were most of the reasons why abortion might be sought. . . . But the more I read, studied, and asked questions, the more I realized that the bill was a fraud. While appearing to promise major relief, it was, I am convinced, really worse than no bill at all because it would simply defer, perhaps for many decades, any real relief.[2]

By the time she went to testify at the Senate hearings in April, Hayes was convinced of the need for complete repeal of the abortion law. She also had new support from the AAUW, which had voted at its state convention to support the repeal position. With her experience as a lobbyist, Joan Hayes did not stop at testifying. She also sought out the several individual members of the committee to find out where they stood. She found that Senator Donald Ching would support change in the abortion law, while Senator Mamoru Yamasaki was opposed. Senator Percy Mirikitani was aware of and sympathetic to the issues, but told her that the people for abortion law repeal were so sure of their views that they did not try to persuade others; this was something they must do if change were to come about. He said his mail was five to one against change, and he thought it would take years for restrictive abortion laws to be repealed. Senator Nadao Yoshinaga, who was not a member of the committee but had personally submitted two abortion law repeal bills, said there were enough votes to pass the ALI model abortion law, but not enough votes to pass the repeal bill.[3]

Hayes then went to Senator Yano, who said he needed more time to consider the issue. She asked, "What would it take to convince you?" He said he wanted to know how all the individual physicians felt about it (as opposed to the formal position taken by the Hawaii Medical Association). She then began on her own to survey local physicians. Senator Yano's desire for a survey of physicians had reached other ears. Dr. Roy Smith, a pediatrician and Associate Professor of Maternal and Child Health in the School of Public Health at the University of Hawaii, together with graduate student Beverly Manner also began to prepare a questionnaire. The three joined forces. Dr. George Goto, legislative liaison officer for the Hawaii Medical Association, made arrangements for the use of the Association's stationery and addressograph and, with AAUW help for the mailing, the questionnaire was sent to every physician in the state.[4]

As these efforts got underway, the legislative session was drawing to a close and Senator Yano still felt he needed more time to study the issue. One of his first readings was an article by Harvey Zipf, "Recent Abortion Law Reforms (or Much Ado About Nothing)."[5] Zipf's argument that the reform law in Colorado had not solved the abortion problem increased Yano's concern over the proposed legislation. Of the other Senate committee members, three favored the House bill (Senators Mirikitani, Ching, and Yee) while one (Senator Yamasaki) was reluctant. Senator Yano, as committee chairman, had a great deal of power over the course of the bill. He discussed the problem with Senator Ching and arranged to have the bill stay in committee when the session ended. This was formally accomplished by Senator Ching's vote against the bill, which created a tie. Senator Yano then cast the deciding vote against release. Because the 1969 session was only the first half of the two-year legislative term, a bill could be held in committee and released the following year. The bill did not necessarily die at the end of the session, but the action was ambiguous.

The committee's failure to release the abortion reform bill was widely interpreted as an attempt by Senator Yano to stop abortion law reform. A few community figures, however, knew that he was still undecided. Representative Loo was particularly piqued because he had been assured that Senator Yano would not block the bill.[6]

THE REPEAL CAMPAIGN'S NEW LEADERS

Senator Yano continued to read and ponder the issue. Shortly after the end of the session, he read *The Terrible Choice: The Abortion Dilemma,* a collection of articles discussing the abortion problem largely within a Catholic framework.[7] There he came upon the philosophical argument of Father Robert Drinan, then Dean of the Law School at Boston College. Father Drinan considered that when a state law permitted abortion for any reason whatsoever, it condoned murder, At the same time, there was little likelihood of passage of legislation which did not permit abortion under any circumstances; the immediate question was whether or not to permit it for additional reasons. Therefore, he argued, there should be no abortion law at all. This was preferable to having the State condone abortion under particular circumstances. The Drinan position was based on a total religious opposition to abortion, but its practical effect was to make abortion available unconditionally by removing all legal restrictions against it.

The Drinan position is often misunderstood to be a pluralistic argument that permits each individual to decide whether or not to utilize abortion, but in fact the argument is much different. Its rationale is the very Jesuitical reasoning that the absence of an abortion law, even if in fact it makes abortion generally available, avoids the worse evil of having the law condone abortion in some specific circumstances.

> Abortion on request—or an absence of law with respect to abortion—has at least the merit of not involving the law and society in the business of selecting those persons whose lives may be legally terminated. A system of permitting abortion on request has the undeniable virtue of neutralizing the law so that, while the law does not forbid abortion, it does not on the other hand sanction it—even on a presumably restricted basis.[8]

Senator Yano was greatly impressed with the argument because it provided a way for him to facilitate change in the abortion law while still maintaining his personal moral conviction of opposition to abortion. He continued to study other articles by Father Drinan and sometime during the summer became fully convinced that the answer to the abortion question was to repeal the abortion law completely.[9]

During the summer of 1969, Joan Hayes began trying to interest powerful local labor unions in the issue of abortion law repeal. Her political sophistication and experience as a Washington lobbyist were evident in this move. The unions were a major source of political support for the Democratic majority. Their endorsement would guarantee a receptive ear in the legislature. In August, Hayes participated in a debate on abortion at a meeting of the United Public Workers. "I wanted to give the ILWU and the AFL-CIO a 'cram course' on what had convinced me. But I couldn't guarantee that they would show up for such a session," she explained. "I needed a better audience." Her solution was to have the American Association of University Women sponsor a citizens' seminar on abortion that was aimed at the community's opinion leaders.[10]

From the Chamber of Commerce she obtained a list of one hundred potentially interested organizations. To these were added the elected officials in city and state government, eighty business leaders, the clergy, and the newspapers. Three hundred handwritten invitations to the September Citizens' Seminar were prepared and sent out by the AAUW. The invitations pressed for participation by saying, "If you will be unable to attend personally, please let us know who will represent you." The public was invited to the seminar through newspaper announcements and by printed flyers put out by the YWCA and distributed by the Episcopal Church Women. The seminar was scheduled in the afternoon in the hope that professionals would attend as part of their working day.

As speakers for the afternoon seminar, Joan Hayes organized a panel including: Dr. Jan Newhouse, an ecologist from the University of Hawaii; Dr. George Goto, obstetrician; Dr. Sharon Bintliff, pediatrician and geneticist; Dr. Kwong Yen Lum, psychiatrist; Dr. Leonard Pepper, psychologist; Earlene Chambers, social worker; Patricia Putman, lawyer with the Legislative Reference Bureau; and Senator Vincent Yano. For dramatic impact, she had also arranged for a woman to present her personal experience with illegal abortion. This was not announced beforehand, however. She decided that the program should emphasize factual information rather than philosophical positions, so no clergymen were included in the panel although many were invited to attend the seminar.

An overflow crowd of two hundred attended the Citizens' Seminar on September 10, 1969, at the AAUW clubhouse. The high point of the afternoon was Senator Yano's announcement that he would introduce an abortion law repeal bill in the next legislative session. Senator Yano had originally been asked to talk about the legal aspects of the abortion problem. However, Hayes had suggested that if he were ready to support abortion law repeal, the seminar would offer him a good public forum for the announcement. Because Senator Yano did not reveal his intentions until the day of the seminar, Hayes had expected the personal testimony of a girl who had undergone an illegal abortion to be the newsworthy event, since such experiences were very rarely reported publicly by women at that time.

Senator Yano's surprise announcement that he would support repeal turned the AAUW Citizens' Seminar into the springboard of a public campaign for abortion law repeal. On one hand, the seminar fulfilled its original purpose of educating important community leaders about the issue. On the other hand, it aroused the hopes and energies of those who were already personally committed to repeal. Many of the subsequent events of the campaign can be traced to that seminar. During the afternoon, for example, Reverend Claude du Teil, an Episcopal clergyman, asked Senator Yano whether he would be violating the existing abortion law if he helped a woman obtain an abortion in Japan. Senator Yano's answer was, "Yes." The subsequent discussion sparked the formation of the local clergy counseling service which, in benign defiance of the existing law, helped many Hawaii women obtain abortions. In addition, the seminar motivated several people to go back to their organizations and seek support for abortion law repeal through formal resolutions and other activities. Both of the unions that had been Joan Hayes' original targets, the AFL-CIO and the ILWU, adopted resolutions supporting abortion law repeal shortly after the seminar.

Joan Hayes and Senator Yano were publicly identified as leaders of the repeal campaign, although they continued to operate independently of each other. Both of them recognized that abortion was a "public conscience" issue—that is, one in which public interest had to be developed first, so that support would come from the public and then be directed toward the legislature. During the fall of 1969, while the legislature was not in session, they both accepted many speaking engagements and encouraged community interest in the issue.

The leaders of the fight for abortion law repeal in Hawaii were an unlikely pair: a Catholic legislator with ten children who had been honored as a Knight of the Pope (a high honor awarded to Catholic laymen for service and leadership) and a middle-aged, middle-class woman with a hesitant manner who had not been aware of the abortion problem six months earlier. Neither of them knew anyone who had even tried to get an abortion. Paradoxically, it may have been their naiveté and the newness of their own decisions that made them such effective spokespersons for the issue. Both had studied the facts of the issue, both knew what had convinced them, and both were thoroughly respectable citizens.

Neither Joan Hayes nor Vincent Yano aspired to the historical role of leader of the first successful campaign for abortion law repeal in the United States. Senator Yano continued to advocate repeal despite his own strong moral opposition to the act of abortion. He was the personal embodiment of the argument that abortion law repeal would leave the decision to the individual's conscience. Since he was Catholic and offered his position on abortion as one compatible with Catholic theology, his presence undercut the Church's opposition more effectively than any amount of anti-Catholic invective could have. He came across as a reasonable, moral man wrestling with his conscience. His example led many other reasonable, moral members of the community, Catholic and non-Catholic, to do the same.

Despite her experience in public relations and lobbying, Joan Hayes' public manner was shy and hesitant. She had stumbled into the abortion issue because of her official duties as an officer in a highly respectable women's organization, the American Association of University Women. She brought a practical, realistic perspective to what had previously been a lost cause for idealistic crusaders. Equally important, she had no personal desire for glory; she just wanted the job to get done. "I kept hoping someone else would pick up the ball, but nobody did, so I kept on doing it," she recalls.[11]

Neither Senator Yano nor Joan Hayes tried to control the abortion law repeal campaign. When people came to them with ideas for activities, they offered suggestions and encouragement. Senator Yano often referred people to his secretary, Betty Becker, who served as an informal clearing-house for the campaign. She, too, saw her role as simply one of helping the flow of information and resources. All three created an atmosphere of encouragement, cooperation, and equality, and they welcomed others who came along to share the work. These qualities of the leaders left the Hawaii campaign for abortion law repeal amazingly free from the petty bickering and partisan antagonisms which have plagued such efforts elsewhere. The handful of community leaders who had already been urging abortion law change were delighted that something was happening and cooperated willingly with the newcomers. There was plenty for each person or group to do. No one even suggested that the movement ought to be centrally organized, and it was not. Everyone understood that the effort was collective and the credit for success would be shared. Indeed, successful change in the law itself was the only reward anyone sought.

In the fall of 1969, abortion was a new issue to the vast majority of the people in Hawaii. The personalities of the repeal leaders and the quality of the campaign were particularly important in creating a favorable first impression of the issue. Very few people had already formed an opinion on the subject, because most had never thought deeply about it before. The idea of repealing the abortion law was presented to the public largely through the channels of existing, respected civic organizations. Senator Vincent Yano and Joan Hayes were accepted by these organizations as respectable social equals. They spoke in terms familiar to their audiences, explaining what had convinced them as individuals of the need for repeal. They made the issue legitimate because they themselves were personally legitimate in background, motives, and style. The two of them neither wanted to accomplish, nor could have accomplished, the change in Hawaii's abortion law by themselves. They served as leaders and catalysts to many others, yet their personal styles set the tone for the tactics and the issues of the campaign.

The first concrete indication that abortion law repeal might be politically feasible came several weeks after the Citizens' Seminar. Governor Burns spoke at a small local Democratic club meeting, with no reporters present. Mark Lester, a member of the audience, asked the governor whether he would favor the kind of abortion legislation Senator Yano had proposed. Burns replied that he believed abortion should not be either prohibited or sanctioned by the law, but should be left as a matter of individual conscience. Questioned by reporters the following day, Governor Burns confirmed the statement. He added that it was an expression of his personal feelings, not a legislative proposal.[12]

The informal comment was important for two reasons. First, Governor Burns was known to be a devout Catholic, so there was a real question of whether he would veto an abortion law reform bill even if it could be steered successfully through the legislature. The governor's remarks raised the hopes of repeal supporters that he would accept a repeal bill. This greatly improved not only the bill's ultimate chance of becoming law, but also the probability of getting legislators to vote for it in the first place. Second, the governor's remark was prized because he was widely respected as a man who always kept his word. The fact that he had once made such a statement, however informally, was regarded as a virtual promise by his political associates and followers, although those outside this circle were not at all sure he would stand by his comment when the bill reached his desk.

THE OPPOSITION EMERGES

Shortly thereafter, the opposition began to emerge on two separate fronts. One source of opposition was maintained almost singlehandedly by Representative George Loo, who still advocated the reform bill which he had successfully steered through the House. Loo did not accept the argument that women had a "right" to abortion. He was also not particularly impressed with arguments about unwanted children. His main concern remained the problem of women who had been raped. Although Representative Loo, a non-Catholic and a bachelor, was willing to accept abortion under limited conditions, he still felt that the fetus was "close to life" and that the issue therefore required very cautious handling.[13]

Although Representative Loo's commitment to the reform bill was certainly a genuine reflection of his personal beliefs, he also appeared to be somewhat piqued at Senator Yano's sudden prominence in the abortion law arena. Representative Loo had been the original hero of the abortion law reformers, and he had successfully steered the ALI model abortion law bill through the House. Representative Loo claims that at a legislative joint session in the spring of 1969, Senator Yano assured him he would not stop the reform bill when it reached his committee, although Senator Yano denies that any promises were made. At any rate, Senator Yano did stop the bill, and when it emerged it was an entirely different proposition from what Representative Loo had intended. Although Senator Yano does not seem to have consciously upstaged his party colleague in the House, it may well have looked that way to Representative Loo.

Throughout the fall of 1969, Representative Loo continued to oppose the repeal bill and argue for the limited reform concept. He was thus soon identified by repeal advocates as part of the opposition. This label was unfair, since he had been one of the original champions of abortion law change. By the fall of 1969, however, he stood for a partial reform that was rapidly being swept aside in the mounting enthusiasm for total repeal.

The second source of opposition emanated from the Roman

Catholic Church, which was already on record as being opposed to the ALI model abortion law reforms.

On October 31, 1969, Bishop John Scanlan published a front-page letter in the diocesan newspaper, The *Hawaii Catholic Herald,* reiterating the Church's position on abortion. He reminded his readers that abortion was "an unspeakable crime" which the Church condemns, and made it clear that this condemnation meant complete opposition to any change in the law.

> There exists in our society an increasing pressure to liberalize the existing laws to the point where abortion on demand would be legally possible. . . . This frontal attack on morality must be vigorously resisted. This is an attack on human life, the preservation of which is the first obligation of human society.[14]

The bishop's statement reached a non-Catholic audience when it was reported in the two Honolulu daily newspapers.[15] A subsequent article in the *Hawaii Catholic Herald* was directed toward the state legislature. The bishop argued that people do not always know what is good for them, and laws provide part of the support man needs in order to be good. He urged the legislators to study the abortion issue carefully, keeping in mind the teaching function of the laws.[16]

These two articles set the pattern for Bishop Scanlan's involvement in the abortion issue. He took a strong stand in opposition to any change in the existing abortion law. Most of this activity was carried out through official agencies of the diocese and was directed at the audience of Hawaii Catholics who were under his authority. In addition to his frequent personal statements in the diocesan newspaper and at ceremonial occasions, the bishop encouraged the Catholic school system and other religious institutions to help transmit the Church's position on abortion.

Although the bishop did not attempt to speak directly to the non-Catholic public, he did focus considerable attention on the legislature. Spokesmen for the Roman Catholic diocese had already testified against abortion reform bills at legislative hearings. This practice was maintained and even strengthened when the debate shifted toward outright repeal of the abortion law. Occasionally, the bishop's statements in the *Hawaii Catholic Herald* were aimed specifically at legislators. Much later in the campaign he requested and received a special meeting with members of the legislature.

In all, the bishop conducted himself as one might expect the head of a large and powerful religious organization to do. He used all of the organizational resources at his disposal to convey the Church's official position both to the Church members under his jurisdiction and to those persons in the larger community who had the power to change the law. His attempts to influence the legislative process by sending his subordinates to testify at a public hearing and by seeking a private audience with legislators incensed non-Catholic supporters of abortion law repeal. From their perspective, he was only a private citizen who demanded special privileges and acted very undemocratically. Considering his position within the Catholic hierarchy and the size of the Catholic community in the state (about 28 percent of the population), however, his behavior was actually circumspect. This may have been a deliberate posture, or it may have happened because the bishop did not think the abortion law would actually be repealed in the near future.

Within the Catholic community itself, Bishop Scanlan's influence was not uniformly strong. Long before abortion became an issue, many Catholics in the state disagreed with the generally conservative tone of the *Hawaii Catholic Herald,* which they regarded as simply "the bishop's mouthpiece." Because the paper is distributed free of charge at all parishes, it is difficult to determine what proportion of the state's Catholics actually read it.

The governor of Hawaii and several state legislators, including Senator Yano, were practicing Catholics. Their behavior and statements indicate that all of them felt duty-bound to reach a personal decision on the abortion issue and not to accept the bishop's pronouncements solely because of his position as an officer of the Church. Certainly, many of these government officials found the bishop's arguments persuasive, but there is no evidence that he was able—or even tried—to dictate to them on the grounds of his religious authority.

A certain degree of independence could also be observed in the private thinking of some priests and nuns who were directly subordinate to the bishop's authority, although they were not usually free to express their views. Father Daniel Dever, superintendent of Catholic schools for the diocese, was frequently called upon to argue the Church's position against abortion. Although Father Dever was an articulate public spokesman against abortion law repeal, he felt privately that the official position was difficult to defend in a civil political context. While presenting the Church's opposition to the ALI model abortion law bill in the 1969 spring House committee hearings, Father Dever had indicated that if some change in the abortion law were inevitable, he (following the Drinan argument) would favor full repeal rather than reform. Once the bishop had articulated the diocese's position of opposition to any legalization of abortion in October, 1969, Father Dever as an official spokesman could no longer espouse this view. Instead, he tried unsuccessfully to get Bishop Scanlan to deal with the political and legal ramifications of absolute opposition to all abortions.[17] Bishop Scanlan's response was to claim support for the fetus' right to life under existing law and to remind legislators of the role of law in teaching and upholding public morality.

Sister Maureen, chief administrator of St. Francis Hospital, was also called upon to serve as an official spokesman for the Church's opposition to repeal of the abortion law, although it was rumored that she did not privately agree with the bishop's position. Indeed, her public statements carefully focused on such peripheral issues as the right of Catholic medical personnel to refuse to participate in the performance of abortions for reasons of conscience.

In sharp contrast to the narrow latitude for public dissent which prominent Catholic religious officials experienced, one lone nun, Sister Mary Heenan, a member of the independent Maryknoll order, felt free to espouse the Drinan argument publicly because she had not been ordered to serve as an official Church spokesman. She spoke as an independent Catholic.

Many Catholic laymen accepted the bishop's position on the issue, however, either because it was Church doctrine or because it coincided with their personal convictions. One Catholic layman who did agree with the bishop's position soon rose to public prominence as a leader of the opposition to abortion law repeal independently of the official actions of the diocese. Robert J. Pearson, Jr., a deeply religious Catholic convert, was a prosperous independent building contractor on the island of Maui. Three of his six children were adopted, and he was strongly committed to the protection of children. He was adamantly opposed to abortion but did not speak out publicly on the issue until January, 1970. A chance event brought him into the anti-abortion law repeal campaign and ultimately changed his life.

In connection with a between-semesters symposium on population and ecology, the Associated Students of the University of Hawaii (the official student government organization) had invited nationally-known birth control and abortion law reform crusader William Baird to the campus. Baird gave a number of presentations that were attended by the public as well as students. He presented educational material on various kinds of birth control, recounted his brushes with the law for helping young women obtain contraceptives and abortions, and encouraged Hawaii students to organize a local abortion referral service.

Pearson heard one of Baird's talks and was struck by the openness of Baird's attack on abortion laws and his forthright manner. He was particularly impressed that Baird was carrying on his crusade as a layman, without any special expert credentials. Pearson telephoned Baird for an appointment to meet and talk privately. The meeting in a Waikiki hotel lasted well into the night. Pearson found it pleasant, invigorating, educational, and motivating. Here was someone with whom Pearson could identify. Both men were about the same age, were laymen, and felt strongly about abortion on opposite sides of the issue. Each had a family. The big difference was that Baird was willingly sacrificing financial rewards and inviting personal abuse by campaigning for a cause he deeply believed in. Pearson decided to do the same. On January 22, 1970, two weeks after Baird came to Hawaii, Robert Pearson initiated his personal campaign to prevent the repeal of Hawaii's abortion law.[18] Baird, meanwhile, had left Hawaii to continue his campaign elsewhere.

The appeal to muster general popular support against repeal outside the Catholic community can be said to have started with the personally motivated, belated efforts of Robert Pearson in late January, 1970. Others had spoken against repeal earlier, but mainly when they had been invited to present the opposition position at various forums. Pearson's leadership was originally unsolicited and for the most part was uncoordinated with any Catholic caucus. Most of his funding came from private donations solicited by Pearson or from his own pocket.

Pearson's commitment was total. Since his home was on a neighbor island, away from the political center of Honolulu on the island of Oahu, he worked locally at first, organizing anti-abortion letter writing efforts and speaking to local Catholic clubs. Most notably, he was able to get financial cooperation from the Aloha Club, a fraternal club on Maui. With their backing, but mostly with his own funds, he began a program designed to combat the argument that abortion was the solution to the problem of unwanted pregnancies among young women. Pearson offered to support totally any pregnant woman throughout her pregnancy. He publicly advertised that any woman was eligible for this support as long as she maintained the pregnancy she did not want and otherwise might abort. She did not need to keep the child, which could be given up for adoption. If the woman needed transportation costs to get to Maui, he would arrange it. This was a sincere offer. He was truly committed to the idea that this effort and similar ones by others would generate sufficient funds and support to sustain any number of women.[19]

The offer to take care of pregnant women was a direct alternative to William Baird's abortion referral plan. Pearson also employed a variety of other tactics, often emulating Baird. His educational presentations included visual aids: enlarged photographs of fetuses at various stages of development. He organized a letter campaign using duplicated form letters, ran full-page newspaper advertisements with pictures of fetuses, and organized demonstration marches to the Capitol.

While his efforts were obviously sincere, their emotional tone and belated appearance contrasted sharply with the reasoned, dignified approach of the local supporters of repeal. Because he opposed all use of abortion, his arguments were sometimes directed at the limited reform bill rather than at full repeal. His work attracted support, but it also probably turned some people toward the repeal camp. Whatever else they accomplished, Pearson's highly visible activities served to keep the issue hotly controversial and in the public eye when the legislature reconvened in January, 1970 and the Senate began to consider Senator Yano's abortion law repeal bill.

CHAPTER 3

Tactics Aimed at the Public

IN THE SHORT SPACE of five months—from September, 1969 to February, 1970—a remarkable transformation took place in Hawaii. The community became aroused, informed, and mobilized about an issue which had been obscure and politically impractical six months earlier. Nearly all of the key figures who accomplished this transformation in public consciousness had been strangers to the issue and to one another twelve months earlier.

The timing of the shift in public awareness and opinion can be identified precisely, but it was not precipitated by any watershed event. There was no public scandal to arouse concern, no one special visitation by an outsider who incited the community to action, no suddenly visible social problem demanding immediate solution. Nor can the phenomenon be attributed to the sheer force of the idea alone. On one hand, the concept of a radical reversal of abortion laws had been around for some time, but little headway had been made toward convincing either the public or the lawmakers of the merits and feasibility of the plan. On the other hand, the issue itself acquired a new depth and breadth as it came to be debated publicly. Each week new arguments and counterarguments developed. The entire range of issues and positions was not publicly and fully displayed until the Senate committee hearing in February, 1970 (which will be discussed in subsequent chapters).

The idea of abortion law repeal became a public issue because a handful of people brought it to the public's attention in particular ways and at an appropriate point in time. It was brought to the public and the legislature through a variety of techniques or tactics. Both the pro-repeal and anti-repeal groups used approximately the same range of maneuvers, but with differences in emphasis and timing which proved important.

To speak of tactics suggests planned elements of an overall strategy. Although most of the individual tactics required advance planning and coordination, there is little evidence of an overall campaign or strategy mapped out from the beginning by a political leader, caucus, or group. Key figures and groups, both those for and those against repeal, were responsible for many of the ideas and organization, but most of the events were conceived and carried out as the special contribution of one group or one person with only loose coodination or sharing of information and manpower among groups. The movement may properly be considered a grass roots response. Despite this spontaneity, each individual tactic built on previous events and provided momentum for the future. Thus it seems appropriate to speak of an abortion law repeal campaign, since all of the efforts contributed to an overall impact on both the public and the legislature.

Each side considered the other to be well organized and working from a plan. The swift action taken by the forces for repeal so surprised those for *status quo* that they thought many months of clandestine planning and much money had been involved in the preparation for repeal. Similarly, the repeal forces thought that Bishop Scanlan and Robert Pearson had spent many detailed caucus meetings and planning hours as well as thousands of dollars in fighting the issue. There is no evidence for either set of beliefs. Both sides misjudged the large amount of popular interest this topic could muster on short notice.

The tactics themselves can be discussed according to their intent and the direction of their effect. For example, some were educational while others were emotional; some were directed toward arousing public support for or against the issue while others were aimed at the legislators to influence the actual legislative decision on whether to keep, modify, or repeal the law. The breakdown of tactics that follows corresponds roughly with the order in which they first appeared in the campaign. Most of the attempts at public education and arousal were necessarily conducted before the attempts to influence the legislature directly. This occurred both because the public had to become acquainted with the issue before there could be any pressure on the legislature, and also because the legislature was not in session until January, 1970.

The first problem of the original advocates of abortion law repeal was to bring the issue clearly to the public's attention. The abortion reform bill which passed the House in the spring of 1969 had generated some public interest but little enthusiasm or activity. Although many predicted that the more radical issue of abortion law repeal would attract even less public support, precisely the opposite was true. In fact, many of the groups and individuals publicly supporting the 1969 reform bill had used that occasion to advocate a much more basic change in the law. By September 10, 1969, when Senator Vincent Yano announced his advocacy of abortion law repeal at the AAUW Citizens' Seminar, a critical mass of support for a repeal campaign had already been reached.

PUBLIC FORUMS

The setting in which Senator Yano made his politically momentous announcement was itself an example of one of the major tactics of the campaign: an educational public forum. The usual format of these meetings was a panel discussion by a series of representatives from different professions. Sometimes the panel was balanced with both *pro* and *con* speakers; other times it was heavily weighted toward a single position. In addition, many other groups planned programs around a single speaker followed by group discussion. Such forums were generally sponsored by private organizations but were open to the public.

A relatively small number of experts circulated among the various public forums as panelists and featured speakers. For the anti-repeal position, two types of experts were available: Roman Catholic priests and physicians. The priests were not parish priests but higher-ranking officials, such as the chancellor of the local Catholic college, editor of the Catholic newspaper, and superintendent of the Catholic schools. Several Roman Catholic physicians were available, including both obstetricians and general practitioners.

Some of the anti-repeal panelists supported liberalization of the law, while others wanted no change. Although he had led the liberalization campaign in the House for several years, Representative George Loo soon became identified with an anti-repeal position. He served on several panels representing the reform or liberalization view. However, because his position was in the middle, and because he had previously been a major advocate of change in the abortion law, he did not serve as a legislative leader of the opposition in the same way that Senator Yano became the focal point of the repeal advocates.

A wider range of experts was available to represent the repeal position. Representatives of several religious denominations, physicians, legislators, psychologists, psychiatrists, social workers, lawyers, and university professors from various fields volunteered or were called upon to speak. Their arguments were occasionally supplemented with case histories presented by community workers or women who had had abortions or had been denied them. The usual strategy, however, was to establish professional experts as opinion leaders. Although the experts offered personal opinions as well as hard data, their opinions were generally presented as conclusions to arguments based on professional knowledge and factual information. Even the religious representatives favoring repeal tended to emphasize their roles as professional counselors for family and social problems and to place moral arguments within a social context.

Later, public forums focused more on tactics and mobilization than on simple debate on the issues. When William Baird visited the University of Hawaii during the January interim session program, he suggested tactics he had been using elsewhere. These tactics included demonstration marches and rallies as well as establishing abortion referral services. Although he knew little of the local repeal campaign and did not put much stock in its success, his vivid presentation helped mobilize student support for abortion law repeal. A direct outgrowth of his visit was the formation of a student group called the University Abortion and Birth Control Committee, which was also supported by several faculty members. The group first organized to carry out Baird's proposal of starting an abortion referral service in conjunction with the local Clergy Counseling Service, but soon shifted to the repeal campaign as a more general solution to the problem.

The local chapter of Zero Population Growth also sponsored a tactical symposium on how to change the abortion law, featuring State Ombudsman Herman Doi and Senator Yano. Both stressed direct contact between legislators and the public rather than demonstrations. They also encouraged qualified persons to testify at the forthcoming Senate committee hearing on the bill, which Senator Yano planned for the new legislative session.

As more people became involved in the issue of abortion law repeal, public forum audiences became more active. While some came for help in learning the issues and forming their own opinions, more and more were present to strengthen their own views and proselytize others. An example of the emotion generated during these forums was provided at an AAUW-sponsored panel at Maui Community College during the heat of the campaign, when half of the audience of one hundred and fifty persons walked out as abortion foe Robert Pearson began making a speech from the floor during the question and answer period.[1]

The forums themselves provided opportunities for advocates to get to know one another and coordinate activities and plans. Legislators were frequently requested to appear on panels to make their positions known and just as frequently attended the meetings in order to evaluate public sentiment. Advocates quickly learned to use the sessions to present their case directly to the available legislators.

The forum technique of using representative experts as opinion leaders was also employed by the newspapers. Feature articles appeared frequently in the newspapers reporting the views of either a range of professional and organization representatives or a range of individual opinions within one category. For example, religious figures, high school students, and physicians would have their opinions jointly or individually presented. The newspapers were able to supplement the fund of local talent with the views of experts in other parts of the country. These materials, in turn, became incorporated into the arguments of the local advocates.

Because the educational public forum often explicitly covered both sides of the issue, it is somewhat difficult to assess its value as a tactic used only by one side or the other. Persons and groups on both sides of the issue utilized single speakers or single-position panels to promote their own views. The forums for and against repeal seem to have been initiated either by supporters of repeal or by groups that were genuinely neutral and uninformed at the outset. Repeal supporters were rarely invited to speak in hostile territory, although of course they frequently encountered individual opponents of abortion law repeal in their audiences. By contrast, persons representing the anti-abortion view were frequently asked to present their views before groups that turned out to be heavily pro-repeal. Anti-repeal spokespersons thus obtained more exposure to potential supporters, but the situations were sometimes more difficult for the speaker because the audience was not sympathetic.

There was definitely more manpower for educational forums available on the pro-repeal side. Both a broader range of professionals and a greater number in each category spoke in support of abortion law repeal. While well informed and persuasive speakers opposing repeal were certainly available, there were not very many of them. This meant that the supporters of repeal could offer audiences a greater variety of arguments and speaking styles, in addition to having the sheer numbers to reach more people. Given the nature of the arguments and the areas of professional knowledge represented by the available speakers, it was much easier to present the pro-repeal position as a broad-based movement supported by scientific evidence in a variety of fields and opposed largely by a narrow religious belief. Had sufficient anti-repeal speakers been available with equivalent professional knowledge to match the repeal advocates area by area, the impact of the educational forums might have been different.

ORGANIZATION ENDORSEMENTS

Another application of this same technique of using experts as opinion leaders was the development of formal position statements by organizations. Both before and during the Hawaii abortion law repeal campaign, various national organizations went on public record for or against abortion law change. Those against abortion had recent history and standing law on their side. The prestige of such national organizations as the American Public Health Association, however, helped to legitimize the position of local advocates on an issue for which official supporting information was difficult to obtain.

Far more important for the state's legislative campaign, however, was the announcement of formal position statements by local organizations. Such statements were valuable for three reasons. First, the process of getting an organization to make the statement required some education and involvement of persons who otherwise might not have thought much about the issue. This was particularly important when organizations polled their membership before issuing their final statement of support. The three thousand members of the Hawaii Chamber of Commerce, for instance, were polled after the organization's Board of Directors initially endorsed the repeal. Since Chamber of Commerce members might not otherwise have become involved in this controversial issue at all, the process of polling the membership for an official Chamber statement served to bring the matter to the attention of a new public. The membership's overwhelming vote for repeal strengthened the endorsement considerably.

Another example is the Episcopal diocese of Hawaii, which began to discuss the issue of abortion reform or repeal as early as 1968. Discussion of the issue reached down to small social groups organized at the parish level and became more formalized in the votes of delegates both to the annual Episcopal Convocation and to the annual state convention of the Episcopal Church Women. This process raised the level of consciousness of individual church members and also reinforced the active participation of Episcopal clergy in the repeal movement. Similarly, the United Methodist Church and the Unitarian Church involved their memberships in discussion of the issue and then took a formal stand for repeal.

Second, endorsement by local organizations as the campaign developed, provided a rough index of public opinion. Although opinion leaders are often more committed than their constituents, the effect of an organization position statement was to suggest that persons in economic and social groups similar to the organization's membership could be expected to take a similar stand. Such an interpretation might be made either by one person determining his own position as part of the group or by a legislator trying to determine where public opinion lay.

Third, the endorsement of professional organizations, like the use of experts in public forums, legitimized a political position which for some persons had previously been associated with very powerful taboos. Up to 1969, abortion was not only illegal, it also bore for many the taint of social unacceptability and the suspicion of sexual license and political radicalism. The endorsement of middle-class churches, the Hawaii Medical Association, the Mental

Health Association, the Chamber of Commerce, the American Association of University Women, and respectable social agencies such as Child and Family Service and the YWCA sharply altered the context of the abortion issue for many people.

This same process of legitimization also occurred among organizations. After some respectable groups had taken the first step, it was much easier for others to come forward publicly. When the liberalization bill was before the House in the spring of 1969, only a handful of community organizations openly supported it. The bill was endorsed by the AAUW, the Hawaii Medical Association, the Unitarian Church, the United Methodist Church, the Episcopal Church Women, the Hawaii Student Nurses' Association, Hawaii Planned Parenthood, and the Hawaii Public Health Association.

As the repeal campaign began in September, 1969 with Senator Yano's announcement, the AFL-CIO,[2] the Unitarian Church,[3] and the Primary Convention of the Episcopal Diocese of Hawaii[4] quickly announced their support as the result of action within their own organizations. The Hawaii Public Health Association and AAUW positions already supported repeal. Within the next two months, the ILWU[5] and Kappa Delta Sorority Alumnae Association[6] announced their support for repeal. The Hawaii section of the American College of Obstetricians and Gynecologists reported its unanimous support for repeal,[7] and the State Judicial Council, an official body charged with preparing a complete revision of the penal code, announced that it would recommend abortion law repeal as part of the proposed criminal law reform.[8]

In January, 1970, the endorsements began to snowball. The Hawaii Psychological Association came out 95 percent for repeal,[9] and the Committee for the Protection of Children (the local child abuse agency) voted unanimously for repeal.[10] The Hawaii Chamber of Commerce Board of Directors,[11] Child and Family Service,[12] the Christian Social Concerns Committee of Hawaii United Methodist Church,[13] the Planned Parenthood Board of Directors,[14] the Hawaii Chapter of the National Association of Social Workers, the Hawaii Council of Churches, and the Mental Health Association all announced their support for repeal before the end of the month.[15] Much of the impetus at this time was to take an official position prior to the legislative hearing coming in February. The active supporters of repeal worked hard to get additional organizations to go on record in support of the repeal position before the hearing.

Endorsements climaxed at the Senate committee hearing on February 3 and 4, 1970, when these organizations and many others testified in support of abortion law repeal. On the first day of the hearing, the *Honolulu Advertiser* reported the names of twenty-three organizations on record as supporting repeal. In addition to those previously noted, they included: American Civil Liberties Union, Democratic Action Group (a liberal Democratic group), Friends of the Earth and the Sierra Club (ecology groups), Moiliili Community Center, Zero Population Growth, Honpa Hongwanji Parent-Teachers Association (affiliated with a large Japanese Buddhist temple), and the YWCA Board of Directors.[16] The Honolulu Community Action Program Board of Directors (a community board affiliated with the Model Cities program) submitted written testimony at the hearing. Its endorsement for repeal was announced publicly several days later.[17]

Endorsements continued after the hearing. The Hawaii Island Chamber of Commerce announced its endorsement of the repeal bill on February 14.[18] A newspaper advertisement sponsored by the University Abortion and Birth Control Committee, which appeared in the two Honolulu daily newspapers on February 16 and 17, listed thirty-three organizations supporting repeal. Besides those previously mentioned, the list included the Associated Students of the University of Hawaii (the official student government organization), Chamber of Commerce of Maui, Clergy Counseling Service (an abortion counseling and referral service run by a group of local clergymen), the Commission on Children and Youth (attached to the Governor's office), the Department of Social Services and Housing (the state welfare agency), Hawaii Government Employees Association, Hawaii Psychiatric Society, the John Howard Association (a social agency which works with prisoners and ex-prisoners), the Salvation Army, and Volunteers from VISTA.[19]

Formal opposition to repeal began with the Roman Catholic Bishop's reaffirmation of the Church's position in October. No other organization positions in opposition to abortion law appeal were reported prior to the Senate hearing in early February. Nor were there any published reports of organizations failing to take a position on the issue because of resistance to repeal, although it is probable that some groups remained silent for this reason. It appears that during this period of time the organizations that did decide to act had memberships that were generally favorable to the repeal position. In groups where such sympathy did not exist, the issue was not broached at all.

A number of anti-repeal organization endorsements were generated in time for the Senate hearing. The Catholic Physicians' Guild, Catholic Social Services, the Knights of Columbus, and the Catholic Women's Guild all took official positions opposing abortion law repeal, and the Roman Catholic diocese of Honolulu reiterated its official opposition. Both the superintendent of Catholic schools and the chief administrator of St. Francis Hospital testified in their official capacities.

The Aloha Club, a fraternal organization on the island of Maui, supported Robert Pearson's anti-abortion efforts financially but did not announce a position publicly or testify at the hearing. Likewise, the (Roman Catholic) Holy Name Society circulated an anti-abortion petition but did not announce an official organization position or send a representative to testify against the repeal bill at the hearing.

After the hearing, some non-Catholic opposition arose in organizations, particularly on the neighbor islands, but it resulted in inaction rather than endorsement of an anti-abortion position. For example, the question of endorsing abortion law repeal was raised at a mid-February meeting of the Lehua (Hawaii island) Jaycees. After some discussion, the group decided not to take a stand.[20] Shortly thereafter, the Presidents' Committee of the State Association of Hawaiian Civic Clubs defeated a resolution proposed by the Kauai Hawaiian Civic Club to urge the Governor to veto any abortion law repeal measure. The organization did not take a public stand on the issue.[21]

Organization endorsements seem to have been used as a means of generating public interest and support only on the pro-repeal side of the issue. Most of the small number of anti-repeal endorsements came from groups which were already officially committed to opposing repeal because of their religious affiliations with the Catholic Church. Opposition in other organizations was apparently either very limited or unorganized. Only at a very late stage did such opposition begin to mobilize, and then it was sufficient only to prevent the announcement of a few organization endorsements for the repeal bill.

Rather than demonstrating a genuine absence of opposition to abortion law repeal in the state, the lack of anti-abortion organization positions seems primarily to reflect the organizational and tactical weaknesses of the opposition. The Catholic diocese concentrated on mobilizing support within its own membership, largely by reiterating the Church's official position. Since the affiliated organizations were expected to follow the official position, there was no point in urging them to take an organization position of their own. In fact, once the Drinan argument had been presented as an alternative Catholic position, it might have been dangerous to do so. Robert Pearson was trying to arouse support outside the Catholic community, but he did not grasp the political significance of endorsements by organizations. Instead, he concentrated on direct mass approaches such as speeches, letter writing campaigns, and demonstrations.

By contrast, the successful use of the tactic of organization endorsements illustrates a key feature of the pro-repeal campaign: the delicate bridge between spontaneous, grass roots activity and the dedicated efforts of a few people. A relatively small number of activists stimulated the consideration of an endorsement for abortion law repeal in a great many organizations. Joan Hayes reports that she raised the issue with everyone she met and asked them why particular organizations they belonged to had not yet taken a stand.[22] Some of the unexpected endorsements can be attributed directly to the presence of one active repeal supporter in an organization. Others came about because a few repeal supporters in an organization argued effectively that the issue was intrinsically related to the group's activities and goals.

Yet for an organization to take a public stand on the abortion issue, the activists in the group had to convince others and bring about a collective decision. The organizations which announced public endorsements were not "front groups" or hastily formed dummy committees. Most were respected community organizations of long standing. All had formal procedures for conducting business and had to follow those requirements to make an official statement of support for abortion law repeal. An endorsement might be instigated by a single person or a small group, but it could not be accomplished without broad support.

Those familiar with abortion law repeal movements elsewhere have expressed surprise that such organizations as major labor unions and the Chamber of Commerce supported abortion law repeal in Hawaii.[23] The small size of the state and of the capital, Honolulu, undoubtedly made possible the quick development of support from formal organizations. Like the legislature itself, the major organizations in the state are small, accessible, and replete with overlapping memberships. If one person does not know anyone who belongs to a particular group, he probably knows someone else who does. This small-town intimacy not only made it easy to raise the possibility of endorsement for abortion law repeal in a variety of organizations, but the element of personal contact as well made it far more difficult for organizations to avoid the issue once it had been suggested.

The impact of an official endorsement from a prestigious or powerful statewide organization was probably as great in Hawaii as in many other states. However, the process of obtaining such an endorsement was much easier in Hawaii than elsewhere because of the state's small and highly concentrated population. Even so, major organization endorsements did not come about by chance. Joan Hayes perceived that the fastest way to mobilize public support for repeal and focus it effectively on the legislature was to get the politically powerful labor unions and other visible, prestigious community organizations to endorse the idea. The tactic was employed deliberately, and it worked.

OPINION POLLS

Another way of gauging public support for repeal and using that support at the same time to influence others was through opinion polls. The most important of these was the poll of members of the Hawaii Medical Association conducted by Dr. Roy Smith and Dr. George Goto at the request of Senator Yano and with the assistance of the American Association of University Women. The mailed questionnaire (which had a 54 percent return) was initiated before the AAUW meeting at which the repeal campaign was launched, and results were announced at the end of October, 1969. They showed that 96 percent of the responding physicians desired some change in the abortion law, with more than a third for total repeal. Among obstetricians in the sample, 56 percent were for total repeal.

This poll's results were well publicized and had considerable impact on opinion leaders. The evidence of broad support within the medical profession for abortion law reform or for outright repeal increased the willingness of medical organization leaders to take a strong stand and undoubtedly encouraged other organizations to act.

The poll also provided a much needed indication of the actual demand for abortion among Hawaii residents. In the same questionnaire the physicians were asked how many requests for abortions they had received from their patients during the previous year. The 425 physicians responding to the questionnaire reported 1557 requests for abortion, 677 of which had been referred for treatment (usually to Japan).[24]

Although Hawaii's sizeable Buddhist community was not too publicly involved in the repeal campaign, a poll reported in January, 1970 suggested that many Buddhists did support it. A survey of 95 members of the Honpa Hongwanji Mission Sunday School PTA was conducted by Dr. Shigeaki Fujitani, a psychologist with the University of Hawaii Counseling and Testing Center. The results were reported at a special seminar on Buddhism, Population and Family Life held at the East-West Center. Seventy percent of those surveyed were in favor of legalizing abortion, and half of the group believed it was right to have an abortion for personal reasons other than danger to health or rape.[25]

Several well timed polls of the general public were also taken. The first of these was perhaps the most significant in terms of influencing the public, although it suffered from serious flaws as an accurate gauge of public opinion. On October 25, 1969, the *Honolulu Star-Bulletin* published a questionnaire form called "Speak Up" that readers were urged to fill out and return to the newspaper office.[26] Over the next two weeks, the newspaper printed partial and then final returns as they were received. Because there was no control over the sample in the first place and persons could examine the partial results before entering their own opinions, the poll was not an accurate estimate of public opinion. In fact, the results differed substantially from subsequent polls using better sampling techniques. Nevertheless, all three reports of the poll showed identical breakdowns: 90 percent supported repeal, 6 percent supported liberalization, and 4 percent wanted no change in the law.[27] These results strongly reinforced the feeling of repeal supporters that the rest of the public was behind them.

The poll was probably more of an indication of the strength of individual commitment to each side of the issue rather than of the numbers of persons voting for each position. That is, more of those who were strongly for repeal may have taken the time both to fill out a questionnaire (or more than one) and turn it in, and perhaps to urge their friends to do the same. Even though partial returns were published early enough for those opposed to repeal to mobilize a counterattack, they did not do so.

Misleading as this poll may have been, it was extremely well timed and well reported for the benefit of the repeal campaign. The poll was conducted early in the campaign, when newsworthy events were not happening too frequently, and thus served to bring the issue of abortion law repeal to public attention at a crucial stage for the mobilization of support. The repeated reporting of both partial and final returns naturally heightened this effect.

Later in the campaign, several more accurate polls of registered voters were conducted. The first of these was conducted by Paul Larson, a student at Leeward Community College, under the supervision of William N. McIntire. This properly designed poll of 1500 registered voters from all precincts on Oahu, reported in mid-December, showed 41.3 percent of Oahu voters in favor of repeal and only 20 percent against any change.[28]

The *Star-Bulletin* conducted two polls of Oahu voters in February and March, 1970. In the February poll, conducted shortly after the widely publicized Senate hearing, 55 percent favored repeal. More men (63.2 percent) agreed with the repeal position than women (46.3 percent), but twice as many women were undecided (8.1 percent of men, 16.9 percent of women).[29]

The March poll was taken too late to be considered a tactic of the campaign, but its results suggest how effective the campaign tactics had been. The poll showed that support for the repeal bill had increased to 58.5 percent.[30] The increase was almost entirely due to women shifting from "undecided" to agreement with the repeal position.

MASS MEDIA

Conducting and reporting opinion polls was but one of many ways that the news media participated in the campaign. Both major Honolulu daily newspapers, the *Honolulu Star-Bulletin* and the

Honolulu Advertiser, supported repeal editorially as well as covering the campaign thoroughly in the news columns. The two newspapers share plant and advertising facilities and publish a combined Sunday edition but otherwise have separate editorial boards; the *Honolulu Advertiser* assumes responsibility for the combined Sunday edition. When the liberalized bill was before the House in March of 1969, the combined Sunday paper supported it editorially.[31]

The *Star-Bulletin* editorialized independently on April 12, 1969 in support of the 1969 reform bill but strongly suggested that it favored even greater liberalization.[32] Another editorial advised government leaders to keep church and state separate in voting on the abortion law. The message was clearly directed at Senator Yano, whose committee was then deliberating on H.B. 61.[33]

When Senator Yano announced in September, 1969 that he would seek repeal, the *Star-Bulletin* immediately supported his position.[34] In subsequent editorials, the *Star-Bulletin* continued to comment on specific events in the repeal campaign, particularly the actions of important persons such as the governor, the mayor of Honolulu, and the Catholic bishop of Honolulu. In all, the paper printed fifteen editorials and three political cartoons supporting abortion law repeal during seven months.

The *Honolulu Advertiser* also covered the campaign thoroughly with news, feature, and background articles. However, it did not endorse abortion law repeal editorially until February 9, 1970, immediately before the Senate vote on the repeal bill.[35] The *Advertiser* subsequently printed six editorials and three cartoons related to the repeal campaign.

Both newspapers gave reasonable coverage to anti-repeal activities, printed anti-repeal advertisements and letters to the editors, and reported major anti-repeal statements from the *Catholic Herald.* Both also provided some editorial page space for the opposition. The *Advertiser* printed a long anti-repeal article by a local social worker in its "Dissent" column[36] and another by local resident Claire Booth Luce.[37]

The two newspapers also devoted considerable space to abortion-related news from outside the state. This material included reports of legislative and judicial activity related to abortion laws, the statements of professionals outside the state, and statistics that could be used *pro* and *con* in the local abortion law campaign.

During the months of the repeal campaign in Hawaii, a number of significant events happened elsewhere that were directly related to the issue. These were brought to the attention of the Hawaii public through newspaper articles. Perhaps the most important to legislators were two judicial actions, in California and Washington, D.C., overturning abortion statutes that were essentially the same as Hawaii's existing abortion law.

On September 5, 1969, the California Supreme Court declared unconstitutional a law that permitted abortion only to save the life of the mother. Although the law in question had already been superceded by California's 1967 abortion reform law, the decision had a major impact because it dealt directly with the constitutional issues and was the first decision of any state high court on the consitutionality of restrictive abortion laws. The court declared that the law was unconstitutionally vague, was not justified by compelling state interest, and denied the rights of both the woman and the physician.[38]

Two months later, this California decision was cited in a Washington, D.C. ruling by Judge Arnold Gesell of the federal district court that struck down the District of Columbia's restrictive abortion law.[39] Although the U.S. Supreme Court subsequently upheld the constitutionality of the District of Columbia statute, with important interpretations, Judge Gesell's decision overturning the then-current abortion law in the District of Columbia created exactly the situation advocated by the abortion law repeal movement in Hawaii. Both cases were thoroughly reported in newspaper articles in the Honolulu dailies.

Another event that had an important impact on the Hawaii situation was the growing concern about the safety of oral contraceptive pills. In September 1969, the Federal Drug Administration reported that although the pills were still considered safe, a definite cause-and-effect relationship had been established between use of the pills and deaths due to blood clotting disorders. The British Drug Safety Commission was also issuing warnings about the greater danger of high-estrogen forms of the pill. Following these disclosures, U.S. Senator Gaylord Nelson began a probe of the safety of oral contraceptives. His subcommittee conducted widely publicized public hearings on the issue from January 14, 1970 through March, 1970. A Gallup poll taken in late January, 1970 found that alarm generated by the Nelson hearings had already led 18 percent of American women on oral contraceptives to discontinue using them, and another 23 percent were considering discontinuation.[40] Public attention to the problem of the safety of birth control pills coincided exactly with the peak of Hawaii's abortion law repeal campaign, and it contributed a great deal to the legitimization of abortion as an alternate means of preventing unwanted births.

In the newspapers, the public had two means of expressing personal opinions on the abortion issue: letters to the editor and paid advertisements. Letters to the editor, printed regularly in both newspapers, played a role in the campaign from early in 1969. During the peak of legislative activity on the repeal bill in February, 1970, the volume of letters to the editor rose dramatically. The *Honolulu Advertiser* published forty-eight pro-repeal letters to the editor during the month of February. In all, the *Advertiser* published sixty-two pro-repeal and twenty-seven anti-repeal letters, while the *Star-Bulletin* published forty-seven pro-repeal and twenty-two anti-repeal letters. The 158 letters were written by 139 different persons. Repeal campaign leader Joan Hayes led the field with seven letters. Gerri Madden, an indefatigable campaigner and colorful letter-to-the-editor writer on moral and spiritual subjects, opposed repeal with six letters.

The letters provided a means for citizens to comment on the events of the campaign and to try to influence the readership. They sometimes served to correct errors or to counteract the effect of particular statements or events. On occasion the letters could be termed educational, but more generally they were a means of keeping the issue alive and of suggesting how private citizens felt.

Newspapers also served to disseminate information and opinions through paid advertisements. During the course of the campaign, four large paid advertisements appeared. One was placed by pro-repeal groups and three by persons who were anti-repeal. The pro-repeal advertisement was primarily a list of the organizations that supported repeal and a brief review of the arguments, followed by an appeal to readers to call or write their legislators. The advertisement was sponsored by the University of Hawaii Abortion and

Birth Control Committee but was paid for by contributions from the listed organizations and other individual donors.[41]

Two full-page anti-repeal advertisements were paid for by Robert Pearson. His first advertisement announced a forthcoming silent march on the Capitol. Most of this ad was devoted to a series of arguments against abortion. The advertisement included a list of legislators and urged readers to write or telephone them to oppose abortion law repeal.[42] It was similar in format and tone to the University Abortion and Birth Control Committee's pro-repeal ad but was much larger.

Pearson's second advertisement and another anti-repeal advertisement paid for by Dr. Douglas Doyle were markedly different in tone. On February 16, 1970, both Honolulu newspapers ran a full-page advertisement sponsored by Pearson which featured enlarged drawings of various stages of fetal development to dramatize the point that the fetus has a right to life.[43]

The final anti-repeal advertisement aroused considerable controversy. It was placed by a Dr. Douglas J. Doyle, who identified himself as a retired Chicago physician. The bottom of the ad carried the additional notation that he was a member of the American Academy of General Practice and the American Medical Association. Dr. Doyle first came to the attention of the public when he offered spontaneous testimony at the end of the Senate hearing.

His half-page advertisement, entitled "History Repeats Abortions," carried a picture of the Biblical scene of Pontius Pilate washing the blood of Jesus from his hands, with a smaller picture of a large crowd of children superimposed upon it. A long, rambling essay followed, beginning with an analogy between the Biblical scene and Governor Burns' position if he did not veto the abortion bill. The text contained questionable descriptions of how abortions were performed and argued that women were safer in the hands of illegal abortionists.

Dr. Doyle also repeated the argument he had made at the Senate hearing, that black women do not make use of abortion or contraception and consequently multiply faster than Caucasians.[44] Aside from its racist implications, the idea that blacks might overpopulate more than Caucasians if abortion were permitted made no sense in Hawaii, where the population in 1970 was only 1 percent black and just under 40 percent Caucasian.[45]

hastily organized march to the Capitol. Only about forty persons participated, and no legislators or government officials were on hand to greet them on arrival. One of the forty marchers was a fourteen-year-old pregnant Roman Catholic school student whose presence was apparently intended to embarrass Catholics.[1] This was the only demonstration by advocates of abortion law repeal. It was organized by an outsider, and it was generally considered a failure. Thereafter, the local leaders of the repeal movement concentrated on more personal forms of contact with the legislators.

Led by Maui businessman Robert Pearson, persons opposed to abortion repeal held two demonstrations at the Capitol. These demonstrations attracted more participation, but little more legislative interest, than the Baird demonstration. In the first demonstration approximately two hundred and eighty persons, including some forty children who were either handicapped or had birth defects, marched silently to the Capitol on February 1, 1970. The participants came largely from the Knights of Columbus and Our Lady of Peace Council.[2] The presence of the handicapped and deformed children was intended to attract sympathy for the right to life of such children, an argument against the clause in the ALI model abortion law which stipulated that abortions could be performed when there is reasonable certainty that the child would be born defective. The local repeal bill, however, contained no such clause, since it did not require any medical conditions for abortion. This anti-abortion demonstration, like the previous pro-repeal march, was widely regarded by supporters of both sides as having been in bad taste.

Pearson organized another demonstration at the Capitol the day before the first Senate vote, but most legislators were not at the Capitol that day. The crowd, estimated at seven hundred and fifty to one thousand people, included senior classes that were released from two Catholic high schools specifically to attend the rally. The demonstrators were addressed by Bishop Scanlan, Monsignor Kekumano, and Robert Pearson.[3]

Comparing all the tactics used by both sides, demonstrations involved the least amount of direct personal contact between the advocates of a particular cause and either their representatives in government or their less-committed fellow citizens. They also seemed to carry the connotation, both with the general public and with the legislators, of being the tactic of unpopular, isolated out-groups fighting minority causes. By avoiding demonstrations, the local advocates of repeal helped enhance the image that abortion law repeal was a respectable issue with a broad base of support in the community. On the contrary, it was the anti-repeal forces that were seen as needing to resort to undesirable tactics.

PETITIONS

A slightly more individualized approach was the voters' petition. One of the first tactics to be organized was a petition campaign conducted by Zero Population Growth. The briefly worded petition forms stated that those signing were registered Hawaii voters who supported repeal of Hawaii's abortion law. Petitions were circulated on the university campus and at many public events in January, 1970. ZPG was very careful to restrict the petition to registered Hawaii voters. By the time of the Senate hearing in early February, five thousand signatures had been collected.[4] A month later, the opposition also began a petition campaign in which three thousand signatures were ultimately collected. The petitions were sponsored by the Holy Name Society and distributed in Catholic churches and through the Catholic schools. They read as follows:

> Whereas abortion is a crime against the human race in that it is the killing of an unborn human being, and whereas abortion is a denial of the Right to Life as guaranteed in the Constitution of the United States, and whereas we are living in an age that seeks to destroy the basic tenets that are the foundation of our Judeo-Christian heritage, and whereas it is ideas such as these whereby we are failing to transmit to the modern generation the VALUES that were handed down to us, thereby causing their dropping out from a corrupt Society, BE IT KNOWN that the undersigned, a voting citizen, is against any change in the present abortion law.[5]

Both sides regarded signature petitions as a reasonable means of convincing legislators of the amount of support their cause commanded among the electorate. They were a cheap, easy, and familiar means of counting noses. Considerable energy was spent distributing the materials and soliciting signatures.

In retrospect, the technique was a relatively ineffective means of persuasion. Even though the signature identified the petitioner personally, the amount of effort and degree of commitment required were minimal. No personal interaction was involved, nor was any serious attempt at argument or persuasion made. Although the persons soliciting signatures may have made some attempt to screen participants, the legislators and politicians who were the recipients of the petitions had only their word that the petitioners were as represented: registered voters, with no duplications. The legislators also did not know how many of the signers, if any, were his own constituents. Since every legislator had personally collected signature petitions as part of the process of filing for election, he was well aware of the amount of screening and checking required to produce a *bona fide* petition. He was not nearly as impressed as the petition circulators were by the volume of signatures collected. In fact, the petition campaigns may have been more effective in keeping the issue alive among the citizenry than they were in influencing legislators.

MAIL AND TELEPHONE CONTACT WITH LEGISLATORS

Somewhat more effective than petitions were organized campaigns to write or telephone legislators as each house of the legislature prepared to vote. Advocates for both sides ran large newspaper advertisements exhorting readers to call or write their legislators. The advertisements conveniently included the names and telephone numbers of the legislators. Anti-repeal leader Robert Pearson also organized a letter-signing campaign on his home island of Maui. Pearson personally delivered to the state Capitol a parcel of approximately 8,000 anti-repeal letters, most of which were duplicated form letters.[6]

To determine the use and efficacy of various tactics on legislators, a questionnaire was sent to all members of Hawaii's House and Senate.[7] The twenty-seven legislators from both houses (39 percent of the total) who responded to the relevant items on the mailed questionnaire reported receiving a high volume of mail and telephone calls on the abortion issue. The figures reported reveal some interesting patterns. There was definitely a higher volume of anti-repeal mail, reflecting the differential emphasis the two sides put on organized letter campaigns. Overall, the legislators reported receiving an average of seventy-seven pro-repeal letters and one hundred and seventy anti-repeal letters each. All considered that this was unusually high compared to mail on other issues. The mail was not randomly distributed, however. The anti-repeal mail seems to have been heavily concentrated on certain legislators. Those who voted for repeal reported receiving somewhat more pro-repeal mail, an average of ninety-four letters for to fifty-one against repeal. Those who voted against repeal were receiving extremely heavy anti-repeal mail, an average of eighteen letters for to five hundred and eighty six against.

For telephone calls, the volume was somewhat reversed, although legislators still received more response in accord with their own final vote. Overall, the legislators in the sample received an average of twenty-four telephone calls advocating repeal and nine phone calls against repeal. However, those who voted for the repeal bill received an average of thirty calls for repeal and ten phone calls against, while those who voted against the bill received an average of four calls for repeal and six phone calls against. It is difficult to say how the letters or phone calls influenced legislators. There was a correlation between a legislator's vote and the direction in which mail and phone calls were running. However, this may reflect basic differences in constituencies or in the previously announced positions of the various legislators and thus cannot be considered an indication of the effectiveness of such letter or phone campaigns.

VISITS TO LEGISLATORS

An even more direct method of influencing legislators was through personal visits. Obviously, such a technique could not be carried out on the same scale as letter writing and telephoning, but the concentration of population in Honolulu, the state capital, was a favorable factor. Once again, both pro-repeal and anti-repeal forces utilized visits to legislators, but with important differences in style. The supporters of abortion law repeal used the visits largely as a tactic for bringing community opinion to the policy makers, although there was some attempt to exert political pressure at the end of the campaign. Those opposed to repeal used visits primarily in attempts to apply high-level political pressure on the lawmakers.

Various groups of abortion law repeal supporters organized four different types of legislative visits. One type was primarily an educational effort. In early January, 1970, the Citizens' Committee for Repeal of Hawaii's Abortion Laws, a coalition of eleven civic, professional, and labor organizations, presented sets of books relevant to abortion law repeal to the chairmen of the Senate and House committees responsible for the repeal bill. Participating organizations included the American Association of University Women, the American Civil Liberties Union, Democratic Action Group, Episcopal Church of Hawaii, Friends of the Earth, Hawaii AFL-CIO, Hawaii Council of Churches, Hawaii Public Health Association, Hawaii United Methodist Church (Committee on Christian Social Concerns), International Longshoremen's and Warehousemen's Union, Local 142, Hawaii Mental Health Association, Moiliili Community Center, National Association of Social Workers (Hawaii Chapter), Sierra Club, Unitarian Church of Honolulu, and Zero Population Growth.

The event was well publicized and served to emphasize the reasonable yet concerned tone of the repeal campaign. Every legislator received a copy of a small paperback book by Alan Guttmacher, *The Case for Legalized Abortion Now.* The cover letter accompanying the gift explained that additional relevant books had been presented to the House and Senate committee chairmen and were available for the use of all legislators. In addition, the letter announced that the legislator would be visited in the near future by representatives of the Citizens' Committee who would seek his "opinions and comments on the abortion issue."[8]

The same tone was maintained in the second type of visit, a virtually complete personal canvas of the legislature. This was conducted primarily by the local chapter of Zero Population Growth. Well-informed representatives spoke with individual legislators both to influence their attitudes and to determine where they stood. A card file was developed that enabled the organization to gauge the repeal bill's voting strength. Later in the campaign this card file was made available to help direct the energies of other repeal supporters toward those legislators whose votes were in doubt.[9]

The canvassing technique was especially valuable because it counteracted the natural tendency of concerned citizens to shower their attention on legislators who already agreed with them and to ignore those unknown legislators whose votes might be won by sound argument and a display of voter interest. The statistics on letters to legislators presented previously suggest that the anti-repeal forces may have fallen into this trap.

As a third type of visit, the local chapter of the American Association of University Women organized a "Visit Your Legislators Day" for its members shortly before the vote was taken in both houses. This event was not a demonstration, and it was not even specifically tied to the abortion issue. Its purpose was to encourage AAUW members to communicate directly with legislators on any issues that concerned them. The AAUW members who participated went to the state Capitol individually or in small groups. The visitors were assisted by the association's organizers in finding their own district representatives. Visitors spoke briefly with the legislators when it was possible and left a personal note to indicate their concern when it was not. About forty AAUW members participated in these visits, covering about half of the Senate and one third of the House.[10] Although this event was not directly linked to the abortion law repeal campaign, many of the participants used the occasion to express their support for abortion law repeal.

In all of these three types of visits, the tone was reasonable social concern based on factual evidence. The aim was to build a dignified, respectable aura around the issue of abortion law repeal, and persons who would damage that image were gently discouraged from participating in the legislative visits.

The final use of the visit technique by supporters of abortion law repeal came during the tense waiting period after the legislature had approved the bill. The governor, having received a bill approved by both houses of the state legislature, had to sign it, veto it, or let it pass without his signature. Although Governor John Burns had previously indicated in an unofficial statement that he would allow the bill to pass without his signature, his personal convictions against abortion were well known, and since that statement he had been subjected to considerable political pressure to veto the bill. To apply additional countervailing pressure and remind him of his statement to let the bill pass into law, several repeal supporters, directed by Joan Hayes, arranged a meeting with the governor. The delegation included representatives of major unions, community organizations, and religious groups, including a Catholic nun. Each had been active in the repeal movement and represented some recognizable constituency. The meeting was reserved and largely symbolic; the delegates announced their concern for passage and reminded the governor of his public comment to let the bill become law. The governor listened to the group but did not reveal his intentions.[11]

The final meeting was the closest the repeal forces came to applying direct political pressure to get the law passed. The meeting was with the highest political official in the state, and participants included representatives of politically powerful labor unions. Yet even in this instance, the union representatives were accompanied by persons from small, nonpolitical community groups and individual parishes. The union representatives had not organized the meeting but had agreed to come at Joan Hayes' request.

On the anti-repeal side, two politically powerful figures attempted to influence the decision by personal contact with lawmakers: the Roman Catholic bishop and the mayor of Honolulu. Each instance provoked cries of outrage from the public.

The first and most celebrated case occurred in February, 1970, shortly after the lengthy public Senate hearing had ended. The Roman Catholic bishop of Honolulu, Bishop John Scanlan, had been invited to testify at the Senate committee's hearing on February 3. He declined this offer and instead sent representatives. The following day, however, he asked to address a special joint session of the legislature. This request was denied, but on February 6 he was granted a special private meeting to which legislators from both houses were invited. The meeting was to be closed both to the public and to the press. It was arranged by the Senate president and the Speaker of the House, and was attended by twenty-three legislators.

Public objection arose immediately to the private nature of the meeting and the special privilege it entailed. Primarily because of the protests, the start of the meeting was delayed, and it was then opened to the press. Besides receiving front page coverage in the two Honolulu dailies, the text of the bishop's remarks was printed in full in the *Hawaii Catholic Herald.*[12] Public indignation continued for some time, with sixteen letters to the editor opposing the visit appearing in the newspapers. A professor at the University of Hawaii wrote to the Senate President and House Speaker requesting equal time, but he was politely refused.[13]

The bishop had not foreseen the furor the private meeting would engender. It was so great that he responded personally with a letter to the editor in both newspapers in which he tried to explain his intent. He explained that he had felt during the Senate hearings that his representatives could "carry the ball, and I naturally felt that if I could talk to the legislators the impact would be greater. The bogey of the Medieval Church never entered my mind and I did not feel I was 'throwing my weight around.' "

After pointing to the precedent that a bishop had once spoken to the United States Congress, he continued:

> As I saw it, this issue was within my sphere of competence, because it had to do with a grave moral problem and I felt that if the legislators would allow me, I should present my case.
>
> I also noted that no constitutional lawyer had come forward to give the trend of law, as exemplified in court cases on this issue, during the last few decades especially. Accordingly, I decided to do some homework on that point, even though it might be inadequate, and present it to the legislators if allowed to do so.[14]

As the furor over the bishop's private audience began to die down, the mayor of Honolulu belatedly became involved in the issue. On February 18, just after the joint Senate-House conference committee had agreed on the final form of the abortion bill, the mayor sent a personal appeal to the legislature not to pass the bill. He asked the legislators to delay the vote to give the public a chance to digest the effects of the change on the community. He announced that he was doing so out of personal conviction.[15] Many observers, however, believed his motives were political. The following week, after the bill had passed both houses in final form, the mayor announced that he would ask the governor to veto it.[16] Mayor Fasi's last-ditch efforts were viewed with suspicion by many but did not arouse the same degree of concern as the bishop's visit. It was widely believed that the bishop might actually influence lawmakers' decisions. In fact, neither the mayor's nor the bishop's appeals at this stage had any appreciable effect on the outcome.

THE PUBLIC HEARINGS

All the ways of influencing legislation discussed thus far were carried out completely on the initiative of citizens. However, the legislators themselves also provided an official opportunity for public expression of opinion. The Senate Public Health, Welfare and Housing Committee held open hearings on the abortion law repeal bill.

The well-publicized hearing was scheduled for February 3, 1970 but continued the following night in order to accommodate all those who wished to testify. An audience of about five hundred persons overflowed the Capitol building hearing room, and the session was also broadcast live on local radio. The audience at home and at the Capitol listened and counted with the legislators to see which way the testimony would go. The reactions of the audience were emotional, and occasionally the testimony was interrupted by applause. Sixty persons, 76 percent of all those who testified, testified in favor of repeal, and eighteen persons testified against repeal. All of the eighteen opposed were identified as Roman Catholics, including both those testifying as representatives of Catholic organizations and those testifying as private citizens.

The hearing provided a natural climax to the repeal campaign. It placed all the various groups and persons committed to the issue in direct communication with key legislators. The distribution of persons and organizations presenting testimony reveals the broad support engendered by the repeal campaign as well as the range of the opposition.

Over half the persons testifying represented organizations that had taken official stands on the issue. Delegates from seven occupational and professional organizations, including two large unions (ILWU and AFL-CIO), testified in favor of repeal. A prominent judge of the family court (Samuel King, who was a leader of the state Republican party), representatives of three government social service agencies, and five other social agencies also supported repeal, with only one social agency (Catholic Social Services) sending a representative to testify against the bill. In addition, eleven political, educational, and social groups had representatives testify for repeal, as did seven representatives from organizations of various religious faiths. Five Catholic organizations had members testify against repeal.

Among all persons testifying as private citizens, twenty-five were in favor of repeal and eleven were opposed. In all, 70 percent of the people and 83 percent of the organizations represented at the hearing advocated passage of the repeal bill. While these figures cannot be projected into population figures, they do legitimately provide a fair estimate of the amount of active support on each side of the argument.

Four religious professionals advocated repeal, including three

Protestant ministers and one Catholic nun; two Catholic priests and one nun opposed it. Eight physicians supported repeal, two of them representing professional medical societies. Three physicians, two in local practice in Hawaii and one a retired visitor from the mainland, all testifying as private citizens, opposed abortion repeal. Six social workers testified in favor of the repeal bill, four of whom represented different organizations of social workers or social agencies. Only two social workers argued against repeal, one as representative of Catholic Social Services and the other as a private citizen.

Nine faculty members from the University of Hawaii testified in favor of the repeal bill as citizens with relevant professional knowledge.[17] The person testifying against repeal on behalf of the Knights of Columbus was also a university faculty member. In addition, five university students testified for repeal as representatives of organizations.

The hearings provided the most direct opportunity for citizens to influence legislators. The Hawaii legislature vests considerable power in its standing committees, and the major deliberation on proposed legislation is expected to take place within committees.

> This is the stage at which most bills die, for many receive unfavorable recommendations and are consequently not reported out. A standing committee has a large measure of responsibility in the legislative process because of its power in deciding which measures to act upon.[18]

Public hearings are one of the key ways committee members learn about both the arguments surrounding a particular proposal and the strength of public sentiment concerning it. Under normal circumstances, the hearings are attended by some or all members of the committee. Other legislators rely on the committee report and other formal and informal systems of information and influence to make up their minds when the bill comes before the entire house for a vote. One clear measure of the importance the abortion issue had assumed was the presence at the public hearings of many legislators who were not members of the Senate Committee on Public Health, Welfare and Housing. Many more listened to the hearings on the radio. These particular hearings served to educate a much broader range of legislators than merely the members of the committee.

The public hearings offered a particularly effective format for influencing legislators. Each person testifying was requested to submit copies of his written testimony in advance so that committee members could study the detailed arguments and supporting evidence. Oral testimony provided an immediate opportunity for persuasion as well as an opportunity for the committee members to pose additional questions and obtain clarification of specific points. Although the length of oral testimony was restricted to conserve time, such testimony provided more opportunity to develop an argument and present evidence than most other forms of communication with busy legislators.

The public hearing is undoubtedly a mere formality for many types of legislation, and the real influence process takes place behind closed doors for reasons unrelated to the intrinsic merits of the issue. For the abortion law repeal issue, however, the public hearing was a genuine point of influence on legislators, and the medium of influence was actually the strength of the arguments.

Even though the hearing was without question the focal point for public influence on the legislature, it attained that significance largely because of the build-up of interest in the issue by means of various other events over a period of five months. Without this period of public education and arousal, the February, 1970 abortion hearing would have been no more spectacular than the 1967 and 1969 hearings on earlier abortion bills.

Similarly, the growing public interest in the issue aroused legislative concern. Abortion law change had become an issue on which each legislator had to form a personal opinion which he could defend. Legislators were actively seeking information, and the public hearings provided an excellent opportunity to obtain it. If abortion had not already become a hot political issue, most legislators would not have felt the need for self-education, and the impact of the hearings would have been limited to those legislators on the committee.

THE EFFECTIVENESS OF THE TACTICS

There is no sure way to evaluate the effectiveness of the various tactics in influencing public opinion, except perhaps to point to the overall increase in opinion poll support for repeal as indirect evidence that, collectively, the tactics had some effect. However, the questionnaire sent to legislators provides considerable information on how effective various tactics were in influencing the men with the power to change the law. Among other questions, the legislators were asked, "How did you respond to the following expressions of public opinion concerning the abortion issue?" Following this was a list of various possibilities, such as petitions, letters, and phone calls. They were then asked to check whether each specific expression "influenced my thinking" or "did not influence my thinking." While the format did not distinguish between positive and negative influence, the pattern of responses suggests that those who were negatively influenced by a particular technique reported that it had not influenced their thinking.

Overall, the single most important influence was the Senate public hearings. While reports on which part of the testimony was influential varied considerably, only two persons in the sample responding to the question reported that they were not influenced by any aspect of the hearings. Moreover, nearly 50 percent of all legislators who responded reported that the hearings were the crucial point at which they made up their minds on the issue.

The aspect of the hearings most frequently cited by the legislators as influencing their thinking was testimony by physicians. This was checked by three fourths of the group. Next most influential were personal experience testimony and statistics presented in testimony. These were each reported by 60 percent of the legislators polled. Half the respondents listed hearing testimony by private citizens, and over 40 percent cited the moral arguments made (on both sides) as influencing them. More than a third reported being influenced by the testimony of clergy, scholars, and organizations.

Among influences on the legislators other than the hearings, personal contacts and educational materials seem to have been most important, along with the positions taken by various organizations. Half of the legislative respondents reported being influenced by educational materials presented by organizations, while over 40 percent were influenced by official organization positions, office visits, and individual letters from constituents. Just under 40 percent reported being influenced by newspaper coverage and editorials, with over one third also being influenced by telephone calls from constituents.

These figures suggest that, overall, legislators were influenced by the educational, factual tone of the abortion law repeal campaign and by the personal efforts of repeal supporters. Although the emphases were somewhat different, the small number of legislators in the sample who reported that they voted against repeal also were largely influenced by a combination of personal contact and testimony presented at the Senate hearings. Five of the six legislators in this category reported that personal visits from constituents influenced their thinking, while two thirds reported being influenced by the testimony of private citizens and physicians. Half said they were influenced by the testimony of people presenting their personal experiences or by moral arguments. Those legislators who voted against repeal and reported that they were influenced by moral arguments also reported being influenced by sermons in their own church and testimony by clergy. The same legislators reported that they were Catholic.

The order of the tactics which did *not* influence the thinking of legislators again emphasizes the lawmakers' preference for personal contact with ordinary constituents. All but one of the legislators responding reported that their thinking was not influenced by demonstrations at the Capitol or by newspaper advertisements. Most legislators (89 percent) said they were not influenced by Bishop Scanlan's audience with the legislature. Mimeographed letters and newspaper letters to the editor did not have any influence on 85 percent of the legislators and three quarters of the respondents reported that their thinking was not influenced by the abortion movie shown on television, public opinion polls, or sermons in their churches.

Those who voted against repeal reported that they were not appreciably influenced (i.e., not more than one person of the six reported influence) by mimeographed letters, the various mass media techniques, public opinion polls, Bishop Scanlan's audience with the legislature, demonstrations at the Capitol, educational materials presented by organizations, statistics in the testimony, testimony by lawyers or organizations, or official positions taken by organizations. In general, they seem to have been less influenced by outside forces of any kind and to have based their decisions more on pre-existing personal convictions.

In sum, the repeal campaign's restrained but active educational approach appears to have been effective in convincing legislators who did not already have a personal moral commitment on the issue. The two key tactical elements in the campaign's success were: (1) the two-stage strategy of first convincing the public and then getting the public to convince the legislature, and (2) the emphasis on calm evaluation of the material presented in evidence. In effect, the public hearings before the legislature represented the same type of educational forum of knowledgeable opinion leaders that had first convinced the public. The strong emphasis on reason and facts helped the repeal advocates avoid both ineffective demonstrations and personal attacks on the opposition. While the opposition tried to make a similar appeal to reason, it made more use of mass demonstration tactics and appeal to emotion as well. It also depended largely on inertia to maintain the *status quo*.

The legislators' own evaluation of what influenced their decision also clearly points up the importance of physicians' support of repeal. Legislators reported that the testimony of physicians at the hearing was most influential to their decisions. The support of physicians followed the same two-stage sequence as the broader educational campaign. The initial poll of physicians served to influence the community and generate support from other organizations, while the participation of physicians at the hearings had a further direct impact on legislators.

The support of physicians at the public hearing was especially important because it demonstrated that reputable physicians would perform abortions and that their colleagues would support them. Without such evidence of how abortion would actually be made available to the public if the law were changed, it is doubtful that the repeal bill would ever have come out of committee.

CHAPTER 5

Pro-Repeal Issues: Human Control of Social Problems

POLITICAL TACTICS do not function in isolation from issues. The abortion law campaign must also be assessed in terms of the issues it raised. The arguments employed by both sides may be evaluated for their persuasiveness and their impact on legislators.

As previously mentioned, the focal event of the abortion law repeal campaign was the public hearing held by the Senate Public Health, Welfare and Housing Committee on February 3 and 4, 1970. The hearing provided an open forum in which both citizens and organizations could present their views on the abortion bill directly to the legislators. Nearly half of the legislators who answered our questionnaire[1] (and over half of those who voted for repeal) reported that the hearing was the crucial point at which they made up their minds on the issue. The hearing testimony, therefore, provides an appropriate vehicle for analysis of the arguments and issues raised in the campaign.

The combined written and oral testimony presented to the committee[2] was analyzed in detail to determine the range and frequency of issues raised. While the discussion and documentation of the issues have been expanded for clarity, neither additional arguments nor subsequently published information have been added. The purpose of this discussion is to set forth the issues as they were raised and debated in Hawaii, not to provide a general summary of arguments that might be advanced or that were later used in other places. Further, the data are presented as given and were not always accurate or substantiated.

Officially, the testimony was requested in written form twenty-four hours in advance of the hearing. This was to allow for distribution of copies to members of the committee and the scheduling of presentations. However, as interest mounted, many persons who were unfamiliar with these procedures decided to testify. Several persons presented their written testimony to the committee at the hearing itself, after having made a telephoned request to testify. A few persons in the audience also obtained permission on the spot for brief testimony.

Because of the requirement of written documentation, the arguments were generally composed as formal speeches or declarations. However, many speakers deviated from their written testimony to raise additional points or to counter the arguments of previous speakers. In addition, speakers were frequently questioned by the Senate committee members and often took that opportunity to elaborate further.

Both sides viewed the hearing primarily as an opportunity to influence the legislators. Because of the extensive press and radio coverage and public attendance at the hearing, they regarded the public at large as a secondary audience to be influenced by the speeches. Although speakers formally addressed the committee, they spoke facing the audience in the auditorium with the committee members on the stage above and almost behind them. Radio, newspaper, and television personnel were positioned in front of the audience, directly beside the speaker's rostrum.

The speakers attempted both to present their own positive arguments and to anticipate and counter the arguments of the other side. Arguments spanned the areas of law, medicine, religion, social problems, ecology, the role and rights of women, and morality. Most of the disputes involved either the interfaces between these various areas or the relative priority of one over another. Moreover, several arguments were frequently linked together—and linked differently by the two sides.

The method of presentation did not provide opportunity for debate. In the main, the speakers refuted specific assertions of the other side or presented specific and pointed issues to be considered. Because the speakers were starting from different assumptions, the presentations of those on one side usually could not shake the faith behind the core arguments of the other side.

Such a stand-off is not surprising when we consider that the two sides drew support from completely different sources and that most people in one group had never heard of, or refused to recognize, the authorities cited by the other side. Neither side was really exposed to the other's sources or respected their value. For example, while the repeal advocates were quoting Paul Ehrlich, author of *The Population Bomb,*[3] the opposition was quoting Norman St. John-Stevas, British author of *The Right to Life.*[4] St. John-Stevas' views were reprinted in the *Hawaii Catholic Herald,* while Ehrlich's book was being distributed locally by Zero Population Growth. People with a previous sympathy for one side of the issue primarily accepted information which supported that predilection and rejected information which did not.

The arguments for repeal of Hawaii's abortion law were based on an unspoken set of assumptions. These basic assumptions are that the problems of life can and should be solved by man, and that the striving for such solutions demonstrates a person's moral worth. A corollary of this belief is the assumption that such striving by private citizens results in general public good. The key to controlling life's problems is the individual's ability to control his own thought and actions. Thus, high value is placed both on the exercise of individual responsibility and on each person's right to pursue his own beliefs even though others may disagree with him. These basic assumptions united the varied arguments put forth by abortion law repeal advocates, which will now be examined in turn.

THE FREQUENCY AND DANGERS OF ILLEGAL ABORTION

Several speakers testified that women faced with unwanted pregnancies seek abortions even when they are illegal, and that illegal abortions are extremely dangerous. As evidence, figures were offered estimating that one to three million illegal abortions were being performed each year in the United States and that about one in five pregnancies was purposely terminated, about 96 percent of them being terminated illegally.[5] Applied to Hawaii, these statistics led to an estimate of about thirty-five hundred women per year seeking abortions.[6] Using data from his survey of local physicians, Dr. Roy Smith of the University of Hawaii School of Public Health arrived at a very similar estimate of about three thousand Hawaii women a year seeking abortions.[7]

Additional statistics placed illegal abortion as the number one cause of maternal mortality in the United States.[8] Criminal abortions accounted for 50 percent of maternal deaths in New York and Pennsylvania, and 40 percent in Michigan.[9] Speakers emphasized that even though illegal abortions were unsafe, abortions performed by physicians under proper conditions were very safe. Dr. George Goto cited research from Czechoslovakia and Hungary showing that mortality from legal abortions was only six per 100,000. He compared this with the higher rate of death from tonsillectomy, which is seventeen per 100,000.[10]

An anonymous young woman dramatized the statistics on illegal abortions by describing her personal experience with a botched drugstore abortion in another state,[11] and a social worker, Mickey Hummer, reported that he knew of at least four unskilled, illegal abortionists operating in one depressed area of Honolulu. He added that those who could not afford even these services resorted to self-abortion.[12]

Making abortion illegal, it was argued, does not prevent abortions from occurring. It simply creates a new public health problem as women resort to dangerous illegal practices instead of being able to obtain safe, legal medical care.

ECONOMIC DISCRIMINATION

Under the existing law, it was pointed out, women with sufficient means could obtain safe abortions, either illegally from qualified physicians, semi-legally through sophisticated use of ambiguities in the law, or legally by travelling outside the state (usually to Japan). The poor, who could not afford the costs of such alternatives, were forced either to bear the unwanted child or to patronize dangerous illegal abortionists. Consequently, the law discriminated unfairly against the poor.[13]

Dr. Roy Smith pointed out that economically disadvantaged women are

> more likely to attempt self-induced abortion, or to resort to abortion by amateurs. In general, this same population has the least access to family planning information and supplies—techniques for preventing conception, and are forced to have most of the unwanted pregnancies. When data from the Hawaii study were analyzed, the disposition of requests for abortion according to economic status indicated that our present system, in circumventing the existing law,

> discriminates against women from the low income group and limits the choices available to them. Three times as many women in the low income group were refused or advised against abortion as were those in the higher income groups. The law was not intended to be applied on an economic basis although this seems to be the effect.[14]

Although no direct testimony was given about the performance of illegal abortions by qualified physicians in Hawaii, there was some testimony from persons who had helped Hawaii women obtain safe abortions. Dr. J. L. Erickson, a physician in general practice, reported that he had sent a number of his patients to Japan for abortions. He testified that after observing the problems caused by unwanted pregnancies and feeling frustrated by his inability to help his patients, he had developed contact with a reputable physician in Japan who performed legal abortions. He testified that most of those he sent to Japan were high school girls whose parents were involved in the decision and paid for the trip.[15]

Reverend Claude du Teil, an Episcopal minister, testified on behalf of Clergy Counseling Service, the group of local clergymen who had organized an abortion counseling and referral service along the lines of similar groups in several other states. He argued that repeal of the abortion law would remove the discrimination

> that now *de facto* exists against those unable to pay the price of a trip to Japan or to pay the price of working through the cumbersome procedure under which therapeutic abortions are available even now in Hawaii.[16]

The latter was a reference to the procedure, used by Clergy Counseling Service, of having a woman obtain two referrals from sympathetic psychiatrists who would attest to the fact that the pregnancy endangered her life because she was suicidal. In 1969 and early 1970, roughly the period from the formation of Clergy Counseling Service to the enactment of the new abortion law, 117 women obtained therapeutic abortions in Hawaii hospitals for psychiatric reasons. This represented an eightfold increase over the two previous years.[17]

CONTRACEPTION AND ABORTION

The advocates of repeal pointed out that birth control does not eliminate the need for abortion, because birth control methods sometimes fail. Failure rates for the most common types of contraceptives were reported to be: coitus interruptus, 15 to 30 percent; condom, 5 to 15 percent; diaphragm, 3 to 15 percent; intrauterine devices, 1 to 3 percent; spermicidal foams and jellies, 4 to 10 percent; and birth control pills, 0 to 5 percent.[18] Thus, even the best contraceptive practice may not prevent all unwanted pregnancies. Several speakers alluded to the U.S. Congressional (Nelson) hearings on the safety of birth control pills.[19]

Most speakers making this point emphasized that expanded birth control use should be encouraged, with abortion as a back-up solution and not as a primary or preferred method of birth control.[20] To allay the fear that greater availability of abortion would reduce the use of contraceptives, statistics from Japan were offered showing that abortion, once the most common method of family planning, was declining, while contraceptive use had increased 40 to 70 percent under an intensive government-sponsored family planning program.[21]

Many speakers also emphasized that abortion alone would not and should not be expected to solve all the existing problems. There would still be a need for more sex education and family planning programs. In addition, services would be needed to meet the new medical and social situations created by the availability of abortion.[22]

SOCIAL PROBLEMS OF ILLEGITIMACY AND UNWANTED CHILDREN

A major argument of repeal advocates was that the continuation of unwanted pregnancies causes serious social problems. One problem is illegitimacy and its many ramifications. Dr. William Hindle, an obstetrician and member of the board of directors of Child and Family Service, presented statistics of a typical day at Kapiolani Hospital, the state's major obstetrical facility. Of the thirty-four postpartum patients in the hospital on February 2, 1970 (the day before the hearings), eight were single. Of these, six were under the care of the Department of Social Services (DSS), while two were private patients. Five of the eight (all DSS patients) were planning to keep their babies. The women's ages ranged from eighteen to twenty-two, plus one forty-two year old. One eighteen year old and one twenty year old each had had three illegitimate children.[23]

It was pointed out that young women who marry to legitimize

the birth of a child also may produce social problems. Statistics from New York were cited showing that pregnancy is a major factor in school dropouts. Other studies found that one third to one half of teenage marriages were due to pregnancy, and half of these ended in divorce within eighteen months.

> Shotgun marriages tend to produce a very high number of broken homes in which a very young, uneducated mother must raise a child by herself, a situation which has been demonstrated in several studies to present a high risk of juvenile delinquency for the child.[24]

William G. Among, Director of the Department of Social Services and Housing, testified that the state welfare agency provides

> services to unmarried mothers, protective services to children, foster care services, adoption services and family planning services. The need for such services are oftentimes the result of an unwanted pregnancy and an unwanted child.
>
> In view of its program objectives, the Department wishes to express a position favoring the repeal of the present abortion prohibiting laws. This position is based on the premise that it is essential that all parents have access to information and services so that they will have the freedom to determine the number and spacing of children.[25]

The poverty cycle, it was stated, tends to perpetuate itself, so that the unwanted children of poor dependent families grow up to produce another generation in similar circumstances. Data were presented showing that 525 mothers in Hawaii who were receiving state Aid to Families with Dependent Children in 1967 had received the same assistance when they were children.[26]

More broadly, it was argued that unwanted children grow up with a variety of social handicaps that lead to problems for the society. As Laurel Kasaoka, speaking for the Democratic Action Group, put it:

> Good motherhood and responsible parenthood are not necessary to comply with compulsory pregnancy laws. The only requirement is that a woman remains pregnant and bear a child. The child resulting from compulsory pregnancy is by such laws guaranteed the right to existence and nothing more. Compulsory pregnancy laws have never been concerned with whether this child will have the physical, mental, and emotional sustenance it needs to develop into normal adulthood with a chance at what we call "the good life."[27]

Dr. Roy Smith, pediatrician and associate professor of maternal and child health at the University of Hawaii, testified:

> There is ample evidence that unwanted children produce an increase in mental illness, an increase in functional and cultural mental retardation, an increase in juvenile deliquency, crime and various other social ills. Every pregnancy and every child should be a wanted pregnancy and a wanted child.[28]

Many speakers referred to evidence associating unwanted children with various social problems. The evidence had previously been presented by speakers at educational public forums, in newspaper articles, and through other information channels so that by the time of the hearing, repeal advocates felt that it was established as fact.

The definitive research on the problem, which was cited during the campaign and which had particularly impressed Joan Hayes in her initial study of the abortion issue, was a Swedish study of the children of women who had been refused legal abortion. This research compared 120 children who were born after their mothers' applications for therapeutic abortion were denied, with a matched control sample (the next child of the same sex born in the same hospital). The subjects were followed from birth to age twenty-one. Based on objective records of child welfare boards, child guidance clinics, and other public documents, the unwanted children were found to have higher rates of juvenile delinquency, crime, mental illness, drunken misconduct, educational subnormality, lower age at marriage, unfitness for military service, and receipt of public assistance.[29]

Some of the speakers could also refer to their own professional experience as a basis for making the connection between unwantedness and social problems.[30] Jean Avery, testifying for the Hawaii chapter of the National Association of Social Workers, reported on a questionnaire which had been sent to the organization's membership. Of the 215 (out of the 307 members) who replied to the questionnaire, two thirds believed that repeal of the abortion law would help to reduce child welfare problems and child abuse cases.[31]

Dr. John Blaylock, psychologist, testified on behalf of the John Howard Association, a social agency involved in work with prisoners and parolees:

> While it is true that the major concerns of the John Howard Association do not normally include such matters, the Board felt that there is a clear and strong relationship between unwanted children and later criminal behavior. In the interest of reducing the crime and delinqency problem, we feel that our interest in abortion repeal is appropriate.[32]

Dr. Charles Stewart, representing the Hawaii Psychiatric Association, testified that

> a greal deal of suffering occurs to the woman who is pregnant against her wish and an ever greater toll results when such a pregnancy is carried to term or the individual is forced to look for an abortionist in keeping with her financial means. The injustice done to a child who comes into the world unwanted, however, is the main issue, for much of delinquency, crime, and later mental illness stem from this early basic unwantedness.[33]

The social problems related to unwanted children were seen as difficulties which could be solved or alleviated, once people understood what caused them and acted to change those conditions. The restrictive abortion laws were perceived as a major stumbling block to the reduction of social problems, because they forced women to bear children they had not planned and did not want. Moreover, the consequences of this situation went beyond the personal hardships of the families involved to affect the entire society.

ECONOMIC COSTS TO SOCIETY

A related argument was downplayed at the hearing, although it was mentioned occasionally among repeal supporters. This was the point that it was cheaper economically for the state to pay for abortions than to support illegitimate and unwanted children on the welfare rolls. This argument was hinted at within the general context of the social costs of abortion restrictions by referring to the antecedents of delinquency and illegitimacy and the poverty cycle, but listeners were generally left to do their own arithmetic. Committee members questioned Edwin Tam, who testified for the state Department of Social Services, regarding the welfare costs of abortion. Tam said that it would be legal for the department to pay for abortions (if the medical procedure were legal) and that the agency would probably need funds for this purpose. When Senator Percy Mirikitani asked which would cost more, the abortion or delivering and caring for the child, Tam replied that the child would cost more, but added, "DSS does not work on the cost factors."[34]

The cost argument was not raised strongly by repeal advocates because it was too politically explosive and would have detracted from the humane approach being emphasized. Senator Yano in particular realized what an emotional impact this argument would have on the Roman Catholic opposition, and he gently discouraged repeal supporters from pursuing it.

RESPONSIBILITY AND PROMISCUITY

While repeal supporters tried to emphasize the most respectable reasons for abortion, such as serious financial hardship, birth control failure, or pregnancy late in life, they were generally sympathetic to any unwanted pregnancy as legitimate grounds for abortion. They tended to regard the unwanted pregnancy as an unpleasant affliction presaging a host of social problems. Consequently, responsible action was equated with eliminating the problem pregnancy, rather than with accepting it.

Social worker Kay Foy testified that:

> There has been much discussion of how women *should* feel about abortion but little acknowledgment of how they *do* feel.
>
> For some women, the loss of a child, as in adoption, is more devastating than the loss of a fetus, as in abortion. For many women in an already precarious situation, to accept a child would be asking him to accept a tragic existence with them.
>
> Do you know that women who have abortions more often experience relief than guilt? That most women releasing their babies for adoption experience deep sorrow? That some parents lose their hope for survival in a family when a child is born?[35]

Community worker Marie Stires reiterated the theme with this comment:

> The people who are so horrified at the thought of interrupting a pregnancy when the fetus is still little more than a blob of ectoplasm think nothing of coercing an unwed mother into giving up her full-term, perfectly formed baby boy or girl—always, of course, for the good of the child.[36]

Sarah Pegg, representing the recent graduate section of the American Association of University Women, testified:

> Most of us have used, are using, or plan to use some form of birth control to allow us to plan our families. We do this because we believe it is important for every child to be born into an environment where he will be wanted, loved and cherished, and that a child is too precious to be allowed, let alone forced, to come into the world without such provision. . . .
>
> Because we want our children to have the best we can provide for them—emotionally, as well as materially—we do not feel it is morally right to continue a pregnancy when we believe the resulting child will be short-changed in terms of the love, care and attention we want to give it. We consider that abortion can and should be a logical addition to the methods available for planning families.[37]

This view was consistent with the general orientation of the repeal advocates toward controlling nature and maximizing the quality of life. Control over one's fertility was desirable. Preconception control was superior, but postconception control through abortion was better (i.e., more responsible) than no control at all. Thus, whatever the circumstances by which the pregnancy came about, the long-term consequences of abortion, both for the woman and for society, were judged superior to those of bearing the unwanted child.

Social worker Earlene Chambers also put the issue in terms of moral responsibility.

> In a society, complex and overburdened by multitudes of social-(personal)-people "type" problems, more and more we are urging that the key to survival is responsibility for one's own actions. In this light, may I call to your attention that in no way does logical reasoning require a person to be "responsible" for duties, obligations, etc., that he does not in full conscience accept.
>
> Every child born into our society desires to be wanted. Every woman, before she bears a child, shoud be urged by society to realize her obligations and privileges in this respect. No woman should be forced to bear an unwanted child. Women are not chattels—nor brood mares—nor pieces of property.
>
> This legislature holds the position of being able to set guidelines in responsibility—by assuring each person protection of his individual right and making it clear that citizenship in a democracy derives its essence by the responsibility of each person for his own acts.[38]

The repeal supporters also clearly rejected the idea that carrying a pregnancy to term could serve as an adequate deterrent to premarital sex. It was argued that despite many changes in birth control practice during the past fifty years, there had been little dramatic change in sexual behavior. Dr. Milton Diamond, associate professor of anatomy at the University of Hawaii School of Medicine and specialist in sexual behavior, testified that all reliable studies showed no precipitously marked change in sexual behavior in the United States since the 1920s. He pointed out that attitudes toward the behavior, however, have changed. "People will now more openly discuss what they do; they don't necessarily do more," and added that modern teenaged and adult women feel less guilty about their sexual feelings.

> Reliable studies show that despite the popular magazine articles, today's teenage girls have premarital experiences about as frequently as their mothers and grandmothers; approximately 50% have premarital coitus by the age of 20 and 3% by the age of 15, and about 12% of these girls have at least one induced abortion by the age of 40.[39]

In response to a direct question from Senator Yano, "Will repeal lead to promiscuity?" Diamond replied, "Not according to the best statistics, sexual behavior does not change drastically due to a change in law."[40]

In general, repeal supporters did not accept the idea that giving birth should be a punishment or a lesson in responsibility. They saw high rates of illegitimacy and illegal abortion as evidence that fear of pregnancy is not a strong deterrent to intercourse. At the same time they pointed to the consequences of both illegitimacy and illegal abortion as too high a price to pay for whatever deterrence might be accomplished by denying abortions to those with unwanted pregnancies.

POPULATION CONTROL AND THE QUALITY OF LIFE

The social problems related to the restrictions on abortion were seen as threats to the quality of life available to the living. The term "quality of life" embodied a strong belief in the capacity of people to improve their environment by controlling nature. It was assumed that people not only could, but should, control their environment and their own behavior, and thereby improve their situation. It was further assumed that, given the proper conditions, people would act morally, voluntarily, and individually to improve the "quality of life." Thus, a good society was one which would maximize the capacity of people to follow their own consciences in improving the quality of life.

Repeal of the restrictive abortion law was seen as a way to increase the capacity of private citizens to act in society's—and their own—best interests. It was moral, repeal advocates argued, to abort an unwanted pregnancy in order to preserve the quality of care for one's existing children. In was moral to abort a premarital pregnancy rather than bring an unwanted, illegitimate child into a poor emotional, social, and economic environment. Conversely, the argument implied that it was less moral to lower the quality of life by an additional birth or to bring a child into an environment where his chances of healthy development were slim. Yet people were forced to make this morally wrong choice because the law did not permit them an alternative. Dr. J. L. Erickson stated:

> Every comment regarding the rights of the fetus ignores the child's basic right to be born with at least one parent wanting him . . . I feel it is a moral crime to kill a fetus, but even worse to bring an unwanted child into the world.[41]

Some argued that the control of population was part of the positive morality of improving the quality of life. Barbara Higbee of the Sierra Club testified:

> Our organization is concerned with preserving a quality environment for this and future generations. Conservation is no longer simply a pleasant hobby for a perceptive few; it is finally recognized as a matter of the survival of mankind.
>
> It is not difficult to see that we have pollution problems; more difficult is the admission that nearly all of these problems stem from the mis-use of our reproductive capabilities. Without control over human population increase, all other efforts at conservation must inevitably fail.
>
> It is, therefore, both prudent and humane to attempt to ensure that every child be a wanted child.[42]

In response to the argument that population is not a serious problem, she added:

> The quality of life is not measured merely in material goods. Solitude, natural beauty, and limitation of stress problems, are also included.[43]

Paul Brumage, graduate student at the University of Hawaii, emphasized the same point:

> Regardless of our ability to feed the world, this is hardly the sole criterion for determining that the world is overcrowded. Each person added to the population places an added burden on all our resources and accelerates the rate at which we are destroying our environment.[44]

A few persons and such groups as Zero Population Growth participated in the abortion law repeal campaign as an adjunct of the ecology and population control movement. Howard Wiig, the ZPG representative, testified that population control was a major part of the organization's program. In answer to the pointed question by Senator Mirikitani: "Then you support abortion as a means of population control, as a method in line with your official policy?" Wiig replied, "Yes, but only as a stop-gap measure. Abortion is not a good means of population control."[45]

Dr. James Dator, futurist and associate professor of political science at the University of Hawaii, testified that legalizing abortion was one of many steps necessary to avert impending environmental disasters caused by population growth. His passing remark that if people will not limit their offspring voluntarily, the state might have to legislate it alarmed the committee members. They questioned him closely about whether he was advocating such state control, and why he was so afraid of population growth. Dator reiterated his belief that population growth was a prime factor in the problem of environmental pollution, and emphasized that he was not advocating state control over childbearing but was rather suggesting that if other steps such as the legalization of abortion were not taken, it might someday become necessary.[46]

Several speakers mentioned population control as one of many social benefits to be derived from repeal of the abortion law.[47] However, other proponents of abortion law repeal wanted to dissociate the cause from the population control movement, which they felt had a narrower appeal to legislators. They testified that abortion should not be viewed as a solution to the population problem, but rather as a method of reducing unwanted births and helping to solve other related social problems.[48]

Dr. Ronald Pion, obstetrician and visiting professor of Public Health at the University of Hawaii, urged that the ideas of population and family planning be kept separate. In response to a question from Senator Yee, he characterized abortion explicitly as a service for women, not a method of population control.[49]

LIBERALIZATION VERSUS REPEAL OF THE LAW

Having established the medical and social problems stemming from the existing restrictive law, the repeal advocates then argued that the liberalized law operating in several other states did not adequately solve the problem. Evidence was offered that only a tiny fraction of the women who sought abortions in those states were able to obtain them, and it was pointed out that most women sought abortions for reasons other than those enumerated by the ALI model abortion law.

Psychiatrist Dr. Charles Stewart testified that of the estimated one million abortions performed each year in the United States, only about ten thousand were legal. In Colorado, North Carolina, and California, legal abortions rose twofold to fourfold after passage of the liberalized law, and the most frequently used reasons were psychiatric. ". . . The new laws have made a very small dent in the existing problem."[50]

Many repeal advocates had read Harvey Zipf's article which argued that the liberalized laws had done little to solve the abortion problem.[51] Alluding to this research, several speakers noted that the liberalized law only aided women wealthy enough to pursue the necessary consultations, left the matter in the hands of physicians who had to make arbitrary decisions unrelated to the woman's real needs, and imposed procedural requirements that were costly and time-consuming.[52]

The issue was put succinctly by Judge Samuel P. King of the family court (a leader of the Republican party in the state):

> The ALI Model is a doctor's bill. It came into being as the result of strong pressure from the medical profession to legalize procedures which doctors felt were medically necessary but which legislators had determined were legally impermissible. . . .
>
> The ALI law has been adopted in several states. In those states

the doctors' problem has been solved, but there has been no significant reduction in illegal abortions. The procedures are too unwieldy, too public, too expensive, and too impersonal. Most objectionable is the implication that a panel of doctors will become arbiters of moral issues.

An alternative proposal is that all statutory restrictions on abortion should be removed. Whether to request an abortion would be a matter of conscience for the pregnant woman to decide in accordance with her own moral commitments. Whether to perform the abortion would be a matter of medical science for the doctor to decide in accordance with his own personal and professional convictions.

This alternative is the woman's bill. It proclaims the right of a woman to decide for herself what shall happen to her own body . . . . I endorse the woman's bill as better legislation than the doctors' bill.[53]

INDIVIDUAL CHOICE

Repeal advocates stressed that abortion was an individual moral choice and that no one should be either forced into, or prohibited from having, an abortion. A number of speakers, including two Protestant clergymen and a Buddhist priest, emphasized that the decision to have an abortion should be a matter of individual conscience.[54]

An interchange between Senator Wadsworth Yee and Dr. George Goto expressed this sentiment clearly.

Senator Yee: How do you feel about the religious factor?

Dr. Goto: It is a matter of conscience on the part of the woman.

Senator Yee: What about people whose faith prohibits abortions?

Dr. Goto: That is none of my business. If they choose to have an abortion despite their faith, it's their own concern.[55]

A Buddhist priest, Reverend Yoshiaki Fujitani of Honpa Hongwanji Buddhist Temple, expressed the moral issue and its bearing on personal conscience in the following way:

There are many arguments set forth in defense of repealing the anti-abortion law.

. . . The most basic and compelling reason for me, at least, is that of individual dignity. It is a question of "to what degree are we willing to recognize the personal rights and the human dignity of the

> individual." Abortion poses essentially a moral question. A question, therefore, that must be answered by the individual . . . .
>
> There are many who consider abortion immoral, but there are as many, if not more, who consider it both moral and therefore, desirable. The repeal of the present law will not only free us all from the unbecoming punitive attitude we seem to harbor against women suffering with unwanted pregnancies, but more significantly, it will also free the women to choose what they wish to do with themselves. If there is love in man we can do no other.[56]

Repeal of the abortion law was seen as adding to the capacity of private citizens to carry out their personal moral imperatives while not forcing a particular morality on anyone who chose not to take advantage of the provision. The usual way of expressing this point was to argue that abortion was a moral and medical problem, not a legal one; therefore, the law should not intervene in the issue.[57]

Unexpected support for this position came from the testimony of two Roman Catholic nuns. Sister Mary Heenan, speaking as a citizen and not as a representative of her Maryknoll order, testified as follows:

> My position is that I am opposed to abortion and, at the same time, I am in favor of the repeal of the abortion law. . . . I do not wish, however, to impose my religious belief and my moral views in this matter on all other members of society. To me, the crucial question here is whether the right of life and the right to a certain quality of life is better upheld by a law restricting abortions, or whether the common good of all concerned would be furthered by the repeal of the law.[58]

Sister Maureen, testifying as administrator of St. Francis Hospital (Roman Catholic), while not approving of abortion, did not personally oppose repeal of the abortion law. She did request, however, that any new abortion bill include a clause which would exempt hospital personnel who were morally opposed to abortion from having to participate in it as part of their occupational duties. (Such a clause was later incorporated into the law.) She added:

> . . . as I respect others and their right to opinions different from mine, I also expect reciprocal respect from them for those who share my own concern for their freedom to act according to their own moral convictions.[59]

Both nuns placed their own opposition to abortion within the context of private morality and saw repeal of abortion laws as permitting free exercise of such private morality for themselves as well as others who disagreed with them.

WOMEN'S RIGHTS AND ROLES

The repeal advocates argued that pregnancy and birth ought to be regulated by the individual woman to maximize the interests of her family, herself, and society. In general, they presented women as intelligent, responsible, and willing to make difficult choices to protect their families and society. Motherhood was generally viewed as one of many female roles, not as woman's destiny or ultimate fulfillment. The role of motherhood was seen as one which women should *choose* and then exercise responsibly.

Mrs. Donald Cundy testified:

> Here in Hawaii we have a law that takes away the female's right to the direction of the most intimate functions of her own body (as one commentator phrased it). No doubt some of you ladies delude yourselves into thinking that this does not really have anything to do with your own aspirations for equality. But can you command respect as an equal when the law of the land regards you as reproductive chattel?
>
> I have heard individuals say that women are society's incubators and that individual women must allow their bodies to be used by fetal tissue regardless of their wishes because the fetus has an obvious right to an independent existence that supercedes her right to an individual existence. Ladies, if you accept this reasoning you are allowing yourself to be considered an object not a human person. I am not against motherhood. It can be one of the most magnificent of human experiences. But what makes it so . . . is that it is a free act out of the human spirit of love.[60]

Abortion was viewed as a means for women to exercise control over their own reproductive functions, a control which women had a fundamental right to be able to exercise. Many speakers referred to a woman's right to control her own body and her right to self-determination.[61]

Laurel Kasaoka, testifying for Democratic Action Group, pointed out:

> Supporters of the present abortion laws go to great length to protect the right to existence of the fertilized egg, a *potential* human being, while disregarding completely the right of an *actual* human being, the pregnant woman, to determine the course of her own life.
>
> In the eyes of the law, therefore, a woman's most useful function is as an incubator with appendages. The degrading and derogatory nature of such an implication on the intellect of woman is anything but equal to the legal and social position enjoyed by the intellect of men.[62]

Community volunteer worker Marie Stires put the issue even more bluntly:

> We submit that since only a female human being can bring forth a human being only that female has a right to determine birth. . . . It would be just as fair for women to demand that all men capable of fatherhood be sterilized after they have fathered two offspring (now that the population growth is being viewed with such alarm) as it is for a woman to be forced to nurture an unwanted seed.[63]

The most militant expression of this argument was presented by University of Hawaii graduate student Karen Lum, testifying for Hawaii Women's Liberation Front:

> The women of the Hawaii Women's Liberation Front recognize the present state law on abortion as one of the many manifestations of oppression that the existing socio-economic system in the United States inflicts upon women. . . . The Hawaii Women's Liberation Front affirms the right of all human beings to control their own physical bodies, and as human beings we demand the right to control our reproductive processes, which includes the right to continue or discontinue a pregnancy. . . .
>
> The social, psychological and economic oppression and exploitation of women in this society must be stopped. Women must be freed from the archaic, restrictive, and inhuman role which has been imposed upon them. All legislation which allows for the perpetuation of the oppression and exploitation of women must be abolished, and for this reason the Hawaii Women's Liberation Front demands that the present state law on abortion be repealed.[64]

Lum's testimony, which also included demands for free abortions, free birth control devices, and free child care centers, deeply offended Senator Wadsworth Yee. He angrily asked Lum if she had come to help the cause of repeal or to hurt it, and began lecturing her about the virtues of the American system of government. The shocked Lum could only protest that she was working within the system by coming before the committee to testify.[65] Senator Yee was apparently upset by the radical economic and political context in which the women's rights issue had been placed, as well as by the militant tone of the testimony's "demands." The incident demonstrated vividly the importance of the repeal campaign's conservative and dignified approach.

Although women's right to control their reproductive functions was linked to liberation from various forms of discrimination against women by other speakers, the issue was usually presented as a simple human right rather than the product of a particular economic or political system. In one case, the women's rights issue was presented optimistically by Dr. Patricia Steinhoff, assistant professor of sociology at the University of Hawaii:

> More than ever before in history, young American women do have a future. . . . They are no longer forced to choose between marriage and a career, but can realistically plan to fulfill themselves through both. Small wonder that they will do everything in their power to protect that future.
>
> They refuse to enter into doomed, hasty marriages because they look forward to a good, fulfilling marriage with loved and wanted children; they refuse to let an immediate crisis destroy their education and their parents' aspirations for them, and so they seek abortions. We, as a society, ought to be supporting them and helping them, because it is in our own best interest to do so. . . .
>
> Why then, do we persist in using the abortion law as a retributive bludgeon against these young women? We don't need the social problems their shotgun marriages give us; we need them far more as educated and fulfilled wives and mothers, raising wanted children in stable, loving homes. We need their talent, their education, their technical and creative potential far more than we need their broken lives as permanent object lessons of what happens to bad girls.[66]

In the women's rights issue, as in other arguments, repeal advocates argued that the law should not be involved in the question, it was a private medical and moral decision to be made in each individual situation and not a matter for general legal control. The existing law was not only causing serious social problems, it was also restricting the fundamental right of a woman to control her own body. The legal prohibitions on abortion were seen as human, not spiritual, products, perhaps appropriate in their time to safeguard life, but now anachronistic, harmful, and unfair. The solution was simply to remove the arbitrary restrictions and permit women to do what they felt was right for themselves.

PHYSICIANS' RIGHTS AND RESPONSIBILITIES

Paralleling this argument for the right of women to control their own bodies was the plea that physicians be allowed to follow their own medical judgment. Testifying physicians pointed out that abortion was the only medical procedure specifically prohibited by law, suggesting that this was undue interference with the practice of medicine.

Obstetrician George Goto, representing the Hawaii Medical Association, testified:

> Obstetricians and gynecologists are the only specialists within the medical profession whose ability to exercise their best medical judgment is restricted by a criminal law. Specifically this applies to the question of aborting women with unwanted pregnancies. Because of this legal sanction against abortions without medical justification, patients are either refused abortions or sent to appropriate medical or psychiatric consultants to explore medical or psychiatric indications for abortions. Approval for abortions from these consultants vary from case to case and the entire procedure is time consuming and expensive. For this reason those patients who cannot present or who do not have convincing, acceptable arguments for abortion cannot have safe abortions in this State.[67]

Psychiatrist Dr. Charles Stewart pointed out:

> There are very few medical treatments or procedures that are specifically regulated by law, and abortion is the *only* situation in which a physician or group of physicians (therapeutic abortion committee) are solely and directly expected to interpret and apply a legal statute. There is some definite advantage to this, of course, in that it allows us a certain degree of flexibility and leeway in handling each case before us. On the other hand, it carries with it the awesome potential that at any time we may be liable for criminal prosecution with the charge of having misapplied or broken the existing law.[68]

Committee members questioned the testifying physicians closely about whether or not medical ethics and existing regulations would provide adequate supervision of abortion law if the law were repealed. In general, the physicians testified that abortions should be performed within existing medical and surgical regulations and guidelines. In response to Senator Donald Ching's question, "Then abortion is not different from any other medical decision?" Dr. Roy Smith replied, "No, especially if the Department of Health and the various medical and hospital groups set the codes."[69]

Several physicians emphasized the generally conservative stance of the medical profession to reassure the committee that abortion decisions would be carefully made. Dr. Smith assured Senator Ching that physicians would accept second trimester or later abortions only in very special cases.[70]

An interchange between committee members and Dr. Ronald Pion, visiting professor of public health at the University of Hawaii, followed a similar vein.

> Senator Ching: Are you then saying that you would perform an abortion irregardless of the laws if the patient required it?
>
> Dr. Pion: No. Especially not in the second trimester. No ethical doctor would ever abort a possibly viable fetus.
>
> Senator Yano: Then you would hesitate to abort a viable fetus?
>
> Dr. Pion: Certainly. I would never do it. We could prevent abortions at a later date by getting women in for tests at the first sign of pregnancy.
>
> Senator Ching: . . . Will the sanctions proposed by the medical profession be sufficient to handle all the situations and consequences?
>
> Dr. Pion: Yes. The medical profession is very conservative and hence careful.[71]

Senator Ching pursued a similar line of questioning with Dr. Goto, and received a surprising answer.

> Senator Ching: Suppose the mother wants an abortion in the third trimester. Is the doctor guilty of illegal or unethical conduct?
>
> Dr. Goto: Because the fetus is viable, this is not an abortion but a delivery. If the baby dies, the doctor is probably guilty of manslaughter.

Dr. Goto added that the procedure would be improper, even if the infant survived, unless it was done to save the life of the mother.[72]

Dr. Robert Noyes, associate dean of the University of Hawaii School of Medicine and chairman of the departments of obstetrics and gynecology and anatomy, pointed out that the medical profession maintains its own sanctions against unethical practitioners, and these would still operate even if the law were repealed. Pressed by Senator Ching as to the nature of these sanctions, Dr. Noyes testified that once he has been censured, a doctor is generally unable to continue in practice.[73]

In his formal testimony, Dr. George Goto made an important related point.

> If the abortion law is repealed the laws governing the practice of medicine would apply to abortions in exactly the same manner as they apply to any other medical procedure. In addition, women seeking abortions will no longer be under the shadow of a criminal law and can expect optimum medical care. Bad results need not be suffered in silence as they are today. For this reason, physicians who are not properly trained and equipped to do abortions will be deterred from wrong doing by the ever present possibility of suit for negligence.[74]

The plea by physicians to be permitted to follow their medical judgment, plus the reassurance that the profession would exercise that judgment carefully, reinforced the general point of repeal supporters that abortion was a moral and medical matter in which the law should not interefere.

In sum, the advocates of abortion law repeal presented a broad and complex set of arguments encompassing medical and social problems, women's rights, and physicians' rights. They argued that repeal of the abortion law would simultaneously alleviate social and medical problems which the prevailing law caused or aggravated, and restore to private parties the rights of individual choice and professional judgment which the prevailing law usurped.

CHAPTER 6

Anti-Repeal Issues: The Right to Life

THE RIGHT TO LIFE of the unborn child was the central argument of those opposed to abortion law repeal. While this belief is found in many religions, it was raised in the context of the abortion issue in Hawaii solely as part of Catholic doctrine and followed a Catholic tradition of religious argument by syllogism. No other religious group in Hawaii took a public stand against abortion law repeal, although other denominations were privately opposed to abortion. Not only was the anti-repeal campaign run almost entirely by Roman Catholics, but, more important, the arguments themselves were based on Roman Catholic assumptions and forms. Like the pro-repeal arguments, the anti-repeal arguments were based on certain unquestioned assumptions and beliefs.

THE FETUS AS HUMAN LIFE

The right to life argument was constructed as a syllogism in accordance with formal deductive logic, with a major and a minor premise upon which the conclusion depended. The major premise of the syllogism is that only God gives man life, so only God has the right to take away human life. Man is both enjoined from taking life and morally bound to protect it. The minor premise is that the fetus is human life and thus deserves protection. The conclusion then follows automatically: abortion is the deliberate destruction of human life, and man is morally obligated to oppose abortion and protect fetal life.

Both the form of this argument and its major premise were accepted by opponents of abortion law repeal as simple articles of faith. It was not considered necessary to prove that only God gives life. At most, repeal opponents sometimes asserted man's moral obligation not to take life. More often, the unspoken assumption structured the anti-repeal argument. This made the issue of whether or not a fetus is a human life the critical one. All other issues, such as social problems and the rights of the mother, were considered to be of much less consequence because they fell outside the train of logic of the major argument. Because the premises were accepted as true on faith, and the form of the argument was deductive and syllogistic, the only really debatable issue as the opponents of repeal viewed it, was whether or not fetal life fit the definition of human life deserving of God's—and man's—full protection. In other words, the critical issue became, "When does human life begin?"

The definition of human life was sometimes given in biological terms, at other times in spiritual terms. Thus, for some speakers the question was, "When does the fetus take on biologically human form?" For others, it was, "When does the soul enter the body?"

University of Hawaii agronomy professor Dr. Peter Rotar, representing the Knights of Columbus, testified:

> Biologically it is clear that life is present from the first moment of conception and all the evidence is in favor of saying that the resulting fetus is a truly human being. Does the being within a mother's womb only become a person when the umbilical cord is cut? Is a newborn baby a person? The living fetus in a mother's womb is a separate human being with its own identity: it is in one stage of development towards becoming a full-grown individual. It is not simply an excrescence of the mother; nor does the mother look upon it as identical with herself. The life within her has a right to existence just as much as a newborn babe and no one has the right to directly destroy it.[1]

Gerri Madden, speaking as an ex-educator and expressing the issue with her usual style, revealed the anti-repeal reliance on formal syllogistic argument:

> Perhaps you members of the committee do not believe that the embryonic fetus *is a person,* protected by our Constitution.
>
> I herewith submit a few facts from science. First of all, there is no formal syllogism proving the actual fact that it is; but there is also no formal syllogism proving the contrary. However, through the marvels of microbiology we see some startling facts. The ZYGOTE (the fertilized ovum), its structural infinitesimal size, its complexity, functional perfection, regulatory mechanism, tremendously complicated membrane, cytoplasm, nucleus, and the magnificent structure even in its primitive stage . . . reveal that it is not a part of the mother, but a distinct life of its own. Yes, there is manifested a living human continuity in the unborn child from the conception to the grave; there is no special time in development that one may say: now it is vegetable, now animal, now rational; therefore, we cannot subscribe to the proposed bill that would fail to protect this precious, fragile life, this masterpiece of God. Yes, this fetus is a person.[2]

Although Madden's testimony emphasized the physical development of the fetus, her comment that one cannot determine the point at which the fetus is "vegetable, now animal, now rational" is a reference to the Aristotelian notion of the gradual development of the fetus from vegetable to rational, which was embodied in early Catholic doctrine concerning the point of ensoulment and the distinction between an "unformed" and a "formed" fetus. This argument is occasionally cited as a doctrinal basis for Catholic tolerance of very early abortion. Her testimony explicitly rejects that notion in favor of the biological evidence of continuity of human life from conception.

Representing the Roman Catholic diocese of Honolulu, Monsignor Francis A. Marzen testified more concisely:

> The Church has consistently and without hesitation supported the position that once human life exists, it has a right to be born. We are not speaking of a spiritual soul but of human life, which today's scientists tell us begins shortly after conception and then develops within the womb of the mother.[3]

Other speakers, however, couched the biological issue more tentatively. They urged that until it was known exactly when life did begin, one had to protect it from the earliest possible moment.[4]

Robert Pearson, who included an eight- by ten-inch color photograph of a greatly enlarged sixteen-week-old fetus to support his argument, argued that:

> When a man is on trial for his life is it not true that if the jury has a shadow of a doubt in their mind that he may be innocent from the evidence given, they are compelled to reach a verdict of not guilty? In this same respect I would question you gentlemen to consider the point of whether you think the fetus which is on trial for its life could be living or not. If there is any question at all in your minds that it is possible that this is living you couldn't under penalty of conscience leave this creature defenseless. Therefore the law would have to stand as it is and not allow the fetus to be aborted as this is killing this life. If you have any doubt in your minds I would like to get down to the gut of this problem by asking you to look hard at the picture I submitted with a copy of my testimony. This picture is taken from Life Magazine of a sixteen-week-old fetus. Think very hard whether you could put that kicking creature into the incinerator.[5]

In his oral testimony, Pearson raised a spiritual question: the time of "ensoulment." When did the fetus acquire a soul?

> Theologians have said many things at different times of when they think the soul does enter the fetus. But here again it has never been pinned down of just when the soul does enter the fetus. So not knowing, we would have to assume that it does enter somewhere between the conception and birth, and being that it is something we don't know, we would have to concede the fact that possibly when we're killing this fetus if it has obtained its soul, it's possible that we are killing another human being.[6]

Having demonstrated within their own frame of logic that the fetus was human, the proponents of the right to life argument logically concluded that abortion was therefore morally wrong because it represented the willful destruction of human life by man. As human life, the fetus possessed a right to life which man could not abrogate. Only God has the power to do this.

Mrs. Edward S. Ehlen testified that the Catholic Women's Guild supported

> . . . the life of the unborn and we oppose any attempt on the part of anyone to terminate it. . .
>
> Senators, I ask myself time and again if your elective office is

higher than the Law of Nature and the Mind of God. I ask this question because the bill and its amendments which you are studying now, if passed, would put you in this position of superceding the Law of Nature and the Mind of God. You are discussing abortion, an act of murdering the unborn within the womb of the Mother.[7]

Monsignor Marzen pointed out that:

> The legislator has the duty in accord with our whole Anglo-American jurisprudence, to insure that human life be protected and to maintain the principle that no human person, whether parent or doctor, can have absolute sovereignty over the life of another human being.[8]

While several speakers tried to contrast the concern of others over war and pollution with what they considered to be the far greater crime (in numbers and moral significance) of killing the unborn,[9] physician Dr. Frederick Dodge won the respect of the repeal supporters for his consistency on this point. A pacifist and strong opponent of the war in Vietnam, Dr. Dodge argued that he was opposed to abortion for the same reason that he was opposed to war.[10]

Many speakers equated abortion with murder, calling it "killing the unborn child," "feticide," or "execution" of the "infant."[11] When Senator Yano told one woman speaker that murder can occur only with respect to a viable human life, she reiterated her belief that an abortion is a murder, which she defined as a "destruction of life."

> You don't recognize that to give quality to life you have to give love, and to destroy life isn't an act of love. And this is one thing that I haven't understood from any of your statements. You seem to think that when a life is conceived, if you destroy it that somehow this is the most loving, kind and wonderful thing to do. You want to save a child from being unloved, unwanted or deformed or something like that, when the first gift you give is life. And you concern yourself with the quality of life. It isn't even an option until you're born.

> Senator Yano: Mrs. Nielson, I think also a basic issue is, some people may not agree with you, your viewpoint, and would you respect their viewpoint?

> Mrs. Nielson: Well, the problem—I've only realized through these hearings to understand the other point of view. But my problem

> here is that if I were to respect their viewpoint and remain silent, how then would I answer to my conscience when the issue is raised to me, a life has been destroyed? It's not defined as a life legally by you, or it probably isn't defined by those who destroy it. But I listen to my conscience, you listen to yours.

Senator Yano: No, I respect your right to express your opinion.[12]

THE FATE OF FETAL SOULS

The importance of protecting the right to life of the fetus is increased because of Roman Catholic doctrine concerning the fate of souls which have not been properly blessed. This reasoning was first introduced into the Hawaii abortion issue as early as 1966, when Hilo physician Dr. William Bergin began an article in the *Hawaii Medical Journal* opposing abortion law liberalization with the following remarks:

> Since the soul of an individual comes into existence at the moment of fertilization of the ovum, interruption of pregnancy at any stage compels a soul to "wander the reaches of limbo" eternally. It is considered that this is a sufficient reason for refraining from interruption of any pregnancy whatever, for any reason whatever.[13]

At the hearings, this Catholic belief was expressed by Robert Pearson, although at the time he was trying to argue that even non-Catholics who did not believe in ensoulment before birth should oppose abortion. He assumed that the doctrine concerning souls was the same, and only the time of entry differed.

> Many of the people . . . believe the soul enters the body at birth and not before birth, so therefore, the fetus is absolutely nothing before birth—with only one exception, that it is the only "nothing" destined to receive that soul at birth. If this is what you believe, that the soul does come at birth, let's think about that a little longer. If we consider the soul as being man's eternal life, unending, and we terminate the fetus before it obtains its soul, it is lost for eternity. Wouldn't we be far better off to let it be born and then kill it, so that at least it would have a soul to live on for eternity?
>
> If we took all of man's life span and put it end to end, we would end up with billions of years, no doubt. At the end of this time eternity is just beginning. So we could consider that that one soul is

> worth the suffering and the time of all man's life here, his existence here on earth.[14]

The singlemindedness with which anti-abortion spokesmen championed the right to life of the fetus can be better understood in the context of this religious belief. The moral imperative was not simply to avoid personal involvement in the practice of abortion, but, more broadly, to prevent it from happening at all, in part because of the consequences for the fetal souls involved.

THE RELATIVE VALUE OF FETAL LIFE

Because the right to life argument was generally expressed as a moral absolute, its proponents were frequently questioned by the Senate committee members about whether or not there were any circumstances at all in which abortion could be condoned. The answers varied both in content and in theological sophistication.

In answer to Senator Yano's question, "If you were in my shoes as a legislator, what would you do? You would prohibit abortion absolutely?" Dentist Neil Bryson replied, "Yes, with the exception of mentally retarded children where it is proven with certainty."[15] This was an exception no other right to life advocate would make.

Robert Pearson was uncertain about whether abortion should be permitted even to save the life of the mother. Pressed by Senator Mirikitani with the example of a woman with cancer of the cervix, he responded, "We cannot make such a decision." When pressed further, he conceded, "If the baby was not removed it would die regardless, so that it would be proper to terminate."[16]

As the official representative of the Catholic diocese, Monsignor Marzen was asked what the Church's position was in cases where the mother's life was in great danger. He replied that the doctors are obliged to save both.[17]

Monsignor Marzen's reply echoes a pronouncement made by Pope Pius XII in 1951 in an allocution to the Association of Large Families. The Pope's statement was:

> Never and in no case has the Church taught that the life of the child must be preferred to that of the mother. It is erroneous to put the question with this alternative: either the life of the child or that of the mother. No, neither the life of the mother nor that of the child

> can be subjected to an act of direct suppression. In the one case as in the other, there can be but one obligation: to make every effort to save the lives of both, of the mother and the child.[18]

Pressed further by Senator Percy Mirikitani about making the choice, Monsignor Marzen replied:

> But—let's go one step further to answer this thing in its entirety . . . if in the final moment the doctor has to make a choice, the choice should be in favor of the new life, in preference to the mother who has had a chance to live, work out her eternal salvation and gain eternity of heaven. So give the child a chance.[19]

This reply also reflects the concern over the salvation of fetal souls pointed out above.

Senator Mirikitani, who pursued this issue with several opponents of abortion, then asked the monsignor:

> Senator Mirikitani: Supposing, say, that the mother was eighteen. Now she can propagate quite a few more children at that point. Even at that very moment you say that the child should be saved and not the mother?
>
> Monsignor Marzen: Because the child is an innocent person. She brought about his existence and he is entitled to live.[20]

Monsignor Marzen's assertion that the life of the fetus should take ultimate precedence over life of the mother follows the logic espoused by such Catholic theologians as Joseph Fuchs, who put the argument in the following way.

> The two obligations concerning a pathological birth, to preserve the life of the mother and not to kill the child, only seem to contradict one another. There is in fact no commandment to save the mother at all costs. There is only an obligation to save her in a morally permissible way and such a way is not envisioned in stating this given situation. Consequently, only one obligation remains: to save the mother without attempting to kill the child.[21]

Father Daniel Dever approached the problem somewhat differently. Arguing that the legislature could not solve the range of moral problems of abortion by a hands-off policy, he pointed to the existing law as having made the necessary compromise between conflicting rights.

> Public policy can never be an abdication of responsibility for awakening and provoking men to respect for life in all of its manifestations.
>
> Obviously, public policy may be forced to compromises beyond the tolerance of individual consciences. The existing law on abortion represents just such a compromise. But in this it cannot be accused of triviality or irresponsibility. It has grappled with the real world where fetal life and conflict of rights are found intertwined. It has faced the supreme value of the individual conscience with the dialectic role of the State. It has bowed to human finitude where decisions cannot escape tragic risk.[22]

The strong implication of Father Dever's comment was that he would accept the existing law's position that an abortion could be justified to save the life of the mother, at least as a matter of public policy.

Some speakers were careful to emphasize that they were opposed to the "direct" killing of the unborn. This was a reference to the Catholic theological principle of double effect, which says that an act which indirectly leads to a moral wrong (such as the death of the fetus) may be undertaken under certain circumstances if it is done in the direct service of a moral good (such as preserving the life of the mother). The principle only applies, however, when the act itself is not directly intended to have a morally bad result. The two officially sanctioned applications of the principle to the destruction of a fetus are the removal of a fallopian tube containing a fetus in the case of an ectopic pregnancy, and the removal of a gravid uterus in the case of cancer of the cervix. Neither procedure is directly viewed as an abortion, but both have the indirect consequence of destroying a fetus.[23]

Dr. Neil Bryson, a dentist, offered a layman's version of the principle of double effect.

> Senator Mirikitani has had the problem for two nights about the situation where it's a mother or a child. And he gave the example of the diseased uterus, with a carcinoma and a cancer and it was necessary to remove this uterus. Well, common sense would tell you that the uterus had to go and the child is just a side effect—no more than bombing a ship to destroy its gunnery would be the killing of people.
>
> Another reason, the mother of course must be chosen, because the child in this particular instance is an unjust aggressor, isn't he, and the physician himself has been retained by the mother and this is

> a case of a toss-up, so certainly the mother would be preferred and the mother certainly at the time is of much more value to society than some child, because she is of more value to her husband and children.[24]

INNOCENT LIFE

Advocates of the right to life of the fetus frequently used the term "innocent" to refer to the unborn child. The term carries three important connotations which lend emotional weight to the basic right to life argument.

The first connotation is that the fetus is innocent as opposed to guilty, innocent of any moral or criminal wrongdoing. This is an important qualification of the right to life argument for anyone who is not a pacifist. As expressed by Dr. Peter Rotar, spokesman for the Knights of Columbus,

> Catholic opposition is based . . . on human rights—that is, the right of every individual to his life unless in some way he has forfeited that right by his actions. No human authority . . . has the right to order the direct killing of the innocent.[25]

A second and somewhat related connotation is that of spiritual purity or religious innocence. The unborn child is seen as God's creation, not yet tainted by the evils of the world. It is therefore an object of reverence and hope. The term "innocent" is used to convey this feeling of respect for something pure and God-given. This special quality of the unborn is implicit in Monsignor Marzen's assertion that if the lives of mother and child cannot both be saved, the child should be saved "because the child is an innocent person." The child is more innocent and pure than the mother, who has sinned in various ways. Dr. Rotar also expressed this view in his testimony.

> We condemn direct abortion because it is the DIRECT KILLING OF AN INNOCENT HUMAN BEING. The child in the womb is a human being with an inalienable right to its life. To remove the foetus from the womb into an environment in which it cannot live, is directly to kill it. The child is innocent because it occupies the place designed for it by nature. By its presence in the womb it does not infringe the right of another. To directly remove the IN-VIABLE foetus from the womb is, therefore, the killing of the innocent.[26]

The third connotation of the term "innocent" is helpless, weak, or defenseless. Because it is innocent of the ways of the world, the unborn child has no defenses against the evil will of others, and therefore requires special protection. More concretely, proponents of the right to life argument often depicted themselves as defenders of the weak or as standing on the side of those who have no voice in actions taken against them. This aspect of their argument did have strong appeal for non-Catholics. The protection of a group that lacked other protection was likened to supporting other unenfranchised groups at personal cost and had overtones of protecting the civil liberties of fetuses.

Dr. Frederick Dodge condemned contemporary society as "sick" and "suicidal," with the unborn becoming society's scapegoats because of their defenselessness.[27] In a similar vein, social worker Catherine Dunn argued that when abortion is permitted in cases of rape and incest, the penalty for the crimes of others is placed "on an innocent, on the weakest person."[28]

All three of these special connotations of the word "innocent" are part of the religious language of Roman Catholicism. The speakers used the word "innocent" in what to them was a familiar symbolic sense, unaware that the term did not carry the same emotional significance for non-Catholics.

Closely related to the religious concept of innocence is another Catholic belief which was frequently expounded by those opposed to abortion: the idea that association with the poor, the handicapped, and the weak teaches people the virtues of love and humility.[29] The argument was intended to counter the idea that abortion should be permitted in order to prevent the birth of a deformed or defective child, an important element in the ALI model abortion law. However, supporters of repeal did not dwell on the problem of the handicapped or defective child; they were concerned about the more common unwanted child.

A further extension of this view was the testimony of social worker Raymond Dorais, executive director of Catholic Social Service:

> The last point relates to poverty.
>
> The poor will always be with us, or at least since the history of man there have been those who have less and those who have more. I

> don't think that that situation will change in the near future and encouraging abortions for the poor is not going to help.
>
> Poverty is a frame of mind according to Senator Barry Goldwater, and I fully agree.[30]

LEGAL PROTECTION OF THE FETUS

Although the argument and the assumptions behind it were essentially religious, the moral imperative to protect the fetus' right to life extended to the realm of law. The repeal movement was viewed as an attempt to deny legal protection to the fetus, and the opposition saw itself as defending that right on behalf of the unborn, who could not speak for themselves. As Dr. Dodge expressed it:

> The unborn children have no voices of their own, no lobby, no votes, no money and no power. They are the perfect scapegoat.[31]

Speakers variously cited the United Nations' Declaration of Human Rights, which refers to the rights of children both born and unborn, the Fourteenth Amendment of the U.S. Constitution (". . . nor shall any state deprive any person of life, liberty, or property without due process, nor deny any person the equal protection of the law . . . "), and the "life, liberty and pursuit of happiness" phrase in the Declaration of Independence as evidence that the law does recognize the rights of the unborn.[32]

More broadly, the abortion issue was seen as the first of many impending attacks on the fundamental principle of the right to life. Several persons warned that if abortions were permitted, euthanasia would come next.[33] The law was thus required not only to defend the rights of the unborn, but also to protect the general principle that man could not take human life. Monsignor Marzen argued that

> law has a certain teaching effect, and . . . the present laws on abortion in our state, teach, to a degree, the respect for human life which our Christian teaching has given us.[34]

Fear was voiced that repeal of abortion laws would lead to a decrease in the general sanctity of life. The argument was that when any life was willfully destroyed it became easier to destroy other lives. If the dividing lines between fetus and person were arbitrary, other lines could be drawn for purposes of euthanasia, such as between normal and subnormal people.

WOMEN'S RIGHTS AND ROLES

An important corollary of the right to life argument was its implication of the role and responsibility of women as mothers. The belief that fetal life is a gift of God which humans must strongly protect implies that pregnancy and birth are not choices women make, but sacred responsibilities which are vested in them.

For married women, Catholic doctrine is clear. Motherhood is woman's primary role, and in becoming a mother she is the vessel which carries and bears God's gift of new life. The married couple is not supposed to interfere with the opportunities by which that new life is implanted by using birth control, because the purpose of sexual intercourse is procreation. The only acceptable means of avoiding conception is through sexual abstinence (which may be accomplished by means of the rhythm method). On the other hand, the privileges of the marriage bed are part of the marriage contract, so the denial of sexual access by a wife is also considered wrong.[35] The overwhelming conclusion is that pregnancy is an honor for which a woman is chosen. Her acceptance and faithful execution of this responsibility provides her fulfillment and is the measure of her moral worth.

A few Catholic speakers recommended expanded programs of contraception or sterilization as alternatives to repeal of the abortion law.[36] Dentist Neil Bryson argued:

> Are there other avenues by which a woman who truly and sincerely and morally and before God has borne all the children she desires, may effectively see fit that she will bear no more children, other than the means of an abortion, by the taking of human life?
>
> Now it has been stated that a woman can regulate her own bodily parts for any just means. Certainly her reproductive system, unlike a human fetus, is a part of her very own tissue. . . . It is surely hers to do with, for a just reason, if she is to exercise her personal right to regulate her own body, and I state that the law should not regulate, the law should be silent, in this private area where a second human being is not involved, unlike the question of abortion. . . .
>
> Let's talk about those women who if they were to have children would have a serious medical problem and maybe a life-endangering

situation. I think all of us would think more of a woman in this situation—not the woman who pushes abortion, the death of a life, but a woman who doesn't want any more children that might undergo sterilization.[37]

Questioned by Senator Yano about whether his own personal beliefs would permit sterilization, since it was against Catholic doctrine, Bryson conceded that he personally did not approve of sterilization but saw it as the lesser of two evils—a compromise that could be made to avoid the far worse alternative of abortion. When Senator Yano pointed out that there were presently no legal restrictions on sterilization, but it did not seem to be effective in preventing the need for abortion, Dr. Bryson countered that he was not proposing it as a total solution, but as a solution for some people.[38]

Other speakers, echoing Bryson's view that people would "think more of a woman" who did not advocate abortion, indicated a general rejection of women's liberation and independence. Attorney Arthur Trask commented:

> I am somewhat dismayed at the way the ladies degrade themselves on this question. They talk about the Magna Carta, they talk about the degradation of—not motherhood but womanhood. They talk about—as though they were by themselves—that man is not a part of their being. We're concerned about happiness, and happiness is a twosome situation. I'm amazed how the ladies really, truthfully, pragmatically, statistically, in search of happiness, seek by their enthusiasm to destroy this bill and get on the bandwagon. . . .
>
> So this violence of feminine enthusiasm and short sightedness, without any historical appreciation, to degrade yourself! I say, for shame!
>
> As a practicing attorney I've handled many cases involving the family. I have yet to know of one case where a woman said she wanted to have an abortion. One case! Women should be encouraged to have children. The question is the morality before the act is done.[39]

This perspective was also expressed by women. Mrs. Edward S. Ehlen, representing the Catholic Women's Guild, testified:

> As women we have been granted the exalted role of cradling this new life within ourselves for nine months. I have used the word, cradling, intentionally, because there are those who have the notion that this new life is the exclusive gift of women to society, women acting

> alone. This is not so. This new life is the blessing of a cooperative act by man and by woman. It is not hers, exclusively, and we acknowledge that the man has as much right over this new life as the woman. For this reason, we feel that a woman cannot indiscriminately dispose of this life without the man's consent and that both of them must share in the guilt of such an act of murder as is the case in abortion. Nor can the man impose his will upon the woman about the future of this new life without the full concurrence of the woman. This whole act of re-creation represents love in the highest order between this man and this woman. We feel that the feminist plea for equality has been exaggerated and in this matter of the unborn child, the feminists have trampled upon the man's rights.[40]

Still others emphasized women's obligation to make the required sacrifices for childbearing and minimized the importance of their personal reservations in the matter. Gerri Madden testified:

> One lady from the AAUW writes: "Must a mother lay her life on the line?" The answer is: from the dawn of creation, mothers have gone to death's door to bring children into this world. It is their duty, their solemn obligation. My mother was told she would die if she had any more children after the fifth; she had twelve, all of whom are living happy, successful lives.[41]

Dr. William Bergin emphasized the same point, testifying from his medical experience.

> The majority of women (some 60%) who request abortion are married women legitimately pregnant, in good health, and feel that they would like an abortion simply because they do not care to have another baby for reasons of convenience or finance and should they have another child it would be unwanted and presumably neglected and even mistreated. Almost any woman who finds herself pregnant is temporarily upset and unhappy during the first trimester when an abortion is feasible. As the pregnancy progresses they adjust to the situation and when the baby arrives they take them into the family and treat them with the same affection they bestowed on the other children.[42]

Although varying degrees of sympathy and rejection were expressed concerning the plight of the unmarried pregnant woman, the anti-repeal speakers were unanimous in feeling that the morally correct response to the pregnancy was to accept it. Several speakers testified to the need to remove the social stigma of illegitimacy and provide social services so that it would be easier for unwed mothers to keep their children.[43] Some emphasized adoption as a solution. Robert Pearson argued that the mother only has to suffer for nine months, after which time the baby will have an independent life for sixty to seventy years.[44]

A rather different perspective on the issue of illegitimacy was provided by the personal testimony of Clarence Kamai, a layman who requested permission to testify. He told the audience:

> You know, if I were to ask a question here, how many of you are really honest, I would be ashamed to see the hands raised. And if I were to ask the question here, how many of you are bastards, none would stand. But I say this to you. You are gazing upon a fellow that was born out-of-wedlock. I am a bastard. . . . The sincerity of this whole question of abortion is repealing the law that my mother lived under, survived, and today you are looking at its product. I am very, very happy, praise the Lord.
>
> And I was the seventh member of my family. . . . We give names, ladies and gentlemen, but the only person who really knows whether you are his or theirs, is the mother. And I thank the Good Lord that my mother had the courage to hang onto such a person as I.[45]

The assumption behind all of these views was clearly that the woman's prime responsibility is to carry the pregnancy to term, regardless of what happens to her or to the child as a result. Since in Catholic theology the right to life position is often extended even to the extreme of saving the child at the cost of the mother's life, it was inconceivable that under normal, nonlifethreatening circumstances anything could take priority over the birth of the child. Social worker Catherine Dunn testified:

> Abortion is unnecessary because there are many, less extreme solutions to unwanted babies: there is adoption, foster care, medical, emotional and social supports—even special supports—for mothers in need; institutional care is available when necessary. A solution of the magnitude and irreversibility of abortion could only be entertained in the absence of all alternatives.[46]

Because the act of abortion was viewed by those against repeal as radical and immoral, several speakers testified that it would have traumatic effects on the woman who underwent the procedure. Social worker Raymond Dorais, testifying as executive director of Catholic Social Service, reported:

> Abortion will create guilt in a conscientious person. A person panicked into encouraging a young daughter to have an abortion will no doubt have a more serious consequence in later years as that daughter grows in wisdom and in guilt. I cannot agree that psychiatric counseling will cure it. When will it be given? Now or later when the ego damaging guilt takes its toll in a poor marriage partner and in poor child raising techniques.[47]

Social worker Catherine Dunn added:

> Abortion is unwise because, in spite of the good it may intend to achieve, it may also produce serious problems. One cannot overlook the emotional factor of guilt and the emotional callousness that can develop as a person compensates for guilt.[48]

The guilt that a woman would feel after undergoing an abortion was viewed as a more serious social problem than any other type of feelings she might have or any adverse social consequences that might stem from giving birth to the child. These were the minor costs of her fulfillment of the sacred responsibility vested in her by the pregnancy.

PERMISSIVENESS AND RESPONSIBILITY

Because abortion itself was viewed as such a profound moral wrong, permissiveness in this area was depicted as unleashing a host of other evils. Gerri Madden predicted general moral decay if the repeal bill passed.

> Of course, since prayer has been removed from our schools, despite the efforts of Senator Dirksen, our youth are deprived of the inner resources and spiritual power that strengthens them against the onslaughts of sexual passion. A society deprived of religious sanctions, largely devoted to pleasure seeking, to permissiveness, irresponsibility, indifference to law and authority is doomed *TO MORAL DECAY*. The New Morality is but Pagan Immorality or A-Morality. Senator Yano, can you not see that you are bestowing a garb of respectability upon a deed that down thru the ages has been stigmatized as evil, shameful, degrading, defiling and debasing. Without prayer, legalized abortion will lead our youth down the path to shame and sorrow.

> Gentlemen, shall we not benefit from history?
>
> "Those who ignore the mistakes of history are doomed to repeat them." The Romans built a mighty power. They became enamored of their success just as we are today. They worshipped a trinity of values: MATERIAL POSSESSIONS, POWER, AND PRESTIGE. They glorified beauty, intelligence, physical performance but, like Hawaii, they exalted QUALITY OF LIFE, NOT SANCTITY OF LIFE. As their affluence grew, there was a decay of their moral values. They practiced abortion and infanticide, and murder of the aged and insane . . . the next step to abortion. AS THEIR MORAL DECADENCE SPREAD LIKE A MALIGNANT DISEASE, THEIR GLORIOUS EMPIRE COLLAPSED. . . . Step by step, is not Hawaii following the same path?[49]

Less graphically, Mary Nielson warned of the same problem.

> I realize that my views aren't shared, to say the least. But I want them heard. Because perhaps when the experiment has gone on, if this law is repealed, then you will find that society, the fabric of our life deteriorates, because you don't recognize that to give quality of life you have to give love and to destroy life isn't an act of love.[50]

Others saw the problem in terms of the deterioration of moral values in the younger generation. As dentist Neil Bryson saw it:

> These young girls that turn for help and that don't want this child and that want an abortion—will you by repeal of this law be actually teaching them that this is the way to live? Won't you be a sham? And won't your younger generation turn on you?[51]

In a similar vein, Mrs. Edward S. Ehlen testified:

> Speaking for myself, I share the views of many of my non-Catholic friends, so many of us feel that this law could do irreparable damage to our already morally confused youngsters. Should we give this child, or some of these children the opportunity to avail themselves of an abortion, we might give them the opportunity to feel that they are justified in acting according to the dictates of their own conscience, rather than the conscience of their Church, their parents or their teachers.[52]

Gerri Madden saw the restrictions on abortion as an important deterrent to sexual misbehavior by the young.

> Girls and young men too, have told me they have planned a lovely evening: music, dancing, a ride in the moonlight. . . . as the eve-

> ning passes, intimacies are exchanged; dressed as they are today the girls are hard enough to resist . . . even without drugs or alcohol. Often, I'm told, in the height of strong passion, when both are about to yield to the complete act of love, the one single thought (not the most noble motivation) comes: I MIGHT BECOME PREGNANT . . . and either the girl or boy puts on the brake. . . . But don't you see, if you liberalize Abortion, you are removing the protection that these young people need. They have not the moral stamina that you and I have to choose between the RIGHT AND WRONG.[53]

Following this same line of thinking, that abortion as an easy way out would lead to general irresponsibility, Dr. Frederick Dodge predicted that abortion would decrease the use of contraception.[54]

In contrast to the repeal advocates, who saw abortion as a responsible solution to various social situations, the opponents of repeal felt that abortion was a way of avoiding responsibility for one's immoral actions. Dismissing the argument that abortion ought to be available to women who have been raped, social worker Raymond Dorais of Catholic Social Service testified:

> True rape is mighty rare. So-called rape is usually the case. That is, "so-called" rape is subtly premeditated, subtly encouraged or a simple lie as a result of guilt.[55]

The implication was clear: if a girl is not really raped, she should not be allowed to avoid paying the penalty for her behavior. Her penalty is to have the baby.

More broadly, social worker Catherine Dunn argued that going through with the pregnancy develops the woman's moral strength.

> Never in my experience as a social worker have I met anyone who grew stronger, solved a problem, or became happier by running away from a problem or sweeping it under the rug. I have seen many who have been progressively weakened by their inability or unwillingness to face a problem and cope with it. I have met others who developed strength facing and meeting problems, serious ones such as illegitimate pregnancies . . . . Abortion as a solution to unwanted pregnancies or children seems to me to be poor mental hygiene. It only fosters emotional flab.
>
> To be responsible for the consequences of one's acts is a valid

> goal of emotional maturity. Abortion as a "way out" of a difficult, even a painful, dilemma works contrary to this principle.[56]

Such an attitude results in part from a theory which sees punishment as retributive and capable of acting as a deterrent. Those who do evil should pay for their sins, and the knowledge of such penalties will in turn deter others from immoral action. More basically, however, the emphasis on accepting responsibility by bearing the child can best be understood in the context of the whole right to life argument and its doctrinal assumptions. When one accepts the assumptions that : 1) life is given by God at conception and must be accepted by man, 2) motherhood is the sacred responsibility of women who have been blessed with this gift of God, and 3) there is a moral imperative that man cannot destroy innocent human life; then any reason for rejecting motherhood naturally appears shallow and irresponsible.

PHYSICIANS' MORALITY AND RESPONSIBILITY

Just as women's reasons for seeking abortion were regarded as petty and selfish, doubts were raised about the motives of physicians who would perform abortions. Dr. William Bergin testified:

> In any abortion there must be a minimum of three individuals involved: the pregnant woman, the doctor, and the living infant to be. The infant is to be executed, albeit cleanly, but nevertheless executed without due process, and only at the will of the other two, one of whom stands to gain financially.[57]

Dr. Keith Kuhlman testified that although he was personally opposed to abortion as a violation of the right to life of the fetus, he generally accepted Senator Yano's position on repeal. However, he wanted to bring two important reservations to the committee's attention. The first was that the procedure would be difficult to supervise from a medical point of view, and it would be difficult to determine whether patients were being abused if abortions were performed in physicians' private offices. Second, he felt that repeal would not necessarily eliminate the nonprofessional practitioners of abortion because they could operate more cheaply than legitimate physicians even under repeal conditions. Dr. Kuhlman suggested that restricting legal abortions to hospitals might alleviate these problems somewhat, and he did not think too many women would be deterred from obtaining hospital abortions because of the resulting lack of privacy.

Senator Yano was opposed to a hospital limitation in part because it would require writing specific legislation to permit abortion rather than letting the law remain completely silent through total repeal of the existing law. He questioned Dr. Kuhlman at length about the effects of a hospital provision and to clarify whether the testimony was intended to support or oppose the repeal position. Dr. Kuhlman insisted that he did support repeal, but that he felt his "second thoughts" deserved consideration.[58]

ABORTION MECCA

Some of those against repeal raised the spectre of Hawaii becoming an "abortion mecca." Speakers cited reports of American women flocking to Britain for abortions as evidence of the impending "abortion mecca" problem. In particular, Dr. William Bergin testified at length on the "nightmare that exists in Britain where in 1968 the politicians literally rammed through their present abortion law." He cited the tremendous demand for abortion as having overcrowded hospital facilities and limited physicians' time to perform other gynecological procedures. The establishment of private abortoria, performance of abortions for high fees, solicitation by physicians and hospitals, and widespread kickbacks for abortion referrals were described, along with the supplementary services of charter abortion flights and special abortion hotels.[59]

Other speakers argued that where abortion laws had been liberalized or legalized, illegal abortions had still flourished, so repeal was not a solution to the problem of illegal abortion.[60]

The abortion mecca argument as well as the prophecies of moral decay and corruption among physicians were presented as corollaries of the basic principle that abortion is a moral evil akin to murder. From this perspective, it followed that the people who participate in this evil, and the society that condones it, are generally immoral. Since the activity is evil to begin with, an increase in the quantity of evil can only make it worse.

LIBERALIZATION VERSUS REPEAL

In general, the proponents of the right to life argument were opposed to any change in the existing abortion law. They raised several arguments against the specific exceptions of the ALI model law, even though that law was technically not under consideration at the hearing. These arguments included the right to life of deformed or mentally defective children and the benefits to society of nurturing such children. Rape was rejected as a reason for destroying the resulting "innocent party."

It was on the issue of complete repeal versus some other degree of liberalization of the law—particularly if some change became inevitable—that the opponents of change tended to split ranks. The Church's official position and that of many lay Catholics was solid opposition to any change at all, including repeal. Some explicitly rejected the Drinan position that it was preferable for the law to remain silent than to spell out conditions under which abortion might be condoned. Monsignor Marzen, expressing the official position of the diocese, testified:

> We have and will continue to oppose House Bill No. 61 which liberalizes abortion in this state. Likewise we oppose the repeal of the existing restrictive law on abortion because it will make abortion-on-demand a reality in this state and will give the seal of approval to abortion-on-demand, not by legislative act but by legislative silence.[61]

A similar view was expressed by Mary Nielson, speaking as a private citizen.

> To say the law by remaining silent will allow a woman to follow her conscience in this matter is absurd. Because by silence it suggests that an intrinsic wrong can be considered and condoned. Silence is not neutral. I think silence shouts.[62]

Among other speakers who expressed a personal belief in the right to life argument, however, there was a remarkably broad continuum of positions regarding the law. Sister Maureen, representing St. Francis Catholic Hospital, did not take a position on abortion as a legislative problem. She emphasized the importance of mutual respect between people of differing opinions, and urged that the public policy regarding abortion include a proviso that:

> No individual, social agency, health agency or hospital shall be required to practice or permit any practice such as sterilization of human beings, euthanasia, abortion or birth control, or any other similar practice contrary to their moral belief.[63]

This statement, as well as several other quotations in her testimony, were cited as being from the book *The Terrible Choice: The Abortion Dilemma,* a source familiar to Senator Yano as the same book which contained Father Drinan's major exposition of the repeal position.

Father Daniel Dever began his testimony by noting that he had previously raised the question of whether no law at all would be preferable to liberalization. He went on to suggest that repeal was not the only alternative, but he proposed a delay in the decision while a citizens' committee investigated the matter more thoroughly and simultaneously attended to the social issues associated with abortion. He urged the legislature to

> Bring public policy in line with the highest and best standard of current medical practice. Support this legislation with back-up legislation that would go to the root of the unwanted pregnancy problem in its multiple aspects.[64]

In his oral testimony, however, Father Dever called attention to his use of the phrase, "bring public policy in line with the highest and best standard of current medical practice," and strongly hinted that he would favor changes in the law even if they violated his personal views.

> We all know, and doctors have mentioned this before in testimony, that the current practice of doctors or the medical profession is wider than the existing legislation. So there is a gap there that may have to be remedied. I myself do not favor this. If I were speaking in terms of my conscience I could not favor this. I would not. I am thinking in public policy you have more than my conscience to deal with and therefore it may be much more liberal and tolerant than my own conscience.[65]

Still farther along the continuum was Dr. Frederick Dodge, who concluded his testimony against the bill by stating:

> If it is inevitable that the abortion laws will be made less strict, I feel that no law is preferable to a poor law—such as liberalization, which in effect spells out who is to die. Conscience, honestly followed, even though it be erroneous, is a sacred thing. Perhaps society must go through a period of increased sickness before it can improve.
>
> I would hope that love of man for himself and his neighbors will eventually result in such a reverence for all life, that any deliberate

> killing, perhaps even all violence, will one day be a thing of the past.[66]

Two other speakers testified that their personal views respected the right to life of the unborn, but that they favored the repeal of the abortion law as public policy. Dr. Keith Kuhlman made this point in the context of expressing two specific reservations about the repeal position, and the fact that he was advocating repeal was only clear in the oral interchange following delivery of his formal testimony.[67]

Sister Mary Heenan explicitly separated her personal beliefs and her advocacy of repeal as public policy in her testimony.

> My position is that I am opposed to abortion and, at the same time, I am in favor of the repeal of the abortion law. I am against abortion because I believe that the fetus is a potential human being. I do not wish, however to impose my religious belief and my moral views in this matter on all other members of society. To me, the crucial question here is whether the right of life and the right to a certain quality of life is better upheld by a law restricting abortions, or whether the common good of all concerned would be furthered by the repeal of the law. I favor the latter position for haven't we citizens in this State and we members of our various Churches evaded involvement, evaded responsibility as long as we felt that the law was somehow magically keeping abortions from being performed?[68]

The opponents of abortion law repeal or reform, that is, the proponents of maintaining the *status quo,* argued that abortion was morally wrong because the fetus is a human life which may not be destroyed by man. In both form and content, the right to life argument reflected Catholic theology on the issue. It led also to subsidiary arguments that various moral aspects of society would deteriorate if the fundamental evil of abortion were permitted. However, some persons testified to their belief in the right to life of the fetus and yet expressed varying degrees of sympathy with the concept of repealing the abortion law. The effect of this diversity of opinion regarding the proper role of law or public policy was to weaken the basic right to life argument as a justification for maintaining the restrictive abortion law. The diversity of opinion did, however, argue against the belief that Catholics could not speak for themselves on the issue and had to adhere to a strict party line.

CHAPTER 7
Give and Take

CLEARLY, the two sides were stressing different aspects of the abortion issue. Repeal advocates emphasized that they viewed repeal as a way to help solve the social problems associated with the existing abortion law. They saw repeal as part of a general approach to controlling and improving the quality of life. The opposition primarily focused on a religious concern with the right to life of the fetus, a point which reduced all other issues to a very minor position. In effect, the two groups were talking past each other. The main concern of one was minor or irrelevant to the other.

The legislators and the public were confronted with two very different arguments, each beginning with radically different assumptions about the nature of the problem and even the nature of man's relation to the world. Spokesmen for each of the two groups presented arguments which they personally found rational, as well as emotionally and morally significant. In turn, they found themselves confronted with arguments that were of much less personal significance to them but that nevertheless had to be rebutted.

THE REBUTTALS

Repeal advocates were not personally moved by the basic theology of the right to life argument. For them, the moral imperative to protect life primarily involved improving the conditions of post-natal life and did not necessarily extend to the fetus. They distinguished between living matter and human life, viewing the fetus simply as potential life. Moreover, they were suspicious of a moral imperative to protect life which applied to fetuses but not to adult women and which did not necessarily apply to people at war. They referred to the lack of agreement among scientists and medical personnel regarding the definitions of life and did not attempt to argue about when life actually began. To them this point was not very relevant to the social and legal problems at hand.

They were equally convinced of the irrelevance of the argument that loss of the right to life by the fetus might eventually be extended to loss of the right to life by other groups. Advocates of repeal generally regarded the references to euthanasia as simple hysteria, because in their own minds abortion and euthanasia were completely different social issues rather than parallel transgressions of a moral principle. They were unable to confront the right to life argument directly, partly because they did not comprehend the emotional significance it held for those who subscribed to it, and partly because they did understand that it was an issue that ultimately reduced to unarguable faith.

The right to life argument was most often rebutted with traditional American pluralism. The issue was the right of each individual to follow his or her own conscience, repeal advocates argued. They contended that a religious minority was attempting to impose its doctrine of morality upon the rest of the society. Repeal of the abortion law would not in any way force members of that religious group to participate in an act they believed to be wrong, but it would permit individuals outside the group to follow their own conscience in the matter. The advocates of repeal stressed that abortion was a matter of private conscience and that it was entirely voluntary. They argued that the law should accommodate differing personal convictions rather than supporting one restrictive view at the expense of others. This argument for individual choice was consistent with the repeal advocates' own morality and its implicit assumption that the sum of individual consciences would equal the public good.

The argument was not convincing to the strong believers in the right to life of the fetus, who believed that certain individual actions are indeed the proper concern of government and the community. The primary concern of those against repeal was with saving the souls of fetuses and maintaining the fabric of society and not simply with their own personal conduct. The opponents of repeal knew that they personally would never undergo or perform an abortion, but their cause was much broader. They felt that they were preventing "the slaughter of the innocents." Moreover, the slaughter was not simply of material bodies; it was the souls that would be denied salvation which were really at stake. And it was clear to them that the repeal advocates could not prove that life did not begin at conception; they had not even tried.

To those against repeal, focusing on social problems missed the major issue of the living fetus. Since for them the whole argument hinged on the fact of fetal life, any social problems which resulted from that life were regrettable but would have to be accommodated in some other way. The real social problem, as they perceived it, was the danger of degrading the value of life, as symbolized by the fetus.

They countered the repeal advocates' argument of the social hardships caused by the restrictive abortion law with three points. First, they argued, there are other solutions to unwanted children, such as adoption or greater social acceptance and support for the unwed mother. Some pointed to prevention through birth control as the solution, ignoring the evidence cited by repeal supporters of birth control failure as well as their own opposition to its use. Others asserted that women become adjusted to their unwanted pregnancies and love the children anyway. All of these proposed solutions, with the possible exception of greater support for unwed mothers, amounted to a denial that unwanted pregnancy was a real problem without a readily available solution under existing conditions.

The second argument for the *status quo* emphasized the redeeming qualities for society of nurturing the products of unwanted pregnancy. It was argued that raising mentally and physically defective or illegitimate children teaches love and humility, which was sometimes expanded to the argument that bearing an unwanted child teaches the mother to adjust to the world. A related argument was that since the poor will always be with us and since they teach us love and humility, repealing the abortion law does not solve the problem and eliminates living lessons. In addition, they argued, unwanted pregnancies provided children for those who could not bear their own.

As a final counter to the medical and social problems argument, the opposition stated that legalization of abortion would not stop illegal abortion because women would want secrecy and because illegal abortionists could always do abortions more cheaply than legitimate physicians could.

In general, these three points were consistent with the theology of the right to life argument. They represented a sincere attempt to handle social problems, given the initial assumption that the births could not be prevented. In addition, they reflected a specifically religious doctrine of love and respect for the poor and weak which is grounded in the belief that the poor, the weak, and the maimed are closer to salvation than others. This belief, a natural concomitant of the initial fatalistic assumption, is a way of making the consequences of that assumption more bearable.

To non-Roman Catholics, particularly to American Protestants who believe that a person's capacity to control and improve his life is a measure of his spiritual worth, this argument appears distorted and hollow. Removed from its natural context of supporting beliefs and assumptions, it appears as another type of denial that a problem exists in the real world.

Some of the arguments used to rebut the social problems issue appeared to be directed at the ALI model abortion law for liberalization rather than against the repeal bill. The argument that raising mentally defective children teaches love and humility, for example, presumes that abortions would be for the purpose of eliminating mentally defective fetuses, as specified in the ALI model law. Likewise, since no statistics were cited by those against repeal, it was not always clear whether their argument that legalization would not stop illegal abortion was actually attacking the ALI model law rather than attacking repeal. To repeal advocates, these arguments simply missed their mark.

The two sides also started from different premises and beliefs in several other arguments, so that there was little possibility of agreement on the facts or the solutions. The advocates of repeal who viewed abortion as a partial solution to the population problem, for example, envisioned that problem as a complex and interrelated set of economic and social forces, ultimately summed up in the notion of preserving a certain "quality of life." The opponents of repeal dismissed the population problem as either nonexistent or hypothetical. They reduced it to the question of whether all the people in the world could be fed. They expressed great faith in the ability of technology to solve any problems of the food supply. This in turn frustrated the repeal advocates who believed that the technology was not adequate and, further, that the problem was not a simple issue of taking the edge off starvation.

Similarly, the issue of women's liberation divided the two camps. Repeal advocates linked the issue of abortion with the idea of a woman's right to control her own body. This disturbed those opponents of abortion for whom motherhood and womanhood were inextricably intertwined. The contemporary image of women's liberation as bra-burning and sexual freedom also reinforced the conviction of opponents of abortion that repeal of the law would encourage sexual permissiveness. Yet to those who advocated abortion as a women's liberation issue, these objections were either absurd, inconsequential, or insulting.

The issue of whether or not Hawaii would become an "abortion mecca" had emotional appeal on both sides because of the strong sense of state pride and personal identification with the state that seem to be characteristic of Hawaii residents. While the proponents of repeal looked forward with pride to the moment when their state would add repeal of the abortion law to its roster of forward-looking civic achievements, the opponents of repeal were genuinely horrified that the taint of being an "abortion mecca" might be visited upon their fair state.

Most repeal advocates found the abortion mecca threat no threat at all. Since they saw abortion as a legitimate medical service which was not available as it should be, their response to the suggestion that Hawaii would become an abortion mecca was often, "So what?" One speaker for repeal even suggested that Hawaii should welcome the term as an honor.

Some repeal advocates, however, saw in the abortion mecca argument a genuine concern that local medical facilities would become overcrowded and were willing to accept a residency restriction as a means of increasing pressure on other states to change their own abortion laws. The residency requirement as an answer to the abortion mecca problem thus became one of the few points of real compromise. Many of those who agreed to consider a residency requirement, however, were convinced it was unconstitutional.

THE EFFECTIVENESS OF THE TWO POSITIONS

From the point of view of those testifying, the purpose of the Senate public hearing was to influence the decision of the Senate committee members and, ultimately, the other legislators. The same arguments were also intended to influence legislators indirectly by increasing the public demand for action on one side or the other. From the legislators' point of view, the hearing gave them a chance to hear all arguments, assess the political ramifications of their stance, and justify their votes to their constituency. Thus the arguments must be evaluated not only for their internal coherence and assumptions, but also for their potential impact on others.

The arguments raised on both sides of the abortion issue dealt with many complex topics. As far as the legislators were concerned, however, two distinct legal questions had to be resolved: 1) how abortion as an act should be evaluated; and 2) what the position of the law towards this act should be. The connection between the answers to these two questions ultimately determined the legislative appeal of each argument.

Answering the first question, the repeal advocates argued that abortion is an acceptable act whose absence or restriction causes serious social problems. This argument held very broad potential appeal because, directly or indirectly, it touched on problems affecting the bulk of the population. Regardless of whether or not one would finally choose to use abortion, the potential desire or need for a discreet, safe abortion was a real possibility for most sexually active men and women, and for their children as well. Moreover, a sizeable proportion of the population had already had direct or indirect experience with illegal abortion in the past. For persons who could sympathetically visualize their own or another's potential desire for the availability of abortion, the problems associated with illegal abortion made a persuasive case for repeal.

Abortion law repeal was also suggested as a potential solution for other more general social ills, such as illegitimacy, the poverty cycle, juvenile delinquency, child abuse, high welfare costs, and overcrowding. These are the everyday concerns of legislators. Supporting abortion repeal thus became a way of contributing to social welfare measures. The appeal was nonpartisan, because this approach was not closely identified with the policies of either major political party and because it appealed to liberals and conservatives alike.

The social problems argument thus contained both a personal and a more social appeal. The main obstacle to its acceptance was the tradition of abortion as a taboo subject, particularly for those who had never had to face the decision personally. The existence of public debate on the abortion issue eroded the taboo and brought to light information showing that a great deal of behavior in violation of the presumed taboo had already occurred. As more and more respected organizations took public positions in support of abortion law reform, more and more people came to feel that abortion was a legitimate solution to a host of genuine problems.

The initial proposal to liberalize the abortion law acted as a catalyst for this breakthrough by raising the issue of which conditions for abortion really were legitimate. Once the magnitude of the problems associated with the *status quo* was revealed by public debate, many people decided that the liberalized proposal did not offer a very satisfactory solution. From there it was but a short logical step to acceptance of the idea that abortion ought to be every woman's right—that she should not have to meet any external set of conditions to make her request for abortion legitimate.

This reasoning made the answer to the second question automatic. If a woman should not have to meet special criteria to obtain an abortion, then the law should make abortion available to anyone who wants it. There was no longer any reason for the law to regulate abortion.

Naturally, the core support for repeal came from people who believed abortion to be an acceptable and even a positive action. They wanted the state to sanction their position. The legal solution they proposed, however, accommodated far more than their own position. In effect, repeal advocates argued that their legal solution met everyone's needs, because it left the question of evaluating abortion to the private morality of the individual.

This argument fits the pluralist ideology that is taught by American public schools as the essence of American governmental institutions. Whether or not pluralism fits the reality, it remains the dominant ideological rationale for domestic political decisions. Consequently, any solution to the abortion issue that could claim to be pluralistic carried an automatic advantage in appealing both to the public and to legislators. Such an argument was particularly attractive in Hawaii, where ethnic pluralism lies at the heart of politics. Besides being convincing on its own merits, any opposition argument would have to show cause for overriding the built-in bias towards a pluralistic solution. In Hawaii, the opposition was unable to accomplish this in its answers to the two basic questions of the abortion issue.

Those wishing to maintain the *status quo* argued in answer to the first question that abortion as an act is wrong because it represents the killing of human life. Yet for this argument to have political appeal, it had to be coupled with the conclusion that the *law* should prohibit abortion as the answer to the second question. This could only occur when the belief that abortion is wrong is coupled with a broader belief that the individual—and the law—must prevent others from doing what one believes to be wrong.

Consequently, the appeal of the right to life argument for opposing abortion law repeal was essentially limited to the Roman Catholic population. The argument required acceptance of the two premises that human life is inviolable and that the fetus fits the definition of human life, as well as acceptance of the supporting doctrinal structure that makes any person's use of abortion a matter of common concern. For practicing Catholics, this support came from specific beliefs about the requirements for the salvation of souls, from the relative importance given to eternal life as contrasted with life in this world, from the system of rewards and punishments attached to absolute religious laws, and from a general concern with the sanctity of life.

To those without Roman Catholic religious training, the very form of the right to life argument was alien, since other religions do not teach faith through syllogistic logic. The form of the argument also seriously hampered efforts to proselytize undecided voters to the side of opposition to abortion. Opponents of repeal accepted without question that man cannot destroy human life and then focused their efforts on proving the validity of the belief that the fetus is a human life. They believed that this would "prove" the conclusion that the fetus should not be destroyed and impel opposition to abortion by force of logic. This reasoning led the most fervent opponents of abortion to produce graphic displays of fetal development in order to prove that the fetus is human life. Non-Catholics who were not accustomed to this type of religious argument did not understand its significance. To them, deduction did not establish faith nor justify the argument. Probably of greater importance, however, was the fact that such displays were simply regarded as bad taste.

There were of course many other people, particularly religious pacifists and women with a strong commitment to motherhood, who were personally opposed to abortion because they could not countenance killing a fetus. However, these beliefs were not so easily translated into general social or legal action when they were held without the supporting framework of Catholic religious doctrine. Non-Roman Catholics who were personally opposed to abortion were much more likely to accept the pluralist argument as protecting their own rights sufficiently while allowing others to pursue theirs. Many Roman Catholics were also sufficiently imbued with the pluralist ethic to feel that the position of their creed need not be supported by the state when other religions disagreed, and they could cite divorce legislation as a precedent.

In addition, the Drinan position mentioned previously cut into Roman Catholic opposition to abortion law repeal. This was the no-law position articulated by Father Robert Drinan, then dean of the Boston College Law School and subsequently a Massachusetts representative in the U.S. House of Representatives. His position was widely known in Hawaii, primarily because Senator Yano espoused it. Father Drinan reasoned that a liberalized abortion law would give legal approval to the killing of the fetus by stating the conditions under which abortions could be performed. Rather than allowing the law to offer the precedent of such approval to killing, he felt it would be preferable for the state to remain completely silent on abortion and remove the issue completely from the realm of law.

The Drinan position did not affect the right to life view as an answer to the question of how abortion as an act should be evaluated. However, it did address the corollary argument that abortion should be outlawed in order to protect the general moral principle of the sanctity of human life. The Drinan position differed from the pluralist argument because it did not really accept the right of others to have abortions, although its effect was to permit this. The Drinan position lent support to repeal as opposed to liberalization, if change became inevitable. Locally it was supported by many influential Catholics. Most undoubtedly accepted the argument on its merits, but some may have supported it because it seemed too extreme to be politically viable.

The extent of latent sympathy for the right to life argument could be estimated roughly by the proportion of Roman Catholics in the population: about 28 percent. This would be an underestimate, however, because some non-Catholics also held right to life beliefs. Not all non-Catholics could be presumed to be sympathetic to the social problems argument. However, when the issue became political support for repeal of abortion laws versus maintaining these laws, there was broader and stronger support for the repeal position. The pluralistic nature of the repeal position satisfied those who were unsure of their own stance, most non-Catholics who were personally committed to the right to life position, and many Catholics who were strongly pluralistic. Even for those who did not accept the positive view of the social problems argument, the pluralist legal position was convincing. The Drinan position cut further into Catholic opposition to repeal.

The existence of these divergent views was dismaying to many Catholic proponents of the *status quo,* who tended to see them as the splinter voices of a dissident, too liberal minority and not worthy of consideration. This was a serious mistake for the anti-abortion forces because it prevented a resolution of the issue using the combined energies of all the best minds among them and split the Catholic anti-abortion forces into weaker subgroups.

These internal conflicts were seen as a bonus for the repeal forces and provided role models for other Catholics who were undecided on the issue or who were for abortion law repeal but were insecure in their confrontation with the dictates of their Church. As a side effect, however, public knowledge of these internal debates proved a benefit to the broad public image of the Roman Catholic Church. It confirmed the reality of the divergence of opinion on the issue among Catholics and also served to weaken the contention that being against repeal meant being Catholic and being for repeal meant being anti-Catholic.

Compared to the subcamps among the anti-abortion forces, where separation led to a weakening of effort and effect, one strength of the pro-abortion groups seemed to be their diversity. The fact that so many different people and organizations could all support repeal for such a wide range of different reasons made the proposal politically very appealing.

Within the legislature itself, the right to life position was even further undercut by pluralism. Among those legislators who replied to our survey question, "What argument impressed you most?" the distribution of results reflects the appeal of both the social problems argument and the pluralist argument that women should have the right to choose for themselves.

Various aspects of the social problems argument (including medical reports of the number of illegal abortions, the unwanted child, and unequal application of the law) were most impressive to about a third of the legislators. The pluralist view that women had the right to a choice was most impressive for another third of the legislators. The opposing right to life argument was the most impressive point for about a sixth of the legislators.

It is not too surprising that legislators were particularly impressed by the pluralist argument, because they must be more professionally sensitive to pluralist ideology than ordinary citizens are. Yet it did surprise many Hawaii residents to find that pluralism was still alive and well in practice, even when a pluralist solution was in actuality politically more extreme than a compromise would have been. Technically, one compromise could have been to adopt a form of the liberalized bill that would have accommodated some of the social problems yet maintained the view that abortion should be illegal. That solution would have pleased few, but it would have fit the common jaundiced view of how politics really works. Instead, Hawaii's legislators upheld the traditional view of how American politics ought to work; they used the law to support the right of individuals to make decisions based on personal conscience.

CHAPTER 8

Legislative Politics

THE OFFICIAL DECISION to repeal the abortion law in Hawaii was based only in part upon the effectiveness of the repeal campaign and the force of arguments. Equally important were the composition of the legislature, the political power of forces on both sides of the issue, and the personal views and power of the governor. All of these factors provided the backdrop against which the abortion law repeal bill moved through the legislative process.

THE COMPOSITION OF THE LEGISLATURE

Before the 1950s, Hawaii politics were heavily dominated by the Caucasian, Republican descendants of early missionaries and businessmen. These men had always constituted a minority of the Islands' population, but they firmly controlled the wealth and political power. During the 1950s, however, a new Democratic coalition of Caucasians and Americans of Japanese ancestry emerged with the backing of organized labor. The new Democratic coalition grew out of the efforts of a small group of men eager to find positions in postwar Hawaii for the new generation of Americans of Japanese ancestry returning from military service. The young Japanese Americans had distinguished themselves fighting in World War II as members of the famed 442nd Infantry Regimental Combat Team, the most decorated combat team in the European theater. The problem was to find a way to use their talents in building a new, more egalitarian society in the postwar era.

The leader of the group with this vision was John A. Burns, a Caucasian who had worked closely with the young Japanese Americans in the early years of the war. Closely allied with him was ILWU organizer Jack Kawano. The vehicle the group chose was the small, underdog Democratic party. After the war, many of the 442nd veterans, taking advantage of the GI Bill, went off to college and law school. When they returned, they were encouraged by Burns, Kawano, and others to begin political careers in the new Democratic party.[1]

In 1954, the Democrats won solid majorities in both Houses of the Territorial legislature for the first time in history. Two years later, Burns won the Territory's most prestigious elective office, territorial delegate to Congress. In Washington, Burns became a minor protegé of Sam Rayburn and Lyndon Johnson and, during his second term in office, successfully steered the Hawaii statehood bill through Congress.

Although Burns lost the first gubernatorial election in 1959 to the former appointed Republican Governor, William Quinn, he came back in 1962 to win the governorship by a landslide. Through the 1960s the Democrats remained in firm control of the state legislature and remained closely allied with Governor Burns. The Democratic party continued to receive strong electoral support from organized labor, particularly the ILWU. Factionalism did develop within the party out of rivalry between those loyal to Burns and a new group backing Lieutenant Governor Thomas Gill (who had been elected against Burns' wishes in 1966), but on most legislative issues the party majority worked smoothly and effectively. By the time of the Fifth Legislature of the state of Hawaii (1969–1970), two thirds of the Senate seats (seventeen of twenty-five) and three quarters of the House seats (thirty-eight of fifty-one) were held by Democrats.

Just as important for the abortion issue was the ethnic composition behind the party line-up. Five of the eight Republican senators, but only five of the seventeen Democratic senators were *haole* (Caucasian). Nearly all of the remainder (ten Democrats and two Republicans) were of Japanese ancestry. The pattern was even more marked in the House of Representatives. Only three of the thirty-eight Democratic representatives and four of the twelve Republicans were Caucasian. The House had twenty-two Democrats and four Republicans of Japanese ancestry. The remainder were a cross-section of Hawaii's smaller ethnic groups: Chinese, Filipino, and part-Hawaiian. About a sixth of the legislature was Catholic, with these delegates more heavily concentrated within the *haole* and Filipino ethnic groups. Except for the heavy overrepresentation of Japanese in proportion to Caucasians, the legislature followed the ethnic and religious composition of the state reasonably closely.[2]

The party, ethnic, and religious affiliations of the legislators suggest their general predilections on the abortion issue and the types of external pressures to which they might respond. The Democratic party had acquired its majority position with the strong backing of organized labor. Although the unions could no longer claim full control over the votes of their members, union support was still a powerful influence in the legislature. Thus, union support for abortion law repeal was politically significant even if the issue was not directly linked to the union membership's needs and goals.

The Democratic party also reflected the views of its Japanese-American constituency. This particular constituency was heavily middle-class by the late 1960s but remained pro-labor and pro-Democratic as a result of the influence these forces had had in combating social, economic, and political discrimination stemming from the plantation era. The plantation memory was also kept alive by active Democratic party recruiting among the Filipino immigrants, who had gradually replaced the upwardly-mobile Japanese Americans in the agricultural labor market.

In the Japanese cultural tradition, abortion is regarded as an unpleasant but necessary fact of life. The peasant ancestors of Hawaii's Japanese Americans are known to have used infanticide to regulate birth during Japan's feudal era.[3] More recently, postwar Japan permitted abortion for loosely defined socioeconomic reasons, and many local women of Japanese ancestry had travelled to Japan to obtain safe, legal abortions. Thus, the presence of such a high proportion of Americans of Japanese ancestry in the state legislature was conducive to favorable consideration of abortion law repeal.

The religious affiliations of the legislators were also a factor to be considered. The majority of the legislators of Japanese ancestry were Buddhist or Protestant. The Buddhists particularly, while against any destruction of life, favored a policy of Church-State separation and a pluralistic philosophy. The idea of a repeal bill where the abortion decision is left to individual conscience thus had inherent appeal. Roman Catholic legislators, on the other hand, were likely to oppose abortion law repeal from a combination of personal belief and sensitivity to official Church views. While Senator Yano's own position was evidence that the Catholic legislator was not inevitably opposed to repeal, the odds were certainly in that direction.

In sum, within the legislature there was a large bloc of delegates with no particular social or cultural reason to oppose abortion law repeal and another smaller bloc likely to oppose it primarily on religious grounds. In addition, a substantial majority of the legislators in the first category received electoral support from organized labor and were thus inclined to support legislation advocated by the major unions.

POLITICAL PRESSURES ON THE LEGISLATURE

Of all the organizations and people publicly involved in the abortion law repeal issue, only three groups could be identified as politically powerful: organized labor (plus, to a lesser extent, the Chamber of Commerce), the Catholic Church, and the specific local constituencies of individual legislators. Obviously, this is not a list of the political powers in the state. Some of the most powerful interests, such as the tourist industry, the sugar and pineapple industries, and the land and development interests, simply did not become involved in the abortion issue.

Two major unions, the AFL-CIO and the ILWU, supported the abortion law repeal bill. In both cases the support consisted of a resolution favoring the bill taken by the union executive board. The resolution was announced publicly and presented in testimony by a female representative of the union at the Senate hearings in February, 1970. The abortion issue was not particularly high on union priority lists because the perceived benefits for the unions' constituencies were indirect and long-range. The unions' primary interest was in the argument that rich women were able to obtain safe abortions despite the law, but poor women either faced the dangers of illegal abortion or the problems of having more children than they wanted. In effect, the unions were making a public service gesture by supporting repeal rather than promoting their own immediate economic interests. The most general effect of such low-key support was probably to serve notice that union backing of legislators would not be withheld if they did support the bill. For individual legislators who campaigned on the basis of across-the-board support for labor-advocated legislation, the effect was somewhat greater.

On the other side of the issue, the Roman Catholic Church constituted a strong political pressure. The Church could claim to represent a constitutency of more than a quarter of the state's population, although of course it could not necessarily deliver those votes. The Church did much more than simply issue public statements opposing the abortion law repeal bill and present testimony at Senate hearings. The Church placed direct pressure on the legislature on three specific occasions. All three occurred while the repeal bill was before the Senate for passage. On February 6, 1970, three days after the Senate hearing and the day the bill went to the floor of the Senate, Bishop Scanlan requested and, after some political maneuvering, held a private audience with legislators. The meeting was arranged by Senate President David McClung as a personal favor for an old friend who requested it on behalf of the bishop. It was attended by virtually all of the Catholic legislators, plus a few non-Catholics. Senator Yano said that he was the only repeal vote present.[4]

Three days later, an anti-abortion demonstration organized by Robert Pearson was held outside the Capitol. Speeches by Bishop Scanlan and Monsignor Kekumano, as well as the presence of Catholic high school students formally released from school and brought to the demonstration by bus, indicated that the event was approved and supported by the Church officialdom.

The third direct attempt to influence the legislators occurred the following day, February 10, 1970, when the bill was scheduled for Senate debate and vote. Each day's Senate session opened with an invocation by a local clergyman, as is the custom in most U.S. state legislatures. Tradition held that the invocation be a general spiritual blessing with no partisan commentary on matters before the legislative body. The person scheduled to give the invocation, and recorded in the *Senate Journal* for the day, was Reverend

Thomas B. Killackey of (Roman Catholic) Sacred Heart Church.[5] However, the invocation was in fact given by Monsignor Francis Marzen, editor of the *Catholic Herald* and director of information for the Diocese of Honolulu. Monsignor Marzen, who had been the bishop's personal spokesman throughout the abortion law campaign, used the occasion to urge the legislators, indirectly but unmistakably, to vote against any move to relax the existing abortion legislation.[6]

In addition to these direct attempts to influence the legislature, the Church also was involved in numerous efforts to encourage its members to voice their opposition to the bill as voters who on election day would remember how their legislators voted on this issue. Because Catholics as voters appealed to their own representatives, it is difficult to distinguish this type of pressure by the Church from the third source of political pressure on the legislature: the specific constituencies of individual legislators.

The perpetual dilemma of any elected official is whether to vote on the basis of what he personally believes is right, what is in the best interests of his constituents, or what his constituents say they want. Although the electorate is rarely unanimous, the legislator who wants to be re-elected must somehow take into account the demands made by voters. The dilemma was particularly acute on the issue of abortion law repeal, for several reasons.

Abortion law repeal was a public conscience issue that received its main support from ordinary citizens rather than from powerful economic interests. On some issues, such as corporate tax write-offs and land use and development arrangements, for example, legislators may respond to heavy pressure from powerful private economic interests and quietly violate the interests of an unaware public. Unless and until the voters organize to express concern about such policies, the legislator may act without much regard for the interests of his constituents and suffer no electoral penalties.

Abortion law repeal was a very different kind of issue. Although the restrictive abortion law had the support of one powerful interest group, the Catholic Church, the law had not been enacted and maintained because of that interest. Likewise, the repeal position was not advanced by a powerful economic interest group to which a legislator could respond without the knowledge of his constituents. Rather, the issue became a concern to the individual legislator precisely because public attention was focused on it. The legislator could not ignore the abortion law repeal issue because a vocal, interested constituency was pressing him to take a stand and watching to see exactly how he voted.

Because abortion law repeal was a public conscience issue, it was also a private conscience issue for the individual legislator. The legislator responded to the issue in the same way the public did, in terms of his personal beliefs and values. The legislator could not regard abortion law repeal at arm's length, as an objective conflict between two sets of competing arguments, because his own beliefs had to side with one of those views. Ultimately, each legislator had to evaluate the issue by the standards of his own conscience, as well as by listening to his constituents.

In a sense, the whole repeal campaign can be viewed as an attempt to put political pressure on legislators. However, many of the groups which were most active had very insignificant voting power. For this reason, their efforts were directed primarily towards the larger voting public and secondarily towards the legislature itself. The direct indicators of political pressure from the voting public were telephone calls, letters and visits to district representatives, and (to a lesser extent) public opinion polls, all of which have been previously described as campaign tactics.

In our legislative survey, more than two thirds of the legislators said that they had voted on the basis of their own conscience. Only 10 percent said that they had voted to support the views of their constituents, while 20 percent said they had voted for their constituency and because of their conscience. Even more interesting is the relationship between the actual vote on the abortion law repeal bill and the legislator's reason for so voting. All of the legislators in the survey who reported that they voted against the repeal bill said that they voted because of their conscience. All who voted for the bill said they voted both because of their conscience and because of their constituency. Likewise, the small number who said they voted for their constituencies also voted for the bill, possibly even against their consciences.

THE POSITION OF THE GOVERNOR

Without some support from Governor John Burns, abortion law repeal was a political impossibility in Hawaii. This was due as much to the governor's personal power and stature as to the legal prerogatives of his office. The governor had the power to veto a bill after it had passed both houses of the legislature, and that veto could only be overridden by a two-thirds vote of the legislature. A safety provision in the law also stipulated that a bill passed by the legislature, but not vetoed, would automatically become law after ten days if the governor did not sign it.[7]

By 1969, Governor Burns was halfway through his second four-year term as governor. The only challenge to his leadership in the state was the beginning of a more liberal faction in the Democratic party, headed by Lieutenant Governor Thomas Gill. Burns still commanded the strong loyalty of the Democratic majority in both houses of the legislature. Even if the legislature were willing to pass an abortion law repeal bill, few legislators would have voted to override a veto by the governor. Even more important, many legislators would not have been willing to vote for initial passage of an abortion law repeal bill if the governor intended to veto it. Thus, Governor Burns' position was critical.

The governor was a devout Catholic who attended mass daily. He habitually signed his official correspondence with the phrase, "Aloha and may the Almighty be with you and yours always." Even more pertinent to the abortion issue, Burns' youngest son had been born despite warnings by physicians that the polio-stricken Mrs. Burns might die if the pregnancy were not aborted.[8]

In the spring of 1969, Dr. George Goto asked the governor if he would permit the abortion law reform bill then under consideration in the House to become law, with or without his signature. The governor would not give him a reply. However, Governor Burns did state for the record that he would not approach the issue on the basis of his personal beliefs, although he frequently expressed reservations about the abortion law reform bill.[9]

The following autumn, several weeks after Senator Yano's announcement that he would introduce a repeal bill in the next legislative session, Governor Burns appeared at a local Democratic club meeting in Honolulu. In response to a question from the floor about whether or not he supported Senator Yano's repeal proposal, Governor Burns replied that he would favor the idea of an across-the-board repeal, although he was personally opposed to abortion. He added that he believed abortion should not be legislated but should be a matter of private conscience.[10] Governor Burns later hinted that the statement had been made in an unguarded moment but said it did reflect his views.

The statement provided clear direction for the legislature. As Dr. Goto put it, "He made it clear that repeal was the only way to go, because he would veto the liberalization bill. Since Governor Burns had been on the opposite side for a long time, this was a big impetus to the legislators."[11] Senator Yano also felt more confident that the repeal bill could succeed after the governor's statement, although he did not talk with Governor Burns about the issue until much later on.[12]

The governor's statement was important both for its content and for its timing. His remark transformed the idea of abortion law repeal into a genuine political possibility. It altered the predictions of all the political pros and greatly encouraged repeal supporters in the community. For the next five months, the governor would say nothing more about the issue publicly. Yet with his October statement Governor Burns had profoundly affected the situation.

THE REPEAL BILL'S FIRST LEGISLATIVE TESTS

When the legislative session began in late January, 1970, Senator Yano introduced his repeal bill. This was accomplished by means of a report from the Committee on Public Health, Welfare and Housing, which still retained control over House Bill 61 from the 1969 session. Instead of introducing a new bill for full repeal of the 1869 abortion law, the Senate committee simply rewrote House Bill 61, Representative Loo's reform bill patterned on the ALI model abortion law, which had been passed by the House in 1969. The committee reported out H.B. 61 with a brief statement:

> The purpose of this bill is to amend the law of abortion by adding additional bases and requirements for justifiable abortion that may be performed by a physician and provisions relating to self-abortion, pretended abortion, and distribution of abortifacients.
>
> Your Committee is in agreement that the existing abortion law, enacted in 1869 and never amended, should be amended now and recommends the following amendments to the bill:
>
> . . . (2) Amend section 1 to provide for deletion of sections 768-6, 768-7, and 768-8, Hawaii Revised Statutes.
>
> . . . omit the remaining sections of the bill.[13]

The report further recommended that the new version be recommitted to the committee after passing second reading. The new version, labelled House Bill 61, House Draft 1, Senate Draft 1, was appended to the report. It read simply:

> Section 1. Chapter 768, Hawaii Revised Statutes, is amended by deleting sections 768-6, 768-7, and 768-8.[14]

House Bill 61, Senate Draft 1, was passed without dissent on second reading on January 29 to allow its formal consideration in committee.[15] By this time the abortion law repeal campaign had already achieved considerable momentum, which Senator Yano successfully exploited by scheduling his committee's rehearing immediately. The public hearing on February 3 and 4 then brought the campaign to a climax and channeled the full range of arguments and facts to the receptive committee.

One week later, the Senate Committee on Public Health, Welfare and Housing submitted its report recommending approval of House Bill 61, Senate Draft 2, which was a minor modification of the repeal version of the bill authored by Senator Yano (Senate Draft 1). The difference between the two drafts was that Senate Draft 1 had also included deletion of the section relating to concealment of the death of illegitimates (768-8). The section required reporting of the death of any "issue" of a woman's body, "whether born alive or not, which if born alive would have been illegitimate." Its aim was to prevent concealment of such deaths "so that it may not be known whether the issue was born alive or not, or whether it was murdered." [16] The committee concluded that this section did not relate to abortion and thus left it intact. This interpretation limited the applicability of the section to infanticide.

The committee report demonstrated the central role of the public hearing in educating and persuading committee members. It also reflected the legal research done by Senator Yano and others. The report began with a firm commitment to the repeal of the abortion law:

> After an extensive public hearing on the proposed bill to repeal the present law on abortion, your Committee concludes that the subject of abortion should not be a matter of legislation but should be left as an individual matter of conscience and choice.[17]

The report then dealt with the principal objection to repeal, the right to life argument. The committee noted that the charge of killing innocent human lives was based on the belief that life begins at or soon after conception. They pointed out that the issue of when human life begins had not been resolved by theologians. They reasoned:

> The right of the unborn child is therefore predicated on the more important question or whether a fetus is a human being and therefore entitled to all rights of human beings. From the standpoint of law, the question of human life is based on viability, that is, the law regards a fetus as a human being only at such time when such fetus can exist individually outside of the mother's womb. Those who are against abortion and insist that abortion is murder and that an embryo is a person conveniently overlook the fact that no state or nation requires the dead fetus to be treated like a dead person and no cognizance is taken of the dead fetus up to five months' prenatal life. Scientists have never regarded such a fetus to be a human being. Whether society has a duty to protect life in the womb during its early stages is a matter of individual opinion and belief and your Committee wishes to leave it as such.[18]

Next, the report considered the legality of the existing Hawaii abortion law in light of constitutional challenges in California and the District of Columbia as well as the related Supreme Court decision in *Griswold* v. *the State of Connecticut* regarding the right of married persons to use contraceptives. The report pointed out that if the Hawaii abortion law were ruled by the U.S. Supreme Court to be unconstitutional, the legislature would have two alternatives: it could either refuse to legislate further laws on abortion, or it could enact a law similar to the ALI model abortion law. The committee favored the first alternative and set forth several objections to the limited reform of the ALI model law.

One objection was Senator Yano's concern, following the Drinan argument, that to legislate the conditions under which abortion would be acceptable constituted the legalization of abortion and the state's approval of the act. Rather, he reasoned:

> Your Committee's position for repeal is *NOT* legalization but rather that we choose not to control or regulate this matter by law and further that we neither approve nor disapprove of abortion.[19]

A second objection, drawn primarily from an article by Harvey Zipf[20] which Senator Yano had found helpful, was that the reform laws do not work, since they have not reduced illegal abortions and have not accommodated very many women.

The third objection to the reform laws raised by the report was apparently based on the testimony presented at the hearing by physicians.

> The present laws also appear to put an unreasonable interference on the personal freedom of a physician to prescribe and administer what is clinically sound by proven medical opinion and scientific findings and the right of the public to the best medical help and treatment to which they are entitled.[21]

A final objection to the reform laws was the possibility that these laws also might raise constitutional questions because of the vagueness of the terms defining the conditions under which abortion is permitted.

The report then briefly outlined the major arguments for repeal which had been presented at the hearing, including the high rate of illegal abortion, the social and economic problems related to unwanted children, the economic discrimination of restrictive abortion laws, and the rights of women with problem pregnancies. To emphasize the reality of the abortion problem locally, the report cited the study of Hawaii physicians conducted by Drs. Roy Smith and George Goto and hearing testimony that therapeutic abortions were available in Honolulu hospitals for those who could afford them and knew the right physicians.

The arguments for repeal were summed up in the following statements:

> Your Committee would also like to stress that the repeal of the abortion law does not in any way infringe upon the right of a pregnant woman to refrain from abortion, but no group has the right to impose its moral code or standards on the rest of society which should be allowed individual choice—a precious right in our present democratic and pluralistic society.
>
> Your Committee feels that in our present society, laws which place criminal penalties for dealing with problem pregnancies are a social injustice resulting in tragic consequences not only to the personal health and welfare of the women involved but also the general

welfare of the State in allowing compulsory pregnancies because an archaic law so dictates.[22]

The report then considered and rejected several compromises or qualifications to the proposed repeal. The first was a residence requirement, intended to counteract the threat of Hawaii becoming an "abortion mecca." The committee presented five arguments against a residence requirement. First, given the likelihood of a Supreme Court decision declaring restrictive abortion laws unconstitutional, the abortion situation would change throughout the country. Second, Colorado's experience with a reform law was cited as some indication that there would be no great influx of nonresidents seeking abortion. Third, a residence requirement might well be unconstitutional, in light of the Supreme Court decision that welfare recipients need not fulfill any residence requirements *(Shapiro* v. *Thompson)*. Fourth, a residence requirement would be "difficult, if not impossible, to enforce." Finally, such a provision would be inhumane, given the humiliation and frustration that citizens of other states suffer under restrictive abortion laws.

Another proposed requirement was that abortion be performed only in hospitals. While acknowledging that the suggestion had merit from a public health standpoint, the committee rejected this restriction because it would raise the cost of abortions and also because of the reduction in privacy.

The committee also rejected the suggestion that a time limit be set within which abortion would be permitted, citing the hearing testimony of medical professionals that the length of gestation and point of viability could not be measured with certainty. The committee added that it

feels real concern for those physicians who may be faced with the problem of destroying a fetus in the later stages of pregnancy due to medical indications, but this problem can be resolved by the fact that this kind of operation will not legally be considered an abortion and immunity can be provided to physicians by amending the present law on murder and wrongful death.[23]

The report concluded by noting that "some moralists have expressed concern that repeal of the abortion laws will lead to increased promiscuity." This argument was refuted by a long citation from the hearing testimony of Dr. Milton Diamond to the effect that sexual behavior in American society had not markedly changed since the 1920s and that abortion was already being used widely despite its illegality.[24]

Committee members Vincent Yano, Donald Ching, Mamoru Yamasaki, and Percy Mirikitani concurred in the committee report. Wadsworth Yee signed with reservations.

THE FIRST SENATE DEBATE

The Senate took up the bill the following day, February 10, 1970. Senator Yano introduced the bill with a speech summarizing the committee report. He also announced the simultaneous introduction of two new bills amending the Medical Practice Act. These bills reflected compromises which were already being negotiated.

Senator Yano was firmly committed to pure and total repeal of the abortion law because his own acceptance of the idea was dependent upon the Drinan interpretation that no law meant no legal approval of the act. Consequently, he wanted any compromises, if they had to be made, to be in other forms of legislation rather than as amendments to the existing abortion statute. This fine distinction was irrelevant to most others on both sides of the controversy, but it explains many of the odd maneuvers in the bill's subsequent history. It was the reason for the introduction of the two new bills on February 10.

The first bill was an amendment to the Medical Practice Act to provide that all abortions be performed in licensed hospitals. Senator Yano introduced it with the comment:

> The suggestion that all abortions be performed in hospitals has been considered by your Committee to have some merit and we have introduced today a bill amending the Medical Practice Act to provide that all abortions must be performed in a licensed hospital. After consultation with the medical profession it appears that this step will greatly insure the safety and welfare of the woman involved whose medical records are confidential and prevent possible abuse by doctors who might take advantage of this situation.[25]

The second bill was a proposed amendment to the Medical Practice Act to ensure that any abortion performed by an unlicensed person would remain a felony. Obviously, if Senator Yano had not insisted that the actual abortion statute be removed from the law, these two items could easily have been included as qualifications in a single permissive abortion law. But that was exactly what Senator Yano did not want: the legalization of abortion.

Senator Yano's proposed compromise of putting the limitations into the Medical Practice Act instead of the abortion law was immediately challenged by Senator William Fernandes. He argued that there was no assurance the bill to limit the practice of abortion to hospitals would pass and that therefore he could not vote for the repeal bill.

Two other senators then spoke against the repeal bill, using the right to life argument. Senator John Hulten argued that since there is no way of proving that life does not exist from the moment of conception, "doubt must be resolved in favor of its existence." He urged his fellow lawmakers to avoid "what may well be a slaughter of innocents."[26]

Senator John Lanham also expressed concern about the civil rights of the unborn child and the overall moral impact of the bill. In his arguments against the bill, Senator Lanham took note of the strong political support for repeal. He said that in opposing the bill he found himself on the opposite side of the issue from churches, labor unions, and others who have helped Hawaii immeasurably.[27]

Aside from those who were totally opposed to liberalizing the abortion law on moral grounds, several senators were willing to accept the basic notion of repeal if certain safeguards were provided. Various senators espoused one or more of four possible safeguards: 1) a provision ensuring that only licensed physicians could perform abortions legally and that unqualified persons who performed abortions could be prosecuted; 2) a provision limiting the performance of abortions to regulated facilities, such as hospitals or clinics, under the supervision of the Department of Health; 3) a limit on the length of gestation at which abortions could be performed; 4) a residence requirement to prevent outsiders from coming to Hawaii to obtain abortions.

Because Senator Yano's advocacy of abortion law change was based on the Drinan argument, he wanted to eliminate the criminal abortion statute completely. He was willing to compromise, so long as the qualifying legislation was incorporated into other statutes and not into a new abortion law. The two bills he introduced to amend the Medical Practice Act were designed to cover the first two problems: preventing unqualified persons from performing abortions and limiting the performance of abortions to licensed hospitals. He believed that a residence requirement would be unconstitutional as well as inhumane, so he did not want to compromise on this point. He also did not want to place a time limit on abortions because that would imply a legislative decision about when abortions were approved, again creating the situation which advocates of the Drinan position wanted to avoid.

Several senators were not satisfied with Yano's offer to compromise by amending the Medical Practice Act. Two attempts were made to amend House Bill 61, Senate Draft 1 on the floor to incorporate the desired qualifications.

The first was an amendment introduced by Republican Senator Hebden Porteus. Senator Porteus proposed to preserve intact the first section (768-6) of the existing criminal abortion statute, which read:

> Whoever maliciously, without lawful justification administers or causes or procures to be administered any poison or noxious thing to a woman when with child, in order to produce her miscarriage, or maliciously uses any instrument or other means with like intent shall, if the woman is then quick with child, be fined not more than $1,000 and imprisoned at hard labor not more than five years; and if she is then not quick with child, shall be fined not more than $500 and imprisoned at hard labor not more than two years.[28]

His amendment would have replaced section 768-7, which said that the only lawful justification for abortion was to save the life of the woman, by providing a detailed set of lawful justifications. The proposal would have made abortion legal during the first fifteen weeks of gestation, as long as it was performed by a licensed physician in a licensed hospital or clinic. From the sixteenth week of gestation, abortion would be permitted if the physician certified the following conditions in writing:

> Continuation of the pregnancy is likely to result in:
> (i) the death of the woman; or
> (ii) the serious permanent impairment of the physical or mental health of the woman; or
> (iii) the birth of the child with grave and permanent physical or mental deformity.[29]

This version covered all of the ALI model abortion law conditions except rape and incest, but the wording came from the Republican senators' 1969 reform bill, S.B. 521. It was more restrictive than the ALI model law version because of the inclusion of the words "permanent" and "grave."

The Porteus amendment not only placed conditions on the performance of abortion, it also reverted to the form of an abortion statute which Senator Yano found unacceptable. It did, however, cover three of the four major qualifications frequently suggested. The amendment aimed to ensure that abortions would be performed only by physicians. This was accomplished by leaving the criminal abortion statute intact and making an exception to the felony for physicians. The amendment limited abortions to hospitals by spelling out the locations in which abortions could be performed without being felonious. The gestation limit was introduced by strict specification of the reasons for which abortions could be performed after the fifteenth week of gestation. The amendment did not include a residence clause.

Senator Yano fought the proposed amendment on the grounds that the limitation of medical sites for abortion was already covered by the separate bill he had introduced. Although Senator Porteus' amendment accepted abortion without medical indications during the first fifteen weeks of gestation, Senator Yano characterized it as a reversion to the original House Bill 61.[30] After some debate, the Porteus amendment failed.

Senator Wadsworth Yee, who as a member of the Committee on Public Health, Welfare and Housing had signed the committee report "with reservations," introduced an amendment at this point. His version reintroduced the first part of the defeated Porteus amendment with the addition of a residence requirement. It read:

> Section 768-7. "Lawful Justification" means the intentional and voluntary termination of the pregnancy of a woman, who has been physically present within the State for a period of ninety days.
> (1) By a physician authorized by law to practice medicine in this State using accepted medical procedures,
> (2) (A) in a hospital licensed by this State; or
> (B) in a clinic or office approved by the department of health; or
> (C) in case of life or death of the woman at the site of such emergency.[31]

Speaking for his amendment, Senator Yee said that he was bothered by the elimination of the criminal section of the abortion statute in the repeal bill.[32] His amendment, like the defeated Porteus amendment, retained the felony provisions for abortions which were not performed by a physician in a hospital or clinic. Senator Yee's amendment had a residence clause but no gestation limit.

Again, Senator Yano fought the amendment in terms of its content, although its form was also objectionable to him. He argued that the residence requirement was unenforceable and probably unconstitutional.[33] The Yee amendment failed to pass.

Debate on the repeal bill continued. Senator Percy Mirikitani, a member of the Committee on Public Health, Welfare and Housing, spoke in favor of the bill. He said that the committee had considered the issue very carefully and thoroughly, and had allowed the matter to sit for a year so that all people concerned would have time to think about it. He pointed out that more than 90 percent of all the organizations and persons who appeared before the committee had supported repeal of the abortion law. The committee, he said, had "efficiently and with deep consideration made up their minds to repeal because it is justified based on sound facts."[34]

Two senators then spoke against the bill on the grounds that it was inadequate legislation. Senator Eureka Forbes cited the lack of a hospital provision, a gestation limit, and a residence requirement. She also raised the issue of protection of paternal rights in regard to the unborn child.[35]

Senator Donald Nishimura also argued that the void created by repeal of the abortion law would lead to serious problems. In particular, he noted that:

> The bill in its present form permits a wife to unilaterally without consulting her husband or without his advise [*sic*] to get an abortion.[36]

Senator Fred Rohlfing then spoke in favor of the bill, citing the civil rights and legal problems raised by the ALI model abortion law alternative. He added that the restrictive abortion law "would not be in the books today if the men were the ones who bore children."[37]

After more than an hour of debate, House Bill 61, Senate Draft 2 passed third reading on a vote of seventeen to seven. Of the two senators who proposed amendments, Senator Porteus voted against the bill, but Senator Yee voted for it.[38]

Thus, the pure repeal bill emerged unscathed from its first legislative test. It had passed by a wide margin, and at least some of the opposition had indicated acceptance of the general concept of a woman's right to request an abortion, but they had couched their objections in terms of the lack of adequate safeguards in the bill.

CHAPTER 9

From Bill to Law

THE SENATE had passed a repeal bill which was actually an amended version of the reform bill passed by the House (House Bill 61). The House could either accept the amended version or reject it. If the House did not accept the amended bill, a conference committee would be selected to come up with a compromise bill acceptable to both houses.[1]

A conference committee usually consists of three members from each house, two from the majority party and one from the minority. The members are appointed by the heads of their respective houses, with the chairmanship of each delegation traditionally conferred on the committee chairman responsible for the bill. The members are supposed to be persons who support the legislation in question but will remain open-minded about the compromises necessary to get it passed.

On February 11, 1970, the House of Representatives rejected the Senate version of the bill. House Speaker Tadao Beppu made it clear that the House decision indicated a desire for some qualifications in the repeal bill rather than a demand for serious revision of the concept.

CONFERENCE COMMITTEE NEGOTIATIONS

The tradition of making the chairman of the responsible committee the head of the conference committee delegation caused some difficulty in the House of Representatives. The majority party leadership supported repeal, but the committee chairman involved was Representative George Loo, who still favored the ALI model abortion law and opposed repeal. Representative Loo feared that he would be bypassed and wanted very much to exercise his influence in the conference committee to tone down the repeal bill. With the help of another colleague, Loo canvassed the House committee chairmen and obtained their support for his appointment to the conference committee, primarily because of the general precedent that this was the prerogative of committee chairmen. Before Speaker Tadao Beppu would appoint him, however, Representative Loo agreed not to stop the bill or stall it in committee.

By this time, Representative Loo realized that he could not stop the movement for repeal. He had polled the House after the Senate vote and found the majority in favor of the repeal bill. Yet he thought he could insist on some modifications. Representative Loo was especially concerned about the danger of Hawaii becoming an "abortion mecca," since it would be the only state in which abortion was available at the woman's request. Loo also feared the overcrowding of local medical facilities and the adverse publicity attached to the title "abortion mecca," as well as the potential overloading of welfare rolls by destitute pregnant women migrating from the Mainland. The solution, as he saw it, was a residence restriction which would limit access to abortion in Hawaii to local residents. Representative Loo had already requested an opinion on residence requirements from the attorney general's office. Deputy Attorney General Thomas Pico had reported on January 23 that while a residence restriction could raise constitutional questions, it was not necessarily invalid.[2]

Representative Loo also wanted abortions to be performed only in hospitals. Although this would increase the load on a limited number of medical facilities, he felt it would afford some measure of control over the practice of abortion. He also wanted a personnel waiver written into the bill guaranteeing the rights of hospital personnel to refuse to participate in abortions without being sued for their refusal.[3]

The other two House appointees to the conference committee were Representative Dorothy Devereux (Republican) and Charles Ushijima (Democrat). Representative Devereux had been involved in the issue of abortion from its first introduction in the House in 1967. Although she had not been active publicly, she had consistently voted for abortion law reform bills in committee and on the floor. A nurse and the widow of a physician, she had arrived at her position on abortion through long familiarity with the problem. Following her appointment to the conference committee, her office screened incoming calls on the abortion issue by reporting that Representative Devereux already firmly supported repeal and suggesting that the callers use their time to convince others. Representative Ushijima had not publicly committed himself on the issue, but he had previously voted for the reform bill and was generally open-minded about the issue.

The House delegation met before the conference committee sessions began to work out their position. Representative Loo said that he would require the hospital provision, a residence restriction, and the personnel waiver. The two House members told him that they were for the repeal bill but would support him on these three demands.[4]

On the Senate side, the conference committee members were Senators Yano, Mirikitani, and Ching. Both Mirikitani and Ching had supported the repeal bill as members of the Committee on Public Health, Welfare and Housing. They agreed to let Senator Yano handle all Senate negotiations in the conference committee. He received their proxies and they did not participate further in the committee meetings.

Democratic Floor Leader Representative Stuart Ho counted votes in the House of Representatives for Yano and found that they were three or four votes shy of a majority for the repeal bill without any qualifications. Yano was willing to accept the hospital provision, because he had already made that concession in the Senate through the auxiliary legislation. He was also very willing to accept the personnel waiver, which Sister Maureen, the chief administrator of the local Catholic hospital, had requested that he include. However, he strongly opposed the residence requirement because he felt it was probably unconstitutional. He also felt he could fight against the residence requirement as a political gesture because he was going to concede the other two points.[5]

The conference committee sessions began with Representative Loo demanding three qualifications in the repeal bill, and Representatives Devereux and Ushijima backing him. Senator Yano, representing all three of the Senate votes on the committee, opposed all three qualifications but was prepared to concede everything except the residency provision. Senator Yano also still hoped to keep the qualifications separate from the actual repeal of the abortion statute. The meetings soon deadlocked on the residency issue, with Senator Yano refusing to accept it and Representative Loo threatening a floor fight if he could not get the provision in the conference committee. Representatives Devereux and Ushijima continued to support their chairman despite Senator Yano's efforts to divide the House delegation. Finally, after days of fruitless negotiation, pressure was building on the conference committee to get the bill out of committee and to the floor. Senator Yano capitulated, much to Representative Loo's satisfaction.[6]

On Feburary 17, 1970, the conference committee reported out a much-altered bill. This version, House Bill 61, Senate Draft 2, Conference Draft 1 retained the Senate draft's section 1, which read, "Chapter 768, Hawaii Revised Statutes, is amended by deleting sections 768-6 and 768-7." However, section 2, which was to replace the old abortion statute in chapter 768 of the statutes, read:

> *Abortion: criminal abortion; penalties; refusal to perform.*
> (a) No abortion shall be performed in this State unless:
> (1) The abortion is performed by a licensed physician or surgeon, or by a licensed osteopathic physician and surgeon; and
> (2) The abortion is performed in a hospital licensed by the Department of Health or operated by the Federal Government or an agency thereof; and
> (3) The woman upon whom the abortion is to be performed is a resident of this State or has in fact resided in this State for at least three calendar months immediately preceding the abortion.
> (b) Any abortion performed in this State that does not meet the requirements of subsection (a) is a criminal abortion.
> (c) Any person who performs criminal abortion on another shall be fined not more than $1,000 and imprisoned not more than five years.
> (d)
> (1) No hospital shall be required to admit any patient for the purpose of having an abortion performed and no hospital shall be civilly liable for its refusal to perform an abortion.
> (2) No employee or member of the medical staff of a hospital shall be required to participate in the performance of an abortion nor

> shall he be civilly liable if he notified the hospital of his election not to participate in the performance of abortions.
>
> (3) No physician or surgeon or osteopathic physician or surgeon shall be required to give advice with respect to, or to participate in, any abortion if he chooses not to do so nor shall he be civilly liable if he notifies the patient of his decision.[7]

Section 3 contained a severability clause, a legal mechanism which would save the major intent of the bill in the event that any portion of the law was declared invalid.

The conference committee report accompanying the revised bill generally followed the arguments set forth in the Senate committee report, with a few key exceptions. Although the conference committee draft was in fact placing new abortion legislation in the same statute where the old abortion law had been located, the committee report still contained the argument:

> Your Committee would like to emphasize that this so-called "liberalized" version [referring to the original H.B. 61] is a misnomer because it actually constitutes 'legalizing' abortions under the conditions set forth. Your Committee's position for repeal is *NOT* legalization but rather that we choose not to control or regulate this matter by law, and further that we neither approve nor disapprove of abortion.[8]

Representative Devereux reports that there was general acceptance of the notion that the bill did not "legalize" abortion.[9] The committee apparently felt that this position was not dependent upon the absence of a specific abortion statute, as in the Drinan view, but rather was true because the repeal law would not bar abortion in general and then specify certain circumstances in which it would be legal. That is, it did not exempt certain abortions from a general criminal category. The fine distinction was that the proposed law distinguished between "abortions" and "criminal abortions." A criminal abortion was defined as one not performed by a licensed physician in a licensed facility on a state resident.

The committee report reiterated the belief that a residency requirement might be unconstitutional, but it added,

> your Committee feels that without a residence requirement the medical services and facilities in this State may be overburdened by residents of other states seeking abortions.[10]

The restriction of abortions to hospitals was explained as follows:

> Your committee also feels that all abortions should be performed in hospitals from the standpoint of public health and safety due to high possibility of infection when performed under septic conditions. Your Committee is aware that the repeal of the abortion laws may well produce abuses both within and without the medical profession and that all illegal abortionists will not be eliminated but also feel at the same time that the removal of criminal sanctions will permit women with problem pregnancies to consult qualified physicians and have the benefit of counseling before deciding on a very delicate and complex problem.[11]

The personnel waiver was simply explained as a protection which should be provided to hospitals, hospital staff personnel, and physicians.

The committee report dismissed the issue of a time limit on abortions with a quote from the report of the Senate Committee on Public Health, Welfare and Housing:

> Another suggestion made is *[sic]* to limit the time within which an abortion is permissible seems to have some merit but testimony indicates that even the medical profession is not certain as to how to measure the time of pregnancy and also measure with any kind of certainty when a fetus becomes viable.[12]

The committee report concluded with some new information concerning the implementation of the proposed new law.

> As a final note, your Committee has been informed by the Hawaii Medical Association and the leading maternity hospital in Honolulu that an outpatient procedure for the performance of an abortion can be worked out at the approximate cost of $200 including the physician's fee, which is substantially less than what it costs a woman today to go to Japan or to go to an illegal abortionist, with reference to cases involving dilatation and curettage within the first trimester of a pregnancy. It is hoped that all women with problem pregnancies will either go to the hospital or to their personal physician and use the best medical facilities available in view of the delicate operation and the added assurance that all medical records are confidential and the further safeguard of a pathological report which will certify the success of every operation. This system will also make possible follow-up

> research and statistics which are vital to evaluate the entire program. The Schools of Public Health, Medicine and Social Work at the University of Hawaii have all volunteered to assist in the follow-up studies to help in determining whether or not further statutory changes are necessary. It is anticipated by your Committee that clinics which can meet standards set forth jointly by the Department of Health and the Hawaii Medical Association will also be allowed to perform abortions in the near future on an outpatient basis. It is your Committee's intention to carefully and constantly evaluate reports and statistics resulting from the removal of criminal penalties on a subject involving a very complex and delicate problem.[13]

Senator Yano may appear to have made a major shift from his original position in the course of the conference committee deliberations. He had not only accepted a series of restrictions on abortion, he had also allowed the restrictions to be written into a replacement to the old abortion statute rather than keeping them separate and removing the abortion statute completely.

Basically, every one of the compromises was a political necessity if repeal was to become a reality. While he was personally committed to the Drinan position of removing abortion from the law completely, Senator Yano was publicly identified with the repeal of restrictive abortion laws, which did not necessarily have to be accomplished according to the Drinan formula. He had to attend to both personal and public needs.

Senator Yano knew beforehand that the real difficulty would be getting the bill through the House, both because of the generally more conservative climate in the House and because of Representative Loo's position. He wanted to bring the strongest bill possible out of the Senate to improve his bargaining position with the House.[14] This meant that in the Senate debate he fought hard against putting in restrictions and also against creating a new abortion statute instead of simply repealing the old one. At the same time, since he wanted the bill to pass by a wide margin as a show of strength, he did compromise on the medical qualifications aspects (limiting performance of abortions to approved facilities and licensed physicians) by introducing supplemental legislation. Thus, by the time the bill reached the conference committee, he had already accepted these two restrictions in principle.

Senator Yano's argument against the residency restriction was primarily that it appeared to be unconstitutional. This argument was undercut by the deputy attorney general's position that although it might be unconstitutional, it also might not be. The obvious loophole of attaching a severability clause further weakened his position against the residency clause.

Representative Loo's argument for a residency restriction was partly to preclude the overcrowding of local medical facilities and the spectre of Hawaii becoming an "abortion mecca." The argument was at least as strong as Senator Yano's and probably stronger. Even more important was the force with which Representative Loo held it. The residence restriction was so important to Representative Loo that he had threatened a floor fight if he didn't get it and had made up three different mimeographed sheets of argumentation for that eventuality. A floor fight led by Representative Loo could have seriously endangered the bill because all sorts of extraneous factors would then have entered into the vote: Representative Loo's personal friendships in the House, House-Senate antagonism, and logrolling on other issues. When Loo escalated his threats, Yano had no real alternative.

On the issue of the repeal bill's form, Senator Yano appears to have become convinced that it was still not "legalizing" abortion. At any rate, he would have had very little support for the subtlety of his argument for the Drinan position, since that was not the basis of support, either for most other legislators or for the public, of the repeal position. In addition, it would have been far more difficult politically for the conference committee to try to steer through a package of abortion legislation consisting of repeal of the abortion statute plus amendments to the Medical Practice Act to incorporate the necessary restrictions. It also would have been nearly impossible to work a residence restriction into such a package.

Although the abortion legislation came up very early in the session, Senator Yano could not realistically hope to gain anything by holding out longer in the conference committee. He had an aroused public behind him demanding that the bill come out for a vote, and he himself wanted to get it to the House floor while the momentum for passage was high. It was Representative Loo who had the most to gain by stalling, and both Yano and Loo knew it.

That, of course, had been the reason the Speaker of the House had placed conditions on his appointment of Representative Loo to the conference committee.

Thus, the bill emerged from conference with a number of qualifications, but it still preserved the essential feature of not making abortion *per se* a criminal act. It was still a repeal bill, radically different from any existing abortion law in the United States. The fight for abortion law repeal, however, was far from over. The revised bill still had to pass both houses of the legislature and avoid the governor's veto.

OBJECTIONS AND REVISIONS

The bill reported out of the conference committee was then to go to the floor of the House. However, before being taken up on the floor, it was discussed in the House Democratic caucus. There it again ran into difficulty. Several House members wanted a clear limit on how late into pregnancy an abortion could be performed. Representative Loo reported to the caucus that Senator Yano flatly refused a time limit. Representative Stanley Roehrig suggested that the term "viability" of the fetus be considered instead, with the understanding that the term could not be defined very precisely in terms of weeks of gestation. Senator Yano was called to the House Democratic caucus, and a compromise on this point was worked out by Yano and Representatives Ho and Roehrig.[15] The bill then went back to the conference committee for redrafting.

Instead of the distinction between abortion and criminal abortion, subsections 2b and 2c of the conference committee bill were redrafted as follows:

> (b) Abortion shall mean an operation to intentionally terminate the pregnancy of a non-viable fetus. The termination of a pregnancy of a viable fetus is not protected by this Act.
>
> (c) Any person who knowingly violates this section shall be fined not more than $1,000 or imprisoned not more than five years, or both.[16]

The issue of viability and the specific wording of subsection b were later to raise new objections, but initially this represented a critical compromise. In keeping with the change, the title of the proposed law was changed from "Abortion; criminal abortion; penalties; refusal to perform" to "Intentional termination of pregnancy; penalties; refusal to perform."

Hospital officials also raised objections about the possibility that they could be held liable for the enforcement of the residency restriction, so a new sentence was added to subsection 3a, the residency clause, stating:

> The affidavit of such a woman shall be prima facie evidence of compliance with this requirement.[17]

In effect, this meant that the hospitals simply had to require a notarized statement of residency from every abortion patient. If the patient perjured herself, the hospital and physician were not liable.

On February 18, 1970, the conference committee issued a second report incorporating these changes in a redrafted bill (House Bill 61, Conference Draft 2). The redrafting also included simplified wording, but no change in meaning, in the personnel waiver. The conference committee report accompanying the second conference draft of the bill again argued against placing a time restriction in the bill, despite the new use of the word "viability." It also offered a new legal justification for the residence requirement. The first argument about the possible unconstitutionality of a residence restriction was based on a 1969 Supreme Court decision *(Shapiro* v. *Thompson)* that welfare recipients need not fulfill any residence requirement. The new report added:

> In said case the Court held that the classification created by the requirement of a specified period of residency touched on the fundamental right to interstate movement and was a violation of the Equal Protection Clause of the Constitution of the United States. Thus, the purpose of deterring the in-migration of persons cannot serve as justification. However, if the waiting period requirement promotes a "compelling state interest," it may be justified. Your Committee feels that the "compelling state interest" on this question would be the over-burdening of medical services and facilities in the State by an influx of residents from other states seeking abortions.[18]

The committee report also revealed that the conference committee had considered, but rejected, legal protection of paternal rights over the unborn child. They wrote:

> As to the question of mandatory consent by a spouse, the general practice in our hospitals presently require the consent of the spouse and two consulting psychiatrists in the case of a therapeutic abortion or sterilization. However, if the present laws on abortion are repealed, your Committee feels that the requirement of consent by a spouse should not be regulated by law. The reason for this suggestion is that the question of consent, if required by law, would present many insuperable problems between spouses because abortions would no longer be illegal and the recent court cases in California and Washington, D.C. support the woman's right to choose whether or not to bear a child.[19]

The implication was that hospitals might require the spouse's consent in practice but the committee did not want it to be a legal requirement.

The bill again went to the House, again met objections, and again was returned to the committee for redrafting. The following day, the conference committee issued a third report and a third version of the bill. This time the only change in the bill itself was a technical one. Because of continuing concern over the possible unconstitutionality of the residence requirement, the severability clause in section 3 was amended to state that the invalidity of any provision "or portion thereof" would not affect the rest of the act. This was considered necessary because, technically, the residence requirement was not a separate section of the bill but rather a "portion thereof."

This final conference committee report also included an expanded explanation of the way in which the time limit problem was handled.

> The bill has been amended to define abortion as the intentional termination of a pregnancy of a non-viable fetus and such definition excludes the intentional termination of a pregnancy of a viable fetus in order to allow the medical profession the legal protection it is entitled to in such cases. The bill has been further amended to require an affidavit from any woman seeking an abortion and also the word "knowingly" has been added to the penalty section to provide further protection for the physician.[20]

The conference committee's work was completed and the bill was ready to go before the floor of the House for a vote. Representatives Loo and Devereux report that the emotions of House members were at a high pitch over the issue. Both said they were subjected to considerable abuse in their party caucuses, an unusual occurrence. The abuse came from persons who were opposed to abortion law change on moral or religious grounds. Representative Devereux reported that legislators who were opposed to the bill looked down on her "for even agreeing to serve on the conference committee."[21] Representative Loo reported that it was the first time in his six years in office that he had been subjected to personal abuse in a party caucus, and he was very glad when it was over.[22]

Two elements were important in the work of the conference committee. Representative Devereux credits conference committee member Representative Charles Ushijima with playing a critical role when committee members were deadlocked. She said that he served as arbitrator between Senator Yano and Representative Loo, and helped the committee examine each issue on its merits.[23]

Equally important in committee decisions was the participation of consulting physicians who met with the conference committee members several times. Dr. Goto reports that he was called several times and dropped all other work to meet with the legislators. Dr. Stanley Saiki, chief of staff at Kapiolani Maternity Hospital (the facility most involved in the legislation) and the husband of Representative Patricia Saiki, also met with the committee during the period. The physicians not only gave technical advice about the medical definitions and measurement of viability, but also made suggestions concerning legal protection of physicians and hospitals. They also reported on current and projected costs of abortions. The physicians' cooperation, and the legislators' trust in them, certainly speeded efforts to produce a workable and passable bill.

FINAL PASSAGE IN THE HOUSE

On its third try, the conference committee bill finally reached the House for consideration on February 20, 1970. The delays had produced several amendments which ensured sufficient votes for passage. Nevertheless, the formal vote was preceded by nearly two hours of colorful debate.

Representative Loo introduced the final version of H.B. 61 with a speech summarizing the conference committee report and elaborating on the issue with which he had been most concerned, the residence requirement. After presenting statistics to show that several local hospitals were already operating at full capacity, he continued:

> Can you imagine what would have happened if unlimited abortions were permitted? The abortions would certainly have burdened our medical services and facilities. An influx of non-residents for abortions would surely have overburdened our medical services and facilities. Thus, in order to insure that our citizens receive proper medical care at all times, your Committee felt that a residency clause was necessary.[24]

In the ensuing debate, many speakers alluded to the high degree of public interest in the bill. For some, this was a negative factor. Representative Bernaldo Bicoy asked:

> To be perfectly candid, Mr. Speaker, is this bill to legalize abortion not a case of over-reaction to the problem of unwanted pregnancy, fanned by the loud and insistent clamor of public emotionalism?[25]

Representative Katsugo Miho compared the public involvement in the abortion issue with the public pressure that resulted in the internment of Japanese Americans during World War II.

> I am reminded that one of our nation's greatest cases of injustice was committed in 1941, when, under the guise of great public necessity and sentiment, an entire segment of its citizens, the members of which were purely and solely determined by their racial ancestry, were interned in American concentration camps without any trial or concern for any of their rights as American citizens.
>
> Public necessity or sentiment alone should not be the only or predominant criteria for voting a measure such as that with which we are faced today.[26]

Other speakers in favor of the bill saw the high degree of public interest as evidence of the thoroughness with which the matter had been considered. Representative Frank Case Judd pointed out:

> Debate this afternoon including my own, will probably change no member's deep-seated convictions on the matter. All that can be said on the subject probably has been said, in public hearings, newspaper articles and letters to the editor, radio and television broadcasts, personal mail we have all received, phone calls, in previous debates and in the debate remaining today.[27]

This sentiment was echoed by Representative Peter Iha:

> Mr. Speaker, I know and fully recognize that considerable pressure has been applied to members of this chamber by both proponents and opponents. I am sure every one of us received numerous letters and telephone calls from concerned and interested citizens. I think this was very healthy because we need to know.[28]

Representative Patricia Saiki saw the public's interest as the main force behind legislative consideration of the issue.

> I am fairly certain that we would not be deliberating this bill here today, if we had not received tremendous support from the people of this State—support from a wide variety of organizations representing a clear cross-section of the entire community.
>
> There have been strong pressures against this bill, but I have every assurance that the voice of this House, in its vote here today, will echo the voice of the people of our State.
>
> I urge every member of the House to make that voice sound strong, clear and unmistakable.[29]

Several speakers explicitly translated the public concern over the abortion issue into votes. Representative Bernaldo Bicoy candidly observed:

> I will not have it easy for re-election this fall, Mr. Speaker, and my negative vote on this bill may well invite my political defeat. But that's the name of the game.
>
> But if I am to be judged by my constituents on this vote, then I wish to be judged by them on the basis that in casting this negative vote, I am being guided by my personal judgment, tempered with what I believe to be in the best public interest.[30]

A similar sentiment was voiced by Representative Katsugo Miho:

> Judged by the overwhelming support of the communications media in support of this measure . . . it would be so easy to vote with the tide and minimize criticism or controversy, or judged by the number of vocal supporters of the measure to vote aye and somewhat assure, as Representative Bicoy said, the prospects of re-election.[31]

A most puzzling reference to the electoral consequences of the abortion issue came from Representative Rudy Pacarro, who announced:

I was one of the fellows here who fought this bill last year, but something happened yesterday. I had a whole slew of mail in my office and I went through every one.

There was one letter that really riled me up. It was from a business agent from a union, and I will not mention his name, threatening me with my defeat of re-election this coming year if I did not vote for this bill. This is the reason why I am speaking today.

After one year of deliberation, Mr. Speaker, and you know my thoughts, I have fought this bill. I was extremely against this bill all the way. The letter threatened me with my re-election this year has nothing to do with this. I had that matter straightened out.

Mr. Speaker, with good conscience, I am proud to say that I am going to vote for this bill.[32]

The House debate covered the major points on both sides of the issue. In comparison with the public hearing and the initial Senate debate, however, relatively more emphasis was placed on the merits and adequacy of the various safeguards and qualifications which had been incorporated in the final conference committee draft.

Most opposition to the bill came from persons who believed that life begins at conception, even though they also raised arguments about the wording of the bill's various provisions. Representative Henry E. Meyer, for example, argued that the bill would not make abortion available to the poor because it would still be too expensive for them.

On top of this, again with the permissiveness of the total repeal, more and more of our youngsters will be participating and if they belong in the "cannot pay" category, the result would be more business for the back alley or self-administered abortions.

If my interpretation of poor is correct, this is the finest toned piece of class legislation I have ever had to consider. Those who could afford and have used their financial position to seek aid in other countries can now stay home and have their problems administered to. The poor have no choice other than the back alleys.[33]

However, he concluded by adding,

Mr. Speaker, in conclusion, I have kept my strongest arguments until now. I feel that life begins at the moment of conception. No one has been able to give me information, even my medical profession friends, as to when the sex of a child is determined. Also, no one

> has given or can give me information as to when from conception to birth, the different organs of a human being are instilled within the human body.
>
> And so, Mr. Speaker, I take the position that life begins at the moment of conception and any abortion that is performed, I feel, is the taking of a human life and this is against the Ten Commandments.[34]

Two other speakers, Representative Barney Menor and Representative Bernaldo Bicoy argued that the legislators ought to attack the causes of the problem of unwanted pregnancy instead of repealing the abortion law. Representative Bicoy argued:

> If we believe that this community, this State, has sufficiently progressed in its social development as to be ready now to accept legalized abortion, then I strongly submit that this community likewise is ready now to accept responsibility and to pay for the idea of in-depth teaching of sex education to our malleable fifth and sixth graders or younger, and to the idea of a comprehensively expanded system of medical facilities and health clinics throughout the State on a program of planned parenthood, and to the idea of the wide publication of and the ready accessibility to contraceptives.[35]

Several speakers opposed the bill at least in part because they felt specific provisions were either inadequate or defective. Representatives Richard Wong and Katsugo Miho agreed with Senator Yano's position that the residency requirement was probably unconstitutional, but they used this an an argument for opposing the bill entirely. Both men viewed the possibility of Hawaii becoming an abortion mecca as a serious problem; they felt the residency requirement would be declared unconstitutional and thus would not solve the problem.

Representative Miho characterized the bill as "dishonest" because the residency clause was being inserted despite the doubts over its constitutionality. He questioned why Hawaii should be the first to change its abortion law, and suggested that the state wait until California had repealed its law, while Representative Wong raised the question of whether the state was prepared to pay for the abortions of indigent women from out of state.[36]

The viability clause also provoked considerable criticism. The issue revolved around section 2b, which read:

> Abortion shall mean an operation to intentionally terminate the pregnancy of a non-viable fetus. The termination of a pregnancy of a viable fetus is not included in this Act.[37]

Representatives Joseph Garcia, Tennyson Lum, Richard Wong, and Buddy Soares were concerned that the wording might mean there was no criminal penalty for the destruction of a viable fetus. They had broached the issue with Attorney General Bert Kanbara, who said the wording did pose "a very substantive question."[38] Representative Stanley Roehrig, the author of the viability clause, explained at length that the felony provision, section 2c, would apply whenever a viable fetus was involved.

> The intent of the felony provision in the bill is to curb those instances wherein the woman would attempt to terminate the heartbeat of the viable fetus while it is within her body, between the sixth and ninth month, by use of a saline solution, as is presently being done in certain illegal abortions. This is the only point at which this penalty provision would apply. Once it is outside of the mother's body after viability, the law considers it is human and then the law with relation to homicide would then apply.[39]

Representative Roehrig insisted that the language of the felony provision was clear, but he also announced that another bill was being introduced which would cover any possible loophole by providing that:

> No intentional termination of a pregnancy of a viable fetus shall be performed except for the purpose of saving the life of a woman.[40]

The four representatives remained unconvinced by Representative Roehrig's assurances and insisted that he had not answered the question of what the penalty was for aborting a viable fetus. On three separate occasions the Chair, Representative Beppu, stopped speakers who kept pressing this point.

The one other area in which opponents felt the bill was defective was the omission of any protection of paternal rights. The arguments were presented with some interesting twists. Representative Anthony Baptiste observed:

> I believe in the rights of women but at the same time, the principal contributing individual to pregnancy is the man and he has a right. This wife can go and have an abortion over his objections. This man

> may want to have a child carry his name and build a family tree, and then the child is gone.[41]

Representative Miho made an even stronger assertion:

> The most important, if not the primary, object and purpose of our institution of marriage is the begetting of children so that mankind itself can survive.
>
> . . . by this measure, we threaten the very foundation of marriage for we are legally, lawfully and completely denying a husband his lawful and legal right to determine whether his child shall be allowed to survive or not.[42]

The opponents of the bill knew the votes had already been counted and the bill would pass, but they argued their case fully and persuasively. By contrast, those who planned to vote for the bill had less need to make their case. The conference committee report, and Representative Loo's oral summary of it, set forth the major arguments for repeal. Only a few representatives added to these reasons for passage of the bill.

Majority Floor Leader Representative Stuart Ho argued that the real issue was:

> There are women who become pregnant in Hawaii for whom pregnancy becomes such a cruel burden because of circumstances not always within their control, that they feel compelled to find a way to rid themselves of this fetus. Thus compelled, our laws, with one exception, deny them the services of the only persons and facilities in our society that could decently grant them relief, thereby forcing them to seek abortions under humiliating circumstances in the back streets of our community.[43]

He emphasized that the problem was to weigh the competing interests of the fetus and the woman, and went on to show the impossibility of spelling out in the law which interest should prevail in each specific situation, concluding,

> I subscribe to the idea that the interest of the mother is a legitimate interest to be considered in addition to the legitimate interest of the non-viable fetus. I believe that these interests cannot be adequately weighed by legislative fiat. Rather, I believe that they can only be weighed by those personally involved, the mother and her physician.[44]

The two conference committee members, Representatives Charles Ushijima and Dorothy Devereux, emphasized that the repeal of the abortion law would leave the matter to each person's conscience. Representative Ushijima noted:

> That is the essence of this bill. Just as you and I are free to declare and act on our own consciences, those who will be affected by this bill will be free to declare and to act on theirs.
>
> I do not pass judgment on any of your moral positions. And it is for the same reason that I do not wish to pass any judgment on the moral position of others that I support this bill.[45]

Representative Devereux added:

> I do not believe we should attempt to do by law what can be accomplished by morality. The issue of morality belongs with the family, the church and our educational system—not with any legislative body. . . .
>
> Mr. Speaker, the intent of this bill is not to encourage the suppression or destruction of human life.
>
> The intent of this bill is to preserve the basic freedom of the individual.[46]

Along the same lines, Representative Frank Judd pointed out that the provisions of the bill were permissive, not mandatory.

> The passage of this bill will in no way interfere with those women who so desire, to continue the pregnancy to childbirth, and I further believe that this will continue to be the case in the vast majority of pregnancies.[47]

Some attempt was made to refute the arguments of those opposed to repeal. Representative Judd reminded the body that the law distinguishes between abortion and murder, and also expressed the belief that

> termination of a pregnancy prior to viability does not terminate life of the complete entity, or the whole man, or life as we know it.[48]

Representative Ho tried to refute the argument that repeal would promote promiscuity by saying,

> Let me place the question the other way. Is there anybody here this morning who feels that to maintain the abortion law on the books will decrease promiscuity?[49]

Several speakers alluded to the historic importance of the occasion and their pride in the legislature for its action. Representative Patricia Saiki commented:

> This legislation is of national significance—lawyers, legislators, medical people, women and progressive leaders all over the United States will be reading about this action today.
>
> I am proud of the House—and of this Legislature—and I take pride in having played a small role in support of this measure.[50]

After all the representatives had had their say, the bill was finally approved in the House by a vote of 31 to 20. All eight representatives from the two smaller islands of Maui and Kauai voted against the bill.

FINAL PASSAGE IN THE SENATE

The bill was then returned to the Senate for final approval of the conference committee version. That debate was held on February 24, 1970. Senator Yano introduced the conference committee version of the bill by summarizing the safeguards which had been added and explaining the revised viability clause.[51]

The Senate debate was brief and focused primarily on the faulty wording of the bill. With passage assured, only Senator Percy Mirikitani spoke in favor of the bill. Following his brief comments, seven senators spoke against it. Senators John Lanham, Hebden Porteus, John Hulten, Donald Nishimura, Nadao Yoshinaga, Eureka Forbes, and Andy Anderson all complained that the bill had been seriously compromised since its initial passage in the Senate. They urged that it be returned to conference to have the language clarified.[52]

Senator Yoshinaga reminded the Senate that he had introduced a bill the previous year which would have provided that abortions could be performed by licensed physicians in licensed hospitals. After further study, he had decided that bill did not go far enough, so he had voted for complete repeal when H.B. 61 had been before the Senate the first time. However, he said that the bill as it had been amended might not accomplish its intended purpose because of defective language. He announced that he would vote against the bill.[53]

After this brief debate, the bill was brought to a vote and

passed, 15 to 9. Although one senator switched to a "Yes" vote because of the new safeguards in the conference committee version of the bill, three others (Senators Anderson, Yee, and Yoshinaga) voted against the final bill because they opposed the changes in wording. The other six "No" votes came from senators who had opposed repeal the first time.

THE LONG WAIT

The state law required that the governor sign or veto a bill within ten working days after its passage by both houses of the legislature. If not acted upon within that time, the bill would pass into law without his signature. Everybody knew that Governor Burns would not sign the bill. To do so would indicate his approval, and his position against abortion was clear. The question was whether he would either veto it or let it pass into law without his signature, as he had suggested he might do in the fall of 1969. Doubts centered on the concern that the bill as passed contained faulty wording and also left much more abortion legislation on the books than the "no law" that the governor had said he favored.

Dr. Goto felt confident that the governor would let the bill stand. "I wasn't worried after the passage," he said. "The governor's word is like gold. He never changes his mind or goes back on his word."[54]

Others were not as certain. Both Representative Loo and Senator Yano went to see the governor after the bill passed. Yano reports that the governor remained neutral and did not declare himself. He gave no hint that he would veto it or let it pass. "I left the meeting feeling that he might veto it personally, but I thought the political implications would make it difficult," he said.[55]

Meanwhile, Representatives Loo and Roehrig were pursuing their follow-up legislation to clarify the wording in the bill regarding abortions on viable fetuses. A bill permitting abortion of a viable fetus only to save the life of the mother was drafted with the help of Dr. Stanley Saiki, chief of staff at Kapiolani Maternity Hospital and husband of Representative Patricia Saiki. This bill, H.B. 1774-40, was reported out of Representatives Loo's committee on Public Health, Youth and General Welfare and passed the House on second reading February 25.[56]

Representative Roehrig then went to Governor Burns to see if the presence of this new bill would expedite the passage of the abortion law repeal bill. According to Representative Loo, the governor told Representative Roehrig he would let the bill before him become law, but he would not take any other bills on abortion.[57] This news, plus other opposition in the Democratic caucus, effectively ended the career of H.B. 1774-40. It was never brought up for third reading in the House, and died at the end of the session. Senator Yano's committee also met with Dr. Saiki and several medical and hospital representatives to discuss whether supplemental legislation was necessary, but these efforts also fizzled out in a few days.[58]

The governor had requested an opinion from the attorney general's office regarding the various problems in the wording and provisions of the bill which had already been noted. Many wondered if this was not an attempt by the governor to find a way to veto the bill honorably. The attorney general's opinion, dated March 2, 1970, covered five points. First, it noted that the bill applied only to the termination of a pregnancy involving a nonviable fetus and concluded that the effect of the bill was to repeal all provisions governing pregnancies involving viable fetuses. It pointed out that the relevant provisions in the Medical Practice Act related only to "criminal" abortions, but that such an act might be punishable if it constituted professional misconduct, gross carelessness, or manifest incapacity by a licensed physician. After citing cases to suggest that the problem would probably not be covered by the homicide laws, it noted that House Bill 1774-40 was designed to cover this omission.

Second, the memorandum pointed out that House Bill 61 would not apply to pregnancy termination obtained by means other than an operation, but noted that this was probably not an important exclusion, given the medically preferred methods of abortion.

Third, it reported that the distinction based on the viability of the fetus did not appear to be unconstitutionally vague, both because similar distinctions had been found acceptable elsewhere, and also because the penalty prescribed in the bill was not dependent upon the definition because the bill only applied to abortion of a nonviable fetus. In effect, the penalty was for performance of such an abortion outside a hospital, or on a nonresident, or by a person who was not a licensed physician.

Fourth, the opinion held that grammatical errors do not affect the operation of the law when the intent is clear. The use of the term "pregnancy of a nonviable fetus" did not affect the bill's legality.

Fifth, the memorandum reiterated the view that while constitutional questions might be raised about the residence requirement, it did not affect the validity of the remainder of the bill because of the severability clause which protects the main bill if part is found invalid. The memorandum concluded:

> While certain provisions do give rise to questions concerning their validity, they do not appear to be fatally defective.[59]

The community leaders who had fought so hard for abortion law repeal were holding their breath during this time. A delegation led by Joan Hayes and including union lobbyists Eddie DeMello (ILWU) and William Abbott (AFL-CIO), representatives of Zero Population Growth, Democratic Action Group, Hawaii Council of Churches, Committee for the Protection of Children, University Abortion and Birth Control Committee, and Sister Mary Heenan, the nun who had supported repeal at the public hearings, met briefly with the governor on March 5. Their mission was to remind the governor of the broad support the bill enjoyed and of his five-month-old statement that he would let the bill pass into law. They emerged from the meeting still uncertain, but feeling that the governor was somewhat sympathetic.[60] Although he had appeared to be most receptive to the Biblical quotations of Sister Mary Heenan, he had also told the group that as a young policeman in Honolulu he had personally seen the damage done by illegal abortions.[61]

As the days wore on, repeal supporters began to feel more confident that the governor would let the bill go through. However, there was new confusion over when the waiting period would end. It was not clear to the public whether the "ten working days" were to be counted from the date the bill passed the Senate, or from the date it actually reached the governor.

Coffman, in his biography of Burns, reports the following incident:

> On the last day of his constitutional deadline for vetoing the bill, Burns had asked a reporter his feeling about the bill, and the reporter said that from a standpoint of social justice he believed it was a good bill—the well-to-do flew to Japan for abortions while those not well-heeled either sought out con artists or reluctantly gave birth. The reporter, thinking of his own child, added that nonetheless he was plagued by a belief that unique life began not at the time a fetus could live outside a mother's womb but at the moment of conception. Tears clouded Burns' eyes, and he thanked the newsman for understanding his moral dilemma.[62]

Finally, on March 11, 1970, Governor Burns released a statement which began:

> House Bill 61, relating to Hawaii's century-old abortion law is now Act 1 of 1970. The measure became law without my signature . . .
>
> I have declined to sign this bill after much study and soul-searching; after receiving competent advice from island and national specialists in law, medicine, theology, human rights and public affairs, and after sincere prayer to the Creator named in our Nation's Declaration of Independence as the Source of our unalienable rights of Life, Liberty and the Pursuit of Happiness.[63]

The statement went on to distinguish between the governor's right to his personal convictions and his obligation to promote "the common good."

> In the recent debates and public controversy over proposed abortion law changes in our State, I have been subjected to pleadings, warnings, even threats from many sources, including clergymen and lay members of my own Roman Catholic Church, and members of other churches and nonreligious groups. I have received all of these with what I hope has been reasonable equanimity, listening to all, judging each argument, and coming to my decision calmly after weighing with the utmost care the sentiments expressed by our distinguished legislators who have borne the brunt of the heated public debate.
>
> I have made my decision. I stand by it. It is the decision of the Governor of Hawaii, not the private and personal whim of John A.

Burns. It reflects my best judgment as Governor, made after consultation with the best minds in the State, in regard to what is in the best interest of *all* the people of Hawaii.

However, I choose now to exercise my right to a personal life, and to freedom of personal opinion and religious belief as an individual citizen. I have felt that in the heated debates over the abortion question, my reputation has been unfairly and seriously attacked, and sadly enough, by a number of my fellow Roman Catholics who do not appear to understand precisely the separate roles of State authority and Church authority.[64]

Governor Burns went on to state his personal abhorrence of abortion and his belief that life begins at conception. He described his own family experience with the problem, when his wife was strongly advised to have an abortion because of her health, but instead carried the child to term. He then expressed his belief in the need for change, particularly when social practice involves the daily breach of an outmoded law.

Stated simply, I believe it best that at this point in time, our laws remain totally silent on the question of abortion. Should this be the condition, the accepted morality of the community-at-large would be the prevailing factor in how abortions are countenanced in Hawaii.

There is reported to be ample evidence that traffic in illegal abortions is considerable in Hawaii—as well as in other jurisdictions covered by restrictive abortion laws. It seems to me that to continue a breach of the law because of a change in the public's attitude on a moral question is inconsistent with the democratic philosophy that the rule of law should prevail at all times. If community standards have changed, we should then change the law rather than continue violating an outmoded law.[65]

The statement pointed out that the governor's power of veto should not be used lightly, as it is not the function of the chief executive to legislate. He referred to the attorney general's opinion that the bill's defects did not seriously impair its main objective, and expressed his hope that

in the future a growing awareness of the dignity and value of human life will develop steadily among our young people as they discuss wars, capital punishment, the "medical moment of death,"

> remarkable advances in biology, genetics and other life-related sciences. . . .
>
> I have a tremendous faith that what the future holds in store for Hawaii and the rest of our Nation is good. I believe freedom of religious and philosophical belief and practice in our "open society" in Hawaii . . . is the best path to an enlightened view of the nature, purpose and value of the fetus.
>
> It is as though we are living in a dark age, fighting each other over religious and philosophical concepts profoundly important now to each combatant, yet all the while progressing through each conflict toward the light, when we shall better understand the mysteries of the beginning of human life now hidden from us.[66]

The statement concluded:

> To summarize, I could not in good conscience condone what the House Bill permits by signing it into law. On the other hand, I do consider the abortion question as a matter involving individual conscience and a proper subject for legislative policy setting and scientific or judicial interpretation.
>
> I appreciate the considerable thought and energies that went into the final development of House Bill 61. Many people—all sincere in their desire to better the quality of life in Hawaii—spoke both for and against enactment of this bill.
>
> Let us now rejoin all our forces and continue to work for a better Hawaii for all our people.[67]

This statesman-like approach to an issue that had so emotionally gripped the populace and the legislature did much to relieve the tension and ease the transition to legal abortion. Hawaii thus became the first state in the nation to permit abortion essentially upon request.

CHAPTER 10

The New Law's Impact

THE PASSAGE of the repeal law without Governor Burns' signature did not close the abortion issue in Hawaii. Instead, March 11, 1970 marked the beginning of a new period of continuing implementation and adjustment. It is not our purpose to examine all of the consequences of the change in Hawaii's abortion law. It is valuable, however, to attempt a general overview of the law's major consequences and present some indication of its continuing history.

The consequences of the new law have been well studied. In addition to official record-keeping by the state Department of Health, a major statewide multidisciplinary study of the effects of abortion law change has been undertaken. The Hawaii Pregnancy, Birth Control and Abortion Study was conducted from 1970 through 1975 by five faculty members at the University of Hawaii: the two authors of this volume; Dr. Roy Smith of the School of Public Health and School of Medicine; Dr. James A. Palmore, Jr. of the East-West Population Institute; and Dr. Ronald Pion of the Schools of Public Health and Medicine. In addition to this project, Kapiolani Maternity Hospital, the facility at which about half of the abortions in the state are performed, also participated in a national surveillance of legal abortion, the Joint Program for the Study of Abortion, directed by Dr. Christopher Tietze of The Population Council. Hawaii's participation was supervised locally by Dr. Roy Smith. Many other persons in Hawaii have also been involved in abortion-related research, including the development and testing of new abortion techniques.

IMPLEMENTATION OF THE LAW

Implementation of the new abortion law required procedures for the performance of abortions, provisions to help women pay for abortions, and agencies to help women make decisions regarding their pregnancy and obtain abortion services. These requirements in turn involved the state's hospitals and medical personnel, the major medical insurance carriers, and a variety of social service agencies, both private and governmental.

The state's hospitals moved quickly to establish procedures and policies for handling the anticipated influx of elective abortion cases. The decisions they made profoundly affected the way the law worked in practice. The first issue raised at each hospital was what abortion cases would be permitted, and which physicians could perform them.

The new law said only that abortions had to be performed in licensed hospitals by licensed physicians. However, every hospital had its own internal system of self-government, involving both the hospital administration and the physicians with practicing privileges. The Hawaii Medical Association had supported the repeal bill, with especially strong support coming from the specialists in obstetrics and gynecology, so that the general approach in the hospitals was to speed and ease the performance of abortions. Yet, as Dr. Ronald Pion had reassured the Senate committee in his testimony at the hearing, the medical profession was indeed cautious and conservative in establishing policies and safeguards.

Most hospitals decided to permit only board-eligible or certified obstetrician-gynecologists to perform abortions on patients beyond twelve or sixteen weeks' gestation. For these abortions of later gestation, one or more consultations with an obstetrician-gynecologist were also usually required. For patients of twenty weeks' gestation, the general policy was to present the case to a hospital abortion board or committee "to determine the necessity of the abortion, and to weigh its medical risks against the need for the abortion."[1] Consultations were not required for abortions early in gestation. These could usually be performed by any physician who had privileges to perform therapeutic abortions and other similar procedures at that hospital.

Every hospital in the state which could reasonably be expected to permit elective abortions did so. Tripler Army Medical Center, however, which has a very extensive obstetrical and gynecological department serving Hawaii's large military population, did not begin performing abortions until several months after passage of the law. Since there was no federal law regarding abortion, the military forces in Hawaii were uncertain about whether to follow Hawaii state law or not. After New York and Alaska repealed their abortion laws, a new federal policy permitted abortions to be performed in military hospitals to the extent provided by the laws of the state in which the hospital was located. In the interim—and even afterwards—women in the military and military dependents were able to obtain elective abortions in civilian hospitals through the CHAMPUS (Civilian Health and Medical Program for the Uniformed Services) insurance program. This is a government insurance plan for medical services received in nongovernment hospitals.

St. Francis Hospital, which is owned and operated by the Catholic Diocese of Honolulu, is the only Catholic hospital in the state. The hospital had already closed its obstetrical ward for other reasons. In any case it would not have permitted abortions to be performed, nor would it have been obliged to under the provisions of the law.

Only one other hospital in the state is affiliated with a religious organization. This is Castle Memorial Hospital, a Seventh-Day Adventist institution. It adopted the most restrictive policy on abortions, permitting them only for "therapeutic" reasons. This policy was later relaxed considerably in practice.

Small rural hospitals throughout the state permitted abortions, but most cases at later gestations were referred to Honolulu gynecologists and performed in the larger city hospitals. The effect of these decisions was to make abortion readily available in the Honolulu area and somewhat less available on other islands. In a 1971 report to the state legislature, the Hawaii Pregnancy, Birth Control and Abortion Study reported that some women from other islands were coming to Honolulu for abortions. The study team observed that the proportion of the state's abortions which were performed on the neighbor islands grew during the first year, suggesting "increased acceptance of the law by physicians and decrease in the stigma of abortion."[2]

The three major Honolulu hospitals (Kapiolani Maternity and Gynecological Hospital, Queen's Medical Center, and Kaiser Foundation Medical Center), anticipating a substantial volume of abortion patients, also had to establish new hospital procedures and fees for abortions. These two issues were complicated and interrelated. They were also affected by the delicate problem of how other persons, both staff and patients, might respond to patients having abortions.

The hospital procedures involved how long abortion patients would stay in the hospital, where to put them, and what type of staff would be required to care for them. All of these decisions in turn affected the hospital charges for an abortion. The aim was to keep hospital costs down by simplifying and streamlining procedures for abortion cases, but not to sacrifice medical safety. Initial procedures were deliberately conservative and cautious, on the assumption that adjustments could be made later when the safety of the procedures had been established.

At all three hospitals it was initially assumed that abortions would be performed under general anaesthesia, which required the services of at least a nurse-anaesthetist. In accordance with the accepted standard for accreditation of hospitals, a pathological report of the removed tissue would be required following every abortion. The abortion procedures were initially to be performed in an operating room. While the three hospitals decided that abortion would be an in-patient procedure, special provisions were made to get patients in and out of the hospital on the same day, so an overnight stay with attendant higher costs for a room and nursing care would not be required. At small rural hospitals where the procedure was performed infrequently, abortion patients even at early gestations were often kept in the hospital for up to three days.

All three major Honolulu hospitals anticipated that they could meet the increased demand for abortion with existing facilities and personnel, unless the residence restriction were overturned and large numbers of nonresidents began coming to Hawaii for abortions. An Ad Hoc Committee on Abortion was formed at Kapiolani Hospital, the state's only specialized obstetrical and gynecological hospital. The committee surveyed all physicians with hospital privileges and estimated that there would be four to eight abortions per surgery day. The committee found that this demand would not tax the operating room capacity or the available nursing, nurse-anaesthetist, and resident staff, but would require additional technical personnel for the pathological examinations.[3]

Ironically, the relatively low demand for abortion services—due to the small size of the state plus the residence requirement in the law—helped to keep the cost of abortion high. There was not a large enough volume in abortion services anticipated to make a specialized, cut-rate abortion service economically feasible. Kapiolani Hospital and Queen's Medical Center established standard hospital charges of around $150 for routine abortions performed early in gestation. These could be handled with a hospital stay of less than twelve hours. For those unable to afford the regular charges, both hospitals also made arrangements to provide for lower-cost abortions, using the resident staff, through their outpatient clinics. In addition to this hospital charge, the typical patient was expected to pay a private physician's fee of $150 to $200 for a total cost to the women of $300 to $350.

Kaiser Medical Center, which is a prepaid medical plan associated with the Permanente Medical Group, decided to charge its members $140 for an elective abortion. Nonmembers would pay $270. This fee included both the physician's and hospital charges and was thus competitive with total costs for abortions at the other two major Honolulu hospitals.[4]

The following year, both Kaiser and Queens hospitals lowered their standard charges for an early abortion. Kaiser dropped the cost for plan members to $40, the same amount charged for a therapeutic abortion or treatment for a spontaneous abortion, while Queens lowered its rate to $90.

In only one aspect of abortion charges do abortion patients appear to have been adversely singled out for discriminatory treatment. At all of the major Honolulu hospitals, it became standard policy to require full payment in advance from all abortion patients not covered by insurance. For no other hospital procedure was this required.

Otherwise, the standard hospital charges were developed by adding up the costs of the specific services rendered. If the charges were high, it was because of the policy decisions that had been made concerning the services required for the routine handling of abortion cases. The decision to consider abortion as an in-patient procedure, for example, meant that the patient was formally admitted to the hospital and given a bed, which added substantially to the cost. One justification for this procedure was medical caution; another was that because the law stipulated that abortions be performed only in licensed hospitals, there was some ambiguity about whether a procedure handled through the hospital's out-patient clinic would be legal.

The issue of how to handle abortion patients and where to put them was also compounded by concern that other patients might respond negatively to them if they were readily identifiable. The well-meaning solution at all three hospitals was not to segregate abortion patients in a separate ward, but rather to mix them with other minor gynecological surgery patients.

While this policy had good intentions, in practice it caused some problems. Some women who had abortions were reluctant to reveal that fact to other women in the ward who might be in the hospital for other reasons. The problem was compounded for women who remained in the hospital for several days while undergoing saline abortion procedures. Unfortunately they were often housed on the maternity floor.

The decision not to segregate the abortion patients meant that hospital personnel would be less likely to single them out and react negatively to them. Yet it meant on the other hand that a much larger number of staff persons might come into contact with abortion patients in the course of their duties. Because the law contained a conscience clause, the hospitals had to allow staff personnel a choice in whether they would handle abortion patients. By and large, the hospital staffs were cooperative and sympathetic. Transfers were made when necessary. Some preliminary staff discussions were held to prepare personnel for anticipated emotional conflicts. At several hospitals, special discussion-rap sessions were later conducted by psychiatrists when it turned out that even staff members who strongly supported abortion were having some emotional difficulties handling the nursing duties involved. Dr. John McDermott and Dr. Walter Char, psychiatrists affiliated with the University of Hawaii School of Medicine, conducted several of these discussions and reported that the small group sessions were quite successful in resolving the staff problems.[5]

Aside from the internal problems of developing abortion services, the hospitals also had to attend to the issue of legal liability for the abortions that were performed on their premises. The new abortion law raised two special concerns. The first was the residence requirement. At the insistence of the hospitals, the legislature had written into the abortion law the provision that the patient's sworn affidavit would constitute *prima facie* evidence of compliance with the residence restriction. This removed from the hospitals the responsibility for questioning or investigating the patient's claim to resident status. On the other hand, it meant that the hospital had to require an affidavit of residence from every abortion patient. Suitable forms were developed at each hospital.

Initially, the hospitals required that the affidavit be notarized. If there were no notary public available at the hospital, the woman had to go somewhere else to get a notary seal on the form, which stated explicitly that the declaration was made for the purpose of obtaining an abortion. This was a source of embarrassment to many women, but the hospitals felt they needed the legal protection it provided.

Within a few months after Hawaii's abortion law was repealed, New York repealed its law and hospitals in California relaxed their administrative requirements under that state's reform law. Even in the first months, when Hawaii was the only state where abortion was legal, there was no large influx of nonresidents. As abortions became available on the mainland, there was even less reason for outsiders to come to Hawaii for abortions, and, indeed, few came.

The Hawaii Pregnancy, Birth Control and Abortion Study estimated that in the first five months under the new law, between 8 and 13 percent of abortions in Hawaii were performed on nonresidents. After New York's law was enacted in July, 1970, the percentage dropped to around 2 percent, and by the end of 1970 it was only about 1 percent.[6]

Most hospitals continued to require some sort of affidavit of residence until the 1973 Supreme Court decision struck down residency clauses in abortion laws.[7] In October, 1974, an opinion by Hawaii Deputy Attorney General Gerald Y. Y. Chang made the

U.S. Supreme Court decision officially applicable to Hawaii.[8] By this time, the hospitals had already quietly dropped the requirement on their own.

The second legal issue concerned the problem of legal consent. To protect themselves against liability, hospitals routinely require the written consent of any patient admitted for any medical service. However, the consent must be given by a person who is legally eligible to do so. At the time the abortion law was repealed, Hawaii law did not permit minors to consent to their own medical or surgical care, and the age of majority was twenty. A 1968 law permitted minors over the age of fourteen to obtain, on their own consent, diagnosis, examination and administration of medication in the treatment of venereal disease and pregnancy. But the law also stipulated that parents had to be notified when the diagnosis was positive. The same law allowed minors to consent to therapeutic abortion under the old abortion law. Because of the placement of the new abortion law under a different number and the repeal of the old section, it was not clear whether this provision applied to the new abortion law. Abortion was not covered under the treatment of pregnancy because it is a surgical procedure rather than the administration of medication. Although one interpretation of the consent statute was that it should apply to all elective abortions, this has not been the prevailing interpretation in practice, and the provision has not been tested in court.[9]

Neither the new abortion law nor any other law required the husband of a married woman to consent to her medical care. However, hospitals frequently required the spouse's consent for sterilization procedures, so a precedent existed for consent of both parties to be required for procedures involving reproduction. The issue was raised when hospital abortion policies were being decided, just as it had come up earlier in the Senate debate on the bill. Because of the obvious problem of wives aborting pregnancies which involved men other than their husbands, most hospitals decided that the husband's consent should be encouraged but not required.

When minors were involved, the hospitals had to require the consent of a parent or legal guardian. However, the hospital was not required to investigate the age of the patient, just as it was not required to investigate her residency status. The solution was the same: the hospitals required the patient to attest to her date of birth. When she reported that she was a minor, parental consent was required. The hospitals usually permitted husbands to give consent for married minors, but parental consent (as stipulated by law) was still required in certain cases.

The requirement of parental consent for the abortions of minors was soon identified as a problem area by the Hawaii Pregnancy, Birth Control and Abortion Study's research on the effects of the law. In its report to the legislature on the first year of the new law, the research team pointed out that

> the greatest delays in obtaining abortions occurred among women who were under 18, women who lived at home, women who were supported by their parents, or women whose abortions were paid for by their parents. These lags seem to result from a combination of financial dependence and the necessity for minors to obtain parental permission for abortion.[10]

They added that this delay led to a longer hospital time and a markedly higher risk of complications, due to different abortion procedures used after the twelfth week of gestation.

There were also indications that some women who were underage were able to "pass" for twenty and obtain abortions without parental consent. The age distribution of abortion patients in 1970 showed an inordinately high peak at age twenty, suggesting some falsification of age.[11]

The hospitals were not the only institutions which had to adjust their policies to accommodate the new law. Several institutions including the state itself, through the Department of Social Services and Housing, were involved in the issue of payment for abortion procedures.

The Director of the Department of Social Services had testified in his official capacity in support of repeal, and there was no question about the department's desire to pay for abortions for eligible women. Still, the inevitable questions arose of which women would be considered eligible and how payment would be arranged. The Department of Social Services took the broadest possible view of the situation and chose to treat abortion like any other medical service, with no special restrictions or policies. This meant that any woman who was receiving welfare assistance could obtain payment of abortion costs under the usual provisions for medical payments. In addition, any woman who was not receiving welfare support but who qualfied as "medically indigent" could also have part or all of her abortion costs paid by state welfare services. The medically indigent category covered persons who were able to support themselves marginally under normal circumstances, but who could not afford any additional expenses for medical care. The eligibility requirements and policies were already established; elective abortion was simply considered as a legitimate medical service covered under the program.

In the first year of Hawaii's new law, the Department of Social Services paid for 9 percent of the state's abortions. More than half of these were for women in the medically indigent category.[12] By the end of 1971, the proportion of abortions paid for by the DSS had increased, and more than three quarters were women not receiving other welfare assistance. DSS paid for nearly one fourth of all abortions obtained by women on the outer islands. This reflects in part the tendency of women from the outer islands who could afford it to obtain their abortions in greater privacy in Honolulu.[13] The policy of paying medical expenses for indigents went well until several years later, when federal legislators and administrators in Washington, D.C. began trying to hamstring the U.S. Supreme Court's abortion decision by limiting the use of federal funds to pay for abortion. A good proportion of the funds distributed by the state were of federal origin. When, in late 1974, an attempt was made to reduce federal payments from 90 percent to 50 percent of the cost for elective abortions, the Hawaii Department of Social Services submitted strong testimony opposing the proposed change[14] and succeeded in preventing it.

During the first year of the abortion law, insurance coverage was not available to most women who had abortions through the state's two major insurance carriers, Hawaii Medical Services Association (HMSA), which is the local Blue Cross plan, and Kaiser Foundation Health Plan, a prepaid plan involving membership in a health maintenance organization. Kaiser, the smaller of the two, set a flat fee for elective abortions for plan members. This was done because the procedure was classified as elective surgery and was thus not covered in the basic insurance package. Kaiser initially requested permission to cover abortions but was turned down by the federal regulatory agency on the grounds that this entailed increasing service without increasing the premium. The fee was set at a rate comparable to the hospital charges at other major Honolulu hospitals. In effect, the plan member was covered for the doctor's fee but not for the hospital charges. This would not have seemed unusual except that a flat fee of only $60 covered complete prenatal maternity care and delivery, including any complications of pregnancy, labor, or delivery, and care of the newborn. The fee for therapeutic abortion or treatment related to a spontaneous abortion was $40. In effect, the plan did not cover elective abortion in the same manner as other related or comparable medical situations.

The problem with HMSA was even more complicated. Any woman whose HMSA policy included maternity benefits was covered for elective abortion. However, maternity benefits were tied to marital status. Only married women had maternity coverage. Moreover, only married women who had had their policies in effect for ten months before delivery were covered for maternity benefits.

Fortunately, both major insurance carriers were responsive to public pressure on this issue. The problem was identified immediately. On March 13, 1970, Kapiolani Hospital's Ad Hoc Committee on Abortion reported that while it had not discussed or explored the problem of insurance coverage in depth, "community awareness and support would be most valuable and effective with spin-off benefits to obstetrical cases."[15]

The coalition of community organizations that three months earlier had distributed reading materials on abortion to legislators again sprang into action. A delegation led by Laurel Kasaoka met with representatives of both HMSA and the Kaiser Plan. After a period of quiet negotiations, both insurance carriers agreed to extend abortion coverage beginning in 1971. The proportion of abortions which were covered at least in part by insurance rose from 26.9 percent in the spring of 1970 to 38.8 percent during the last quarter of 1971.[16] The figure remained rather low because of the high proportion of abortions performed on young women who did not have health insurance through the state's major carriers. In 1973, after more quiet pressure had been applied, the University of Hawaii negotiated a new optional insurance plan for its students which included abortion coverage. These figures do not include abortions paid for by CHAMPUS, the military insurance program, which included abortion coverage for all insured parties from the beginning. During the first year, no evidence was found that physicians were attempting to report elective abortions as therapeutic so that their patients could qualify for insurance coverage.[17]

A variety of social service agencies were also involved in implementing the new law. All of the existing agencies whose clientele included single, pregnant women were affected by the law. In addition, some new services were developed specifically to handle problems raised by the legalization of abortion.

In the forefront was Hawaii Planned Parenthood, whose network of family planning clinics provided pregnancy tests and related pregnancy counseling as well as contraceptive services. The agency, which had supported the repeal bill at the Senate hearing, soon became heavily involved in arranging abortion referrals. In addition to helping eligible women make use of Department of Social Services assistance to the medically indigent, Planned Parenthood social workers arranged for reduced-cost abortions through hospital clinic facilities and referrals to sympathetic physicians.

When the new abortion law went into effect, the University Abortion and Birth Control Committee became concerned that young women would need financial assistance to obtain abortions without insurance. The group tried to develop a revolving abortion loan fund and collected a small sum of money for that purpose. The committee itself soon died a natural death, and the collected money was given to Hawaii Planned Parenthood, which agreed to use it for the intended purpose. In 1975, Planned Parenthood representatives obtained permission from the only remaining members of the University Abortion and Birth Control Committee to use the loan fund money for other purposes; in five years, it had never been necessary to use these funds because the agency's social workers had always managed to arrange an abortion within the woman's ability to pay.

Other groups and agencies besides Planned Parenthood also offered abortion counseling and referral services. Child and Family Service, a private social agency which had strongly supported the repeal bill at the Senate hearing, offered a full range of pregnancy counseling services including pre-abortion and post-abortion counseling as well as referral services. Clergy Counseling Service, the group of clergymen who organized in the fall of 1969 to provide pregnancy counseling and abortion referrals before the old abortion law was repealed, continued in operation to provide pastoral counseling to women with pregnancy problems. Some physicians also arranged for routine pre-abortion counseling for their patients, usually with a psychiatric nurse or social worker.

If anything, the agencies overestimated the demand for abortion counseling services. The initial assumption was that most women would need help in deciding whether to continue a pregnancy or terminate it. While some women did need this type of assistance, particularly young teenagers who also needed help in presenting the problem to their parents, the number of women who were really ambivalent about what to do was much smaller than expected. The Hawaii Pregnancy, Birth Control and Abortion Study found that most women who obtained abortions had made their decision as soon as they knew they were pregnant. Many women had even decided beforehand that they would resort to abortion if they became pregnant.[18] The situation was similar for women who carried their pregnancies to term after abortion was available as an alternative. Only 6 percent of women who gave birth had even considered abortion. Once a pregnancy was diagnosed, the overwhelming majority of women knew very quickly which option they intended to take.[19]

This finding helps to place in perspective the conflicting testimony offered at the Senate committee hearing regarding the degree of guilt which women would experience after having an abortion. Those favoring repeal argued that women had few psychological aftereffects, and that guilt and sorrow were experienced less with abortion than when a child was given up for adoption. Those opposed to abortion contended that women would suffer from extreme guilt afterwards. In fact, those women who were likely to have experienced great ambivalence or guilt about abortion did not choose to have abortions. The women who did utilize abortion usually saw it as the only feasible solution to their problem. Consequently, there was also less need for post-abortion counseling than had been anticipated. Good pre-abortion counseling also helped to reduce the need for post-abortion counseling.[20]

Some agency help was specifically directed toward helping

women maintain their pregnancies. Catholic Social Service was opposed to abortion and continued to provide counseling and services to women who chose to continue their pregnancies. All of the agencies which provided abortion counseling or referral services also continued to counsel and provide services to women who chose to continue their pregnancies.

Robert Pearson began to get responses to his offer to support any woman through her pregnancy as an alternative to abortion. In the first year after the abortion law passed, he accommodated about forty women in his own home on Maui. As the demand rose, he expanded his home. In 1973 he moved the main office of the Pearson Foundation to Honolulu and began to devote his full time to the provision of services for pregnant women. The foundation opened an office and began offering free pregnancy tests and counseling in addition to support for pregnant women. The foundation's services included some assistance in arranging adoptions, but it did not offer any help to the woman after she had given birth.

Agencies on both sides of the abortion issue advertised their services through the public service announcement columns in the daily newpapers. The Pearson Foundation also used small paid newspaper advertisements to make the public aware of its services.

After he moved the foundation's main office to Honolulu, Robert Pearson also began unofficially making the rounds of the public schools with a strong anti-abortion presentation. This he coupled with an offer of services to pregnant women as an alternative to abortion. Since the Department of Education requires that both sides of controversial issues be presented, Planned Parenthood representatives and other professionals involved in abortion services or research were also drawn into the schools to do outreach work on abortion. Finally, in 1974, after Robert Pearson had sought official permission to establish his program in the schools and had been refused, the Department of Education solved the growing problem by developing its own materials for education on abortion, presenting all sides of the issue.

Before the legalization of abortion, one important way in which social agencies assisted women with unwanted pregnancies was to arrange for their prenatal care, including housing, delivery and the subsequent adoption of their babies. Although only about

10 percent of the women who had illegitimate births before 1970 gave up their babies for adoption, the social agency resources devoted to this problem were substantial. Child and Family Service, Catholic Social Service, the state Department of Social Services, and Queen Liliuokalani Children's Center were involved in arranging adoptions. The Salvation Army maintained a home for unwed mothers, the Booth Home, which cared primarily for women who planned to give up their babies.

Although the number of babies available for adoptions was declining even before 1970, the repeal of the abortion law added to this tendency. Among single women who became pregnant in July and August 1970, shortly after the abortion law change, only 4 percent had the baby and gave it up for adoption. This was concentrated almost completely among unmarried women under the age of twenty.[21] Whatever the degree to which legalization of abortion contributed to the decrease in the number of babies available for adoption, the overall reduction was substantial. A 1971 study prepared for the Aloha United Fund by the Health and Community Service Council, an umbrella council of social service agencies, found that many agency resources previously devoted to adoptions were no longer necessary, and staff time devoted to adoptions was being reduced by either reassignment or attrition, or both.[22]

The drop in the number of women giving up babies for adoption led to major changes in the state's facilities for the housing and care of unwed mothers before delivery. The demand for the type of care offered by the Salvation Army Booth Home dropped substantially following repeal of the abortion law and the service was moved to a much smaller facility, still serving the same clientele. In 1972, a second small facility was opened to accommodate unwed mothers who intended to keep their babies. Six months later, the two services were merged into one small facility which accommodated six to ten women at a time. These accommodations serve both women who plan to give up their babies for adoption and those who plan to keep them.[23]

Meanwhile, Robert Pearson's private efforts were also accommodating some unwed mothers. Since he was actively recruiting women to utilize his offer of an alternative to abortion, he continued to have a small but steady demand for these services. The majority of the women he accommodated planned to keep their babies. In 1974, Pearson and the Roman Catholic Diocese of Honolulu jointly announced plans to raise funds to establish a new home for unwed mothers.[24] The Mary Jane Home was later opened and now cares for unwed mothers.

At present two facilities for unwed mothers provide shelter, emotional support, professional counseling, and training for child care. Many of the women who use these two facilities are eligible for, and use, welfare assistance through the state Aid to Families with Dependent Children program of the DSS after the birth of their babies.

THE LAW IN OPERATION

The most specific prediction made during the debate on abortion law repeal concerned the anticipated demand for abortion in the state. A frequently cited figure was a prediction of three thousand to thirty five hundred abortions per year, extrapolated from the survey of Hawaii physicians conducted by Drs. Smith and Goto and Beverley Manner.[25] This estimate was actually reached by a certain amount of prestidigitation. Questionnaires had been sent to all physicians in the state, and slightly more than half responded. The relevant question asked how many requests for abortions the physician had received during the previous twelve months. There was no control over whether the same women had requested an abortion from more than one doctor and, of course, many women who wanted abortions might not have asked a physician. On the assumption that these two errors might cancel each other out, the total number of requests received from the physicians who responded was doubled (to account for those who did not respond) to produce the figure of thirty five hundred.[26]

The number acquired additional credence when Fumi Ige of the AFL-CIO arrived at the same figure by an entirely different procedure. She applied to Hawaii birth figures a reported worldwide ratio of one abortion for every four to five live births and estimated the demand at thirty five hundred abortions per year.[27] This figure was also no more than an educated guess, since the world ratio was based on widely ranging ratios of abortions to live births in many different countries.

The actual number of abortions performed in the first twelve months after the repeal law went into effect (March, 1970 to March,

1971) was amazingly close to the predictions: 3,643. This represented a ratio of one abortion to every 4.5 births.[28]

During the next few years the figure rose slightly; then, in 1973, it leveled off. There were 4,275 abortions performed in the state in 1971, 4,632 in 1972, and 4,658 in 1973.[29] By 1974, use of the new procedure of menstrual induction for performing abortions before eight weeks' gestation had begun to reduce the number of abortions performed. It may be performed within two to four weeks of a missed menstrual period, before pregnancy can be diagnosed accurately by readily available means. Since pregnancy was not usually diagnosed, and in fact the woman was not always pregnant, the procedures were not officially counted as abortions.

During the first year the new procedure was used, menstrual inductions were performed only in hospitals. When those cases were added to the number of abortions, there was no decrease in total abortions for that time period.

Although the total number of recorded abortions in Hawaii remained relatively stable over the first four years under the new law, considering the population increase during the same time period, this actually represented a slight decline in the rate of abortion. The volume of abortions, about ten or eleven per day for the entire state, did not prove to be a serious pressure on existing medical facilities.

As the advocates of repeal had argued, the use of abortion services was much greater than would have been permitted under the American Law Institute model abortion law alternative. If the original abortion law had been liberalized only to permit abortion in certain stipulated health-related circumstances, it would have accommodated only about 5 percent of the women who actually had abortions. Less than 1 percent of the abortions performed after the law changed would previously have been legal (i.e., could have been justified in order to save the life of the woman).[30] This, however;

> represents a higher rate of abortions to save the life of the mother than were actually performed during the last decade when that was the only condition under which abortion was permitted. This suggests that when abortion is generally illegal, it may not be available even to those who are legitimately entitled to it.[31]

Legal abortions have been performed safely in Hawaii. In five years, over twenty thousand abortions have been performed with only one death due to complications. Overall, only 7 percent of all abortions have resulted in any medical complications, and most of these (more than 90 percent) have been minor. Nearly 90 percent of Hawaii's abortions were performed in the first twelve weeks of gestation, when the procedures are relatively simple and safe. Only 1 percent were performed beyond twenty weeks gestation.[32]

About half of Hawaii's abortion patients were young, single, and terminating a first pregnancy. This corresponds to the picture seen in other parts of the United States.[33] The average age of abortion patients was 24.6, with about 20 percent under twenty and another 20 percent thirty or older. This age range is also in keeping with national statistics. Slightly over half of the women who had abortions had never been married, and about one third were married at the time of abortion. Half were terminating a first pregnancy, while less than a quarter were ending their fourth or higher pregnancy.[34]

All of Hawaii's ethnic groups were represented in the abortion population, but the way the groups used abortion differed considerably. Caucasians and Japanese Americans used abortion at the highest rate and had a higher proportion of young, single women obtaining abortions. Women of Filipino and Hawaiian or part-Hawaiian ethnic background were somewhat less likely to use abortion, and those who did were more likely to be older women with completed families. Of all the ethnic groups studied, Samoan women were least likely to use abortion.[35]

The religious affiliation of abortion patients is of particular interest because of the organized opposition to the repeal law by the Roman Catholic diocese. Nearly 30 percent of the state's abortion patients have been Catholic. This closely parallels the proportion of Catholics in the state's population, and suggests that Catholic women did not differ from non-Catholics in their use of abortion. In reality, however, it was found that Catholic women were more likely to be pregnant than non-Catholic women. Thus Catholic women chose to continue more of their pregnancies and terminated a smaller percentage of them by abortion. Those Catholic women who did utilize abortion did not differ from non-Catholics in their reasons for abortion or in the time it took them to decide on abortion.[36]

Based on earlier reports of women who sought illegal abortions, it was predicted that most abortion patients would be married women with completed families. It became clear, however, that a distinction had to be made between women who would have resorted to illegal abortion and those for whom abortion became a new option when the abortion law was repealed. The Hawaii Pregnancy, Birth Control and Abortion Study found:

> Among the women who now use abortion, legal abortion appears to have been a more probable alternative for the single or divorced, and for younger women without children. These women represent the majority of legal abortion patients, and they probably represented an even larger proportion of the former invisible illegal abortion population. The women who utilize legal abortion now, but would not have sought illegal abortion, are primarily older, married women who already have children.
>
> Seen in this light, the estimates of potential demand for abortion were not really wrong. They accurately reflect most of the demand which was not being met by existing services prior to the legalization of abortion. The rest consists of women who would have utilized illegal abortion, plus a substantial number of young women who would have married and begun their families earlier.[37]

This same comparison between women who would use abortion legally or illegally also applies to the evaluation of the effect of the abortion law on population growth. Because many women previously obtained illegal abortions, legalization of the procedure will not necessarily reduce population substantially. Any evaluation of the effect of abortion on population growth in Hawaii is further complicated by the fact that birth rates were already declining in the state even before the change in the law. The crude birth rate had dropped from 28.2 births per thousand women in 1950 to 26.8 in 1960 and 22.9 in 1970 (only the last quarter of 1970 could have been affected by the new abortion law). A more precise measure, the general fertility rate, had dropped substantially from 128.0 births per thousand women aged 15–49 in 1960 to 106.5 per thousand in 1965 and 96.4 per thousand in 1970.[38]

Births definitely continued to drop after the legalization of abortion. The crude birth rate dropped steadily from 21.3 in 1971 to 20.2 in 1972 and 19.8 in 1973.[39] The general fertility rate per thousand women aged 15–44 (a slightly different denominator than that used for the rates reported above) declined from 93.0 in 1971 to 83.0 in 1973.[40]

Some opponents of abortion law repeal had predicted that the change would be followed by a rise in promiscuity and a decrease in the use of contraception. Although this situation could only be assessed in very general ways, neither of these predictions was borne out.

While it was found that only one third of the women having abortions were married, another third were involved in a continuing relationship (engaged, going steady, or living with a man). A 1971 report to the state legislature by the Hawaii Pregnancy, Birth Control and Abortion Study noted:

> Another possible indicator of morality is the age at which girls first engage in intercourse. Our data for the first three months following abortion [law] repeal show 18 as the mean age of first coitus. For the last three months of the first year, 18 was still the mean age of first coitus. No significant change in sexual behavior is revealed by this measure, but we do not know if the proportion of women who engaged in intercourse has changed.[41]

The study also found no change in birth control usage during the first year. However, the use of birth control among abortion patients was generally low; only about one-third of the women had been using birth control at the time they became pregnant.[42] It was later reported that nonuse or failure of contraception was not a predictor of abortion. Among women who experienced unplanned pregnancies, there was virtually no difference in the proportion choosing abortion between those who had used contraception and those who had not. About two-thirds of the women in both groups continued their pregnancies, and one-third had abortions.[43]

Passage of the 1970 abortion law had been possible in part because of the support of physicians for the change. A 1969 survey of physicians' attitudes on the abortion issue had found nearly all physicians in favor of some change in the old, restrictive abortion law and over one-third in favor of full repeal.[44] A follow-up survey of physicans' attitudes in 1973, conducted by Dr. Roy Smith and Alice Beechert, found that support for the repeal position had doubled. Three quarters of the responding physicians reported that they approved of the U.S. Supreme Court decision which essentially paralleled the Hawaii repeal law.[45]

ATTEMPTS TO CHANGE THE NEW ABORTION LAW

The repeal of Hawaii's hundred-year-old restrictive abortion law was evidence of the impermanence of legislation. Similarly, the repeal decision itself is not irreversible. Every year since 1970, resolutions and bills aimed at changing the new abortion law have been introduced into the Hawaii state legislature. To date, none has been reported out of the committee to which it has been assigned.

Interest in changing the abortion law has increased since the 1973 Supreme Court decision which struck down all restrictive abortion laws in the United States. The Supreme Court in two related decisions on January 22, 1973 declared that abortion during the first three months of pregnancy is a matter for medical judgment of the woman and her physician and that, for the stage subsequent to approximately the end of the first trimester, the state may, if it chooses, regulate the abortion procedure (not the grounds) and then only in ways that are reasonably related to maternal health. Only subsequent to viability may the state, if it chooses, regulate and even proscribe abortion, but even during that period it must allow abortion where necessary in appropriate medical judgment to preserve the life or health of the woman.[46]

Since the Supreme Court decision, opponents of abortion have not been able to propose simply restoring the old abortion law or tightening the new one. Instead, they have had to shift tactics. Now they primarily argue for a more fundamental change: an amendment to the U.S. Constitution extending protection of life to the fetus from the moment of conception.

In Hawaii, the anniversary of the Surpeme Court decision, January 22, has become the focal date for an annual demonstration at the state Capitol by opponents of abortion. The 1975 rally was the largest to date, reflecting a climax in the growth of the organization of the right to life movement both in Hawaii and nationally.

A week before the planned March for Life rally in 1975, Bishop John J. Scanlan again used the front page of the diocesan newspaper, *Hawaii Catholic Herald,* to make a strong anti-abortion statement. Calling for strong Catholic participation in the rally, Bishop Scanlan urged Catholics to

> realize our moral obligation to reverse by lawful and legal means the abortion decision of the Supreme Court.[47]

On the weekend preceding the rally, the sponsors, Hawaii Right to Life, distributed anti-abortion pamphlets to homes throughout Oahu. The professionally produced pamphlets were marked "Adults Only" on the outside and contained a number of full-color photographs of aborted fetuses and fetal parts at various stages of gestation. The pamphlets sparked a number of public protests, both because they had been distributed door to door where children could easily pick them up, and because many of the pictures were enlarged or had misleading captions.[48]

The rally itself was well attended. The crowd grew from an estimated five hundred persons at the start to about twenty five hundred for the march two hours later. Besides Roman Catholic Bishop Scanlan, participants included Bishop Lani Hanchett of the Episcopal Church and clergy and laypersons from Our Redeemer Lutheran Church, First Assembly of God, Ka Makua Mau Loa Church, and the International Bahai Yaka Society (a Krishna group).[49]

Two anti-abortion bills were introduced into the state legislature the same week. One, offered by Senator John Hulten, who had voted against the repeal bill in 1970, was a resolution seeking to extend to the unborn the protection to life offered by the state constitution. The other, by first-term Representative Richard "Ike" Sutton, was to make abortions punishable by a maximum fine of $5,000 and five years in jail. The latter measure would be unconstitutional. Neither measure was expected to find much legislative support. Leaders of the House and Senate made public statements supporting the 1970 repeal law on the day of the rally.[50]

Senator Hulten's bill did get as far as a committee hearing in March, 1975. The hearing went almost completely unnoticed by supporters of the 1970 abortion law, but was well attended by opponents of abortion. Thus virtually all of the testimony supported the bill. However, since the bill was simply a resolution seeking to initiate the machinery for a state constitutional amendment, which would probably not be valid in light of the U.S. Supreme Court decision, the effort was largely symbolic.

Nevertheless, it raised once again the problem of the inherent separation between the opposing sides of the abortion issue. When the issue was repeal of a restrictive abortion law, the repeal supporters could muster a broad range of social arguments and statistics to demonstrate the rationality of their cause. They could present evidence about the empirical effects of the restrictive law. Opponents protested on the basis of a strong personal conviction about a metaphysical phenomenon, which did not affect the practical case presented by repeal advocates.

When the issue is a constitutional amendment to extend legal protection to the fetus from the moment of conception, the positions are reversed. Now the opponents of abortion are in a position to argue directly for the set of values which underlies their opposition to abortion, because the issue is whether those values should be embodied in the law. Those who support the availability of abortion can only apply their practical, pro-abortion arguments indirectly and are hard pressed to develop as strong a case against the right to life amendment. The battleground this time is belief, not facts and reason.

While the greatest interest in changing the abortion law presently comes from those who oppose abortion, others have also shown some desire to change the wording of Hawaii's law to conform to the guidelines laid down by the Supreme Court decision. The major areas of nonconformity involve the Hawaii law's residence and hospital restrictions.

In February, 1974 it was announced that a bill would be introduced to substitute for Hawaii's repeal law the Revised Uniform Abortion Act prepared by the National Conference of Commissions on Uniform State Laws. In addition to following the Supreme Court guidelines, the Revised Uniform Abortion Act includes a provision giving minor women the right either to consent to, or refuse to consent to, an abortion.[51] However, the bill was not introduced, apparently because legislators preferred not to open the issue again.

Somewhat concerned by the growing pressure on legislators from the vocal Hawaii Right to Life, representatives for the coalition of community groups which had supported the 1970 repeal movement and subsequently had pressed successfully for changes in insurance coverage met again in 1974. The group wanted to have the Hawaii law adjusted to reflect the broader provisions of the U.S. Supreme Court decision but decided not to mount a major public effort in that direction. Instead, a letter was written to key legislators reminding them that a large number of community organizations still supported the 1970 legislation and expressing hope that the law might be brought into conformity with the Supreme Court decision.[52]

Supporters of the repeal law, both within the legislature and in the community, preferred a flawed abortion law to opening up the entire issue to debate again. It was largely for this reason that no bills were introduced to correct the segments of the law which had clearly become unconstitutional. At the same time, no one wanted to inititate a test case in order to get the provisions nullified by court action. The problem was finally solved in fall of 1974, when State Director of Health Dr. Walter Quisenberry requested an attorney general's opinion on whether the ninety-day residence requirement for abortions in Hawaii was still valid, in light of the U.S. Supreme Court decision. The opinion, written by Deputy Attorney General Gerald Y. Y. Chang, concluded that the residence requirement

> . . . limits the general (public and private) medical care available in this State and is . . . unconstitutional and invalid.[53]

The main reason the requirement was held to be invalid was that it applied indiscriminately to both public and private medical facilities. Deputy Attorney General Chang found that the state had the right to establish a residence requirement applicable to state (public) medical facilities, for the purpose of ensuring that sufficient medical facilities were available to the residents of the state. However, it could not prevent private facilities from extending their facilities to nonresidents. Since the law did not make this distinction, it suffered from the same defect as the Georgia provision which the U.S. Supreme Court had found to be unconstitutional.[54]

Although Dr. Quisenberry's request was for a ruling on the residence requirement, a footnote at the end of the ruling noted that in the same Georgia case in which the residence requirement had been declared unconstitutional, a requirement that abortions be performed only in hospitals was found unconstitutional as applied to the first trimester of pregnancy. The opinion continued:

> We are therefore of the opinion that the hospital requirement . . . is unconstitutional and may not be enforced during the first trimester of a woman's pregnancy. After the first trimester of a pregnancy, however, said hospital requirement is consitutional and the State may require that the abortion be performed in a hospital.[55]

Following the U.S. Supreme Court decision, but before the attorney general's opinion, there had been only slight indication that physicians were performing abortions in private offices. In a 1973 study of physicians' attitudes toward abortion, Dr. Roy Smith and Alice Beechert found that slightly over half of the physicians disapproved of office abortions. This was true even for physicians in the medical specialties which performed abortions (general practice, obstetrics and gynecology, and surgery). Only four physicians (0.7 percent) indicated that they had or would perform first trimester abortions in their offices. However, the physicians reported receiving a high volume of requests for office abortions, estimated at about six hundred in the preceding year. Most of these were referred for hospital abortions.[56]

Before the attorney general's opinion, physicians who wanted to perform early abortions in their offices (to lower the costs and to simplify the entire procedure, as well as to provide greater privacy to patients) were legally in limbo. They could still be prosecuted under the state law if they operated within their office, even though they most certainly would have won the case. The question was whether anyone wanted to risk the expense and time of a court test to clarify the situation. The attorney general provided a neat solution to the problem and even resolved the problem of who might have standing to request such an opinion. He did this by tacking the opinion onto the closely related and legitimate request from the state health director regarding the application of the law to the operation of hospitals under his jurisdiction.

The attorney general's ruling declared that the hospital requirement was invalid insofar as it applied to the first trimester of pregnancy, but would still be applicable for abortions at later gestations. Several months later, in an article in the *Hawaii Bar Journal,*

Nasser and MacDougall argued that because the hosptial provision did not distinguish between the three trimesters of pregnancy, the entire clause was nullified. In addition, they pointed out that the clause of the Hawaii law which would allow someone on the medical staff not to participate in an abortion because of personal beliefs—the conscience clause—could be invalid if it were used by a public hospital to justify a refusal to permit the performance of elective abortions. They also followed the interpretation that the Hawaii statute applies only to abortions prior to viability and, therefore, the state has no law which applies to abortion of viable fetuses (except for the homicide statutes). After noting all of these defects, plus the invalidity of the residence requirement, Nasser and MacDougall concluded that Hawaii does not have any abortion law at all.[57]

The argument is only theoretical. In practice, all parts of the law remain in force until either a court or some other legal opinion or ruling accepts new interpretations and specifically renders the old clauses invalid. Ironically, if this were all to happen without the legislature's stepping in to write a new abortion law, Senator Yano's original aim of removing abortion completely from the realm of the law would finally be accomplished. By means of the attorney general's opinion, this has happened for the residence requirement and the hospital requirement in the first trimester.

Nullification of the residence requirement relieved the hospitals of the burden of demonstrating that they had not knowingly permitted nonresidents to obtain abortions and eliminated one element of paperwork for patients and hospital staff alike. However, it did not appreciably alter the provision of abortion services or the volume of abortions performed. Nullification of the requirement that first trimester abortions be performed in hospitals, on the other hand, had a potentially much greater effect.

To date, there is no evidence on the impact of the invalidation of the hospital requirement. It is difficult to keep track of the volume of office abortions, and a smaller proportion of them are likely to be recorded on official fetal death certificates. Further, we have no specific knowledge of how many abortions were previously being done in offices. Lifting of the prohibition on office abortions also happened to coincide with the greater availability of the new technique of menstrual induction. This technique is an effective way to abort an early pregnancy and is very easily performed as an office procedure. The major effect of the ruling has probably been to increase the number of early first trimester abortions performed in offices as menstrual inductions, and thus to reduce the number of later first trimester abortions performed in hospitals.

WHERE ARE THEY NOW?

One final area in which the abortion law had some effect was on the lives of those who were involved in the campaign. Some lives have taken new directions as a direct result of the events of the abortion law repeal campaign. It is more difficult to assess whether that issue made any difference for others.

The person whose life was probably most profoundly changed by the abortion issue was Robert Pearson. His strong conviction and his chance meeting with William Baird, the pro-abortion layman with whom he identified, have led to a new career of providing alternatives to abortion for pregnant women in need. Five years after the abortion law repeal campaign, Robert Pearson is devoting full time to the abortion issue.

Pearson's local counterpart on the repeal side of the campaign, Joan Hayes, has gone on to use her organizational and lobbying skills for other issues. She has used many of the same techniques which proved so effective in the abortion law repeal campaign to develop public pressure for anti-noise legislation. The anti-noise campaign was never as emotional or as popular as the abortion issue, but it has had some major successes.

The two key legislators involved in the abortion issue, Senator Vincent Yano and Representative George Loo, have both left the legislative arena. George Loo lost his bid for re-election in 1970. He has not sought re-election since and has been working as a lawyer for the state and in private practice. Vincent Yano did not run for re-election to the same office in 1970. He did, however, run for lieutenant governor as the running mate of Thomas Gill in his effort to unseat Governor John Burns. Both men lost in the primary, and John Burns went on to win election to a third term. Yano returned to his private law practice. In 1974 he ran for the Senate again, from a different district, and lost by an extremely narrow margin.

It is difficult to say whether any of these elections were influenced by the abortion issue. Certainly it was not raised as a major campaign issue either for or against any of the men. Just as certainly, most of the voters knew what each man's role had been in the abortion law repeal campaign. It is not at all clear to what extent Loo's constituents were responding to his stand on abortion nor, if they were, whether they were opposing him for having supported some change, or for not having gone far enough. In Yano's case, he probably would have been re-elected had he chosen to run for his same seat again in 1970. Instead, he chose to seek another office in alliance with a controversial underdog. There was some indication at the time that Yano was seeking a way out of politics. His 1974 comeback attempt appears to have been wholehearted, however, and he barely missed election. The abortion issue does not appear to have either made or broken the career of any other legislator.

Many of the other persons who participated in the abortion law repeal campaign are still involved in the area of abortion. However, this is largely a function of their professional activities. As an obstetrician and gynecologist, Dr. George Goto is one of the state's most skilled and experienced performers of induced abortions. Dr. Ronald Pion, who testified at the hearing as a visiting professor from the University of Washington, has since joined the faculty of the University of Hawaii and Kapiolani Hospital, where he has been a leader in research into new techniques for performing abortions. Many of the social workers who testified in support of the repeal bill have become experienced abortion counselors. The authors of this book, along with their colleague Dr. Roy Smith, have devoted most of their research efforts during the past five years to evaluating the effects of Hawaii's abortion law through the Hawaii Pregnancy, Birth Control and Abortion Study.

Many of the lay persons who joined in the abortion law repeal campaign have maintained a vigilant interest in the topic and have also utilized the lessons of the campaign in support of other community causes.

CHAPTER 11
Analysis and Evaluation

WE HAVE TRACED the history of Hawaii's successful campaign to repeal a restrictive abortion law. We have examined the personalities, the tactics, the arguments, and the politics. In less detail, we have also reviewed some of the aftereffects of the change. Throughout, we have pointed to various elements which seemed to have particular significance for the campaign's success. While it is most unlikely that another social issue in another time and place would ever have exactly the same combination of elements, some of these factors, or their equivalents, are likely to occur in other contexts. Abortion, too, remains very much a contemporary issue. The lessons learned here may be appreciated elsewhere.

THE CONTEXT

Two external factors were critical to the success of the abortion law repeal campaign: its timing, and the prevailing political conditions.

Timing

The concept of "timing" covers a number of different elements which were indirectly important in the campaign's success. Repeal of Hawaii's abortion law became conceivable because of a series of historical events which took place in the decade of the 1960s. These events were not necessarily related to one another, but all of them bore on the issue of abortion and helped to create a favorable climate for change in Hawaii.

During the decade of the sixties, there was a change in physicians' attitudes toward abortion due to two medical tragedies: the rubella epidemic in Hawaii and elsewhere, and the thalidomide tragedy in Europe. Both of these events led many physicians to view abortion as the solution to a medical problem or, in medical jargon, as the "method of choice" for handling a specific medical situation involving a pregnancy. As a result, abortion became a possible alternative within the medical profession.

At the same time, the experience in Colorado and a few other states with abortion law reforms along the lines of the American Law Institute's (ALI) model abortion law, followed by Britain's experience with a considerably more liberal new abortion law, led to a new understanding and appreciation of the demand for abortion. Once it was known that large numbers of women sought abortions for a variety of reasons, the inadequacies of the ALI model abortion law became apparent. The issue of abortion law reform shifted from, "When is abortion medically acceptable?" to, "How can the actual demand for abortion best be met?"

The demand for women's rights also gained both legal standing and greater public acceptability during the 1960s. This led to a natural convergence of women's rights arguments with the issue of abortion law reform, and a new perspective on abortion laws. The old argument that restrictive abortion laws were a means of protecting women's health was turned upside down on two grounds. First, the illegal abortions to which women resorted were a greater danger to their health; second, women began to argue that protective legislation for women was generally unacceptable because its effect was to prevent women from exercising their full individual freedoms.

Simultaneously, the decade that had begun with high hopes for an adequate contraceptive solution to the problems of controlling family size closed on a new note of caution. Numerous reports of medical complications associated with the use of birth control pills culminated in the U.S. Senate subcommittee hearings on pill safety in early 1970. There was a growing recognition that contraception was not yet a completely satisfactory answer to the problem of preventing unwanted births. The pill and intrauterine devices had first raised expectations, then let them down. The effect was a change in women's assumptions about the degree to which fertility was controllable, and an increase in the demand for alternatives to unwanted births.

By the end of the 1960s, all these historical factors were converging in the issue of abortion law repeal, and they profoundly affected the force with which the issue developed. The combination produced an especially powerful effect. If all of these developments had occurred sequentially over a longer period of time, the impact on abortion law change would have been greatly reduced.

Against the background of these events of the sixties, the idea of abortion law repeal arose suddenly as a reasonable and obvious answer. In this sense, the repeal of Hawaii's old abortion law was an idea whose time had come. Individuals and small groups throughout the country had been arguing for repeal for many years before the late 1960s. They were the vanguard, but they did not make a great deal of headway until other world events helped them along. While the experience in other places may have been different, abortion law repeal in Hawaii did not develop into a public issue because of the efforts of long-time abortion law reform crusaders whose efforts finally bore fruit. Neither was there evidence that abortion law reform movements elsewhere directly influenced the situation in Hawaii. Rather, there was a sudden quantum leap, a moment in which many new people were independently and individually coming to the conclusion that repeal of the abortion law was the right answer.

Political Conditions

A second extremely important factor in the success of abortion law repeal in Hawaii was a highly favorable set of political conditions. Hawaii's political structure was very conducive to the sort of political action involved in the abortion law repeal campaign. Because the state is small, political activity is personalized and face to face. Both government and powerful interest groups are relatively small and accessible. This helped make the low-key, personal, educational campaign an effective strategy.

At the time of the abortion law repeal campaign, the Democratic party had a strong and well-organized majority in the legislature and worked in close cooperation with the second-term governor. The party caucus worked very effectively to steer legislation through the two houses. The fact that the Democratic party was in control is far less important than the nature of that control and the way in which it was exercised. Although the party was in some sense an efficiently operating "political machine," it was not the private fiefdom of one all-powerful individual. It was the party, collectively, that could get things done. This was accomplished through the cooperation of many individuals, some of whom exercised personal political power even independent of position, and others who derived their power primarily through being incumbents of some strategic official position. This functioning majority greatly assisted the passage of the bill once basic support for it was established.

Coupled with these two aspects of the political structure is the related factor of the legislature's responsiveness to public pressure. One source of this responsiveness was the state's postwar political history described earlier. The size and scale of state politics was certainly also part of the explanation. Since statehood, when political participation had been broadened so that power was exercised by locally-elected public officials, the state has remained small and centralized enough to keep those officials publicly accountable and responsive. This factor, too, made the particular type of campaign waged appropriate and effective.

In addition to the favorable political structure, basic political sympathies were also relatively favorable for the abortion law repeal issue. The state's public officials maintained a strong concern with public welfare and a readiness to use government policies to enhance the quality of life. Although more recently some of these policies have been criticized for not living up to their original aims, the state has a record of leadership in public service issues such as land use planning, maintenance of open and public shoreline areas, and innovative government involvement in employment opportunities and housing. Thus legislators had previously shown themselves receptive to the idea of using legislation as a way of alleviating local social and health problems.

Because of the state's unique multiethnic, multicultural society, public officials possess a keen sensitivity to cultural differences and the resultant need for pluralistic tolerance. At the time of concern, Hawaii had no majority ethnic group. The two largest groups, Caucasians and Japanese Americans, had pluralities of 30 to 40 percent. The part-Hawaiian, Chinese-American and Filipino-American ethnic groups were substantial minorities. A number of smaller ethnic groups were also very visible. Virtually all of these groups had representation within the legislature, often in both parties. The result was a strong preference for social and legal arrangements which permit every group to maintain its own beliefs and customs. This belief in pluralism established a receptivity to the argument that repeal of the abortion law would permit members of every religious group to exercise their personal beliefs about abortion.

The relatively high proportion of working women in Hawaii also contributed to the favorable climate for abortion law repeal. The greater prevalence and acceptance of working wives meant that men in the state, and particularly in the legislature, were more likely to understand the economic and social consequences of an unplanned and unwanted pregnancy. They may also have been more willing to listen to such arguments from women, both at home and in public. By the same token, neither men nor women in the state had much of a vested interest in maintaining an image of women as full-time housewives or mothers. Thus, in a variety of ways, the concept of allowing women to request an abortion was less threatening to prevailing ideas and sex roles in Hawaii than it may have been elsewhere.

A final important political attitude conducive to abortion law repeal was the general deference Hawaii legislators expressed toward physicians. Medical doctors had high credibility when they testified, and legislators generally assumed they would behave responsibly and act in the public interest. Although some of the anti-repeal testimony hinted at the possibility of unscrupulous behavior and economic interests on the part of physicians, legislative sympathies were clearly on the side of the medical profession. Consequently, the argument that abortion should be left to the judgment of the woman *and her physician* implied that the decision would be reached responsibly and legitimately.

These factors of timing and of political structure and sympathies established conditions favorable to abortion law repeal. However, they were not in themselves sufficient to produce the legal change. They simply made the public and legislature more receptive to the arguments of repeal supporters and then made possible legislative approval once the campaign had put those arguments across successfully.

THE ISSUE

In a similar way, certain properties of the issue of abortion law repeal also helped the campaign for repeal. The first was the ideological vacuum within which the old abortion law persisted; the second was the ease with which repeal could be linked to basic shared American cultural values.

Having won their case, at least for the present, some advocates of abortion legalization believe that their success was inevitable because of the righteousness of the cause. Although the authors share their belief that the cause was just, we explicitly reject the notion that it succeeded for that reason. We believe that the situation was far more problematic than that, and that the arguments on both sides of the issue were rational and "right" within a particular framework of values and assumptions. The real question is what values and assumptions lay behind each side, and what segments of the population might therefore find one side of the argument rational and right for them.

Initial Neutrality

Until various movements for abortion law reform began to appear in the 1960s, abortion itself was a taboo topic. Most people not only did not talk about it much, they did not even think about it unless an immediate personal need arose. There was a negative sentiment about abortion, but one with little moral or ideological force behind it. It was primarily the illegality of the act and the circumstances associated with its *sub rosa* availability that generated the sense that it was evil or immoral.

Consequently, when the taboo was broken and the issue of abortion was brought to the surface, most people did not have a strong basis for, or vested interest in, their negative feelings. The only clearly developed argument against abortion was the official Roman Catholic doctrine, but its strength was heavily dependent upon the acceptance of a number of other tenets of Catholicism.

In effect, most people started from a neutral position once they began to consider seriously the issue of abortion. This meant that the repeal campaign did not have to expend its resources challenging people's basic beliefs or trying to break down the connection between this issue and some deeply held negative convictions or values. Once the campaign had succeeded in the far simpler task of getting people to think about the issue, all energies could be devoted toward making a positive case for repeal.

Abortion and Basic Values

This initial neutrality meant that people were open to new arguments on either side of the issue. In itself this was not necessarily an advantage to the repeal side. It became an advantage because there was also an easy and natural connection to be made between the repeal position and some basic American cultural values. The particular beliefs involved are so general that they transcend virtually all ethnic and religious differences in American society. The first set of beliefs forms the ideological basis for the inclusion of these differing groups in American political and social life. The second set is closely related to the upward mobility of various religious and ethnic groups in American society.

The first set of values to which the repeal position could be connected includes the conviction that a person has a right to act according to his own conscience, plus the related belief that pluralistic tolerance of diversity is essential to the operation of a democracy. Because of the deeply rooted belief in the rights of private conscience, the preferred American solution to a conflict over religious or moral beliefs is not to have the law decide between the two, but rather to have the law protect the exercise of both by means of a pluralistic framework. Repeal of the abortion law could be viewed as an attempt to bring the law into line with these basic values, because it would permit private decision making according to conscience. In addition, reference to these values offered a very powerful argument against an anti-repeal stance that was based on a particular set of religious beliefs. Such anti-repeal opposition itself seemed to constitute an attack on basic pluralistic values.

The second cluster of values to which the issue could be related was the very American emphasis on getting ahead or achieving success by actively mastering situations, and the concomitant belief that the public good is served by allowing private citizens to pursue improvement in this way. The implication of these values is that persons should actively combat adversity rather than passively accepting it and that a successful end result may be more important than strict attention to the niceties of means. Thus it was easier to condone the use of abortion than to condone the passive acceptance of an unwanted pregnancy. Moreover, the private use of abortion could be seen as promoting the public good because of its effect on a variety of social problems. Reference to these private and public values made opposition to repeal seem like an unwarranted interference with each person's right to master private problems and generated sympathy for those who resorted to what had previously been taboo behaviors associated with illegal abortion.

These values offered a strong ideological and moral justification for repeal. Once the connection had been made between the repeal position and values which a person already espoused, his neutrality could be quickly transformed into active support of abortion law repeal. Because the values to which the appeal was made were conservative and traditional, the transition did not even require a personal moral confrontation.

A parallel process of attempting to relate the issue to basic values went on among those opposed to abortion law repeal, but with markedly less success. Catholics were reminded that opposition to abortion was strongly rooted in their basic religious and moral values. This was a powerful argument to many believers. However, the repeal supporters were simultaneously appealing to another set of values which the same people espoused as Americans, independent of religion. The result was a state of cross-pressure for many.

Perhaps partly in response to the obvious conflict between the religiously based opposition to abortion and the basic American values of pluralism and individual initiative, the anti-abortion forces also began trying to link their cause to explicitly American values. Their aim was to present the right to life argument not solely as a religious group's belief, but as an American political and cultural value. They did this by referring to the advocacy of the "right to life, liberty and the pursuit of happiness" in the Declaration of Independence and to the Constitutional protections of life, liberty, and property. While the 1973 Supreme Court decisions have rejected the concept of constitutional rights for a nonviable fetus, the subsequent effort to enact a constitutional amendment affording legal protection of life from the moment of conception may be viewed as a continuing attempt to legitimize the opposition to abortion in terms of American cultural values.

THE CAMPAIGN

The particular tactics and style of the repeal campaign have already been discussed at length and the support the campaign received both inside the legislature and in the community has been reviewed. Several specific features must also be considered important factors in the campaign's success.

Campaign Style and Content

For the most part, abortion law repeal was presented in Hawaii as a conservative issue, despite the radical degree of change it entailed. The repeal campaign was aimed at the middle-class mainstream of the society in a sympathetic and thoroughly acceptable way. The tactics used were dignified and low-key. They tried to appeal to reason rather than to emotion. They were persuasive rather than combative or argumentative. They assumed an identification and a basic equality between the repeal supporter and the audience. The arguments appealed to traditional values already supported by the middle class.

It is important to recognize that all of these features of the campaign were choices rather than intrinsic properties of the issue. If different persons had been involved, the issue of abortion law repeal might just as easily have been presented as a radical cause, using a wholly different set of tactics and emphasizing different arguments. Had this happened, the campaign probably would not have succeeded despite all the favorable conditions which existed.

The campaign also assumed that the political process worked and that the people to whom it was appealing had the power to make things happen. The early supporters of repeal treated every potential supporter of the cause as someone who could have a genuine effect in the halls of government. To some extent, this assumption helped to create the reality. It promoted in ordinary citizens the confidence to approach their legislators and present their views.

As the campaign shifted toward convincing legislators, the same attitudes and assumptions that had been applied to the public were used to persuade the legislators. Again, the appeal was reasonable, low-key, and essentially conservative. Legislators were approached within the context of shared values, as sympathetic equals who would respond to the same arguments which had convinced their constituents. The citizens approached them with the assumption that they could and would make a decision on the basis of the merits of the issue. The legislators were also presumed to have the political power to bring about the desired change in a straightforward manner, because it ought to be done. Naturally, not everyone was convinced that the legislators would respond, but the simple faith in the workability of political institutions probably helped make them work. The legislators were treated as honest men, men with practical concerns but not without a certain amount of moral courage; they acted accordingly.

Political Support

Largely as a consequence of the tactics and style of the campaign, abortion law repeal soon had the right political support to succeed. In the community, important political support came from two quarters: physicians and other professionals with high social status, and labor unions with broad membership and considerable political power. Both groups commanded a great deal of public respect. Their support created a broad climate of acceptability for the abortion law repeal issue and also brought considerable pressure to bear on legislators. The combination was a difficult one to disagree with.

Within the legislature, political support for abortion law repeal was also strategically located. From the point in early September, 1969 when the issue gained the support of a committee chairman in the majority party, it became a political possibility. Without that support, Hawaii might well have been among the states which achieved abortion law repeal by means of the U.S. Supreme Court decision rather than by local legislative action.

AND A LITTLE BIT OF LUCK

In one sense, most of the factors which proved favorable to repeal may be regarded as fortuitous, since most of them were not within the realm of deliberate individual control. In another sense, they are all concrete and stable features of the situation. It may be possible to assess whether these factors or their equivalents are present for every issue, regardless of time and place, and to develop a strategy accordingly. In the case of Hawaii's abortion law repeal campaign, two additional factors were present which do not have this measurable quality. They seem to fall more into the category of historical accident or sheer luck. Both must be given credit in any assessment of why the campaign succeeded, even if they are not variables that could be reproduced or anticipated in another situation. These bits of good fortune for the success of abortion law repeal were the timing of certain events in the campaign and the particular cast of characters involved.

Fortunate Timing

The fact that the repeal campaign had time to develop before there was a response can largely be attributed to luck. Since no restrictive abortion law had ever before been repealed in the United States, the Roman Catholic Church and others opposed to abortion did not believe that it would occur. The Church's initial response was a complacent belief that it was still dealing with an old, tiny minority that had pressed ineffectively for abortion law repeal a decade earlier. By the time the Church realized that there had been a real shift in public attitudes toward abortion and that the level of public interest in the topic was high, it was already late in the campaign.

It was also a stroke of luck that the issue reached Senator Yano near the end of the first year of a two-year (1969–1970) legislative term. This enabled him to hold the issue in committee at the end of the 1969 session without killing it. This timing, coupled with the fact that the Hawaii legislature only convened for one sixty-day session annually, meant that between sessions Senator Yano had time to study the abortion issue thoroughly and arrive at his own decision while the measure was still in his hands.

Even more important, there was time after Senator Yano's support was ensured to conduct the public campaign. Support for repeal was built up during months when legislators were clearly identified; moreover, all were experienced, since they had all served for one session. Yet because the legislature was not in session during those intervening months, the legislators had more time to observe the growing public interest and begin to evaluate their own positions.

The repeal campaign reached its highest momentum just as

the second legislative session opened, when legislators were fresh, other business had not yet piled up, and there was not so much pressure for political trade-offs. Senator Yano capitalized on this favorable timing by moving the issue through the legislative process quickly.

A final critical aspect of fortuitous good timing was the signal from the governor which increased the political possibility of a repeal bill. It was given, albeit inadvertently, at an optimum moment: just after the goal had been set by the appropriate legislative figure, Senator Yano, and early enough to legitimize the entire undertaking.

Personalities

The combination of people who figured in the abortion law repeal campaign in Hawaii also was important for the movement's success. This involves not only the people who were present, but also those who were not.

The presence of Joan Hayes, who had special lobbying experience coupled with a quiet, unassuming personal style, was of inestimable value. Had another leader appeared on the scene, she would willingly have stepped aside, but the results probably would not have been the same. It was her personal background and manner which largely set the tone for many aspects of the campaign.

A different leader might have opted for the more expressive tactics of demonstrations, rallies, and marches and thus lost the bulk of the public support. In this vein, although it is important that William Baird came to Hawaii in January, 1970 and aroused a great deal of student interest in the issue of abortion, it is probably equally important that he quickly returned to the mainland and left the students to turn to Joan Hayes. Baird's greatest contribution may have been to arouse Robert Pearson to action.

Senator Yano's association with the issue was also fortunate. To have a key committee chairman actively supporting abortion law repeal be a Japanese-American Roman Catholic with ten children is a stroke of political fortune that would never be believable in a novel. Beyond these demographic facts, however, Senator Yano's personal style and convictions also contributed greatly to the campaign's success. The issue caught Senator Yano at a critical turning point in his life. It came at a time when he had developed both the values which made the repeal position attractive to him and the moral courage to act on his convictions. It is not so much that he was willing to stake his political career on such a risky issue, but rather that he had reoriented his life in a way that made political career considerations less relevant to his decision. His political talents were applied in the service of the issue, not the other way around. Had he been more politically ambitious, the repeal issue might well have been subverted along the way.

In general, the repeal campaign was fortunate to have had the modest, dedicated leaders it did. The absence of internal bickering and of self-aggrandizing leaders certainly helped the campaign both in its organization and in its public image.

The forces opposed to abortion were not as fortunate in their leadership. For several months the campaign for repeal did not face any organized lay opposition, and the official opposition was directed almost entirely within the Catholic community and not at the general public. When an opposition leader finally did emerge to organize the public, he was someone relatively new to such political action.

Probably most fortunate of all, however, was the nature of the opposition in the legislature. George Loo was a strong opponent, but since he supported the limited reform position, he was not totally opposed to abortion. There was room for negotiation, and he eventually came to accept a repeal bill. Had he been totally opposed, it is doubtful that the legislation would have passed.

THE RELEVANCE OF HAWAII'S EXPERIENCE

The U.S. Supreme Court decisions of January 22, 1973 have removed the pressing need for state action to eliminate restrictive abortion laws. However, Hawaii's experience may still be relevant to the continuing cause of abortion law reform.

The Supreme Court decisions nullified the great majority of existing state anti-abortion laws but did not preclude the establishment of new ones designed to circumvent the ruling (although they, too, would be subject to challenge). In addition, there are still states where prevailing practice is not yet in conformity with the Supreme Court decisions because an aroused public has not yet pressed for change. In either of these circumstances, the experience of Hawaii's repeal campaign may be instructive.

Since the Supreme Court decision, there has been a growing

movement for a right to life amendment to the U.S. Constitution. Our analysis of the tactics and issues of the repeal campaign in Hawaii suggests that this would be a more difficult issue for repeal supporters to handle with the techniques that proved so effective the first time around. As the topic of abortion continues to be debated, the arguments, motives, and emotions of both sides need to be understood in terms of the basic values and beliefs which underlie them.

More broadly, Hawaii's experience with the abortion law repeal campaign may have relevance to other movements for social change. Although the reasons for Hawaii's success were manifold and not always either deliberate or replicable, the general strategy of the campaign could certainly be applied elsewhere. This includes: using a low-key, educational approach to reach the public through existing voluntary organizations; linking the specific arguments for the issue to basic values already held by the general public; actively seeking support from organizations and persons with high prestige (such as professionals and respectable community groups) and political power (such as the chamber of commerce, labor unions, political parties, and key legislative figures); and directing initial efforts toward the public and then getting the public to bring pressure to bear on legislators.

There is nothing new about these tactics. They follow classic political rules. However, they are sometimes overlooked in contemporary society because the people who seek change often feel alienated from the political process. Hawaii's experience demonstrates that radical change can sometimes be brought about by very traditional means. Support for such change may turn up in highly unlikely places, if the right tactics are used to create an appropriate environment.

Perhaps the most important finding of this study is that participatory democracy is still alive. The repeal of the abortion law was accomplished by working within the system and by applying in practice an idealistic definition of how the system works. The campaign succeeded because avenues for political participation were open and legislators were responsive to public concerns. We cannot help but feel that the repeal campaign also helped to open and to strengthen these routes to political participation by proceeding in the simple confidence that the political system was accessible and responsive.

APPENDIX

Questionnaire to Legislators

TO DETERMINE how various aspects of the abortion law repeal campaign had influenced legislators, a questionnaire was sent to every Hawaii legislator in July, 1970. This was five months after final passage of the abortion bill and three months after the end of the legislative session. These were mailed to every legislator at his home address. Accompanying each questionnaire was a cover letter. Also enclosed was a postcard to be signed by the respondent and mailed back separately. This provided a means of following up nonresponse without compromising the anonymity of respondents. After four weeks, a follow-up letter and a second copy of the questionnaire were sent to all those who had not returned postcards; the number of postcards returned equalled the number of questionnaires returned. Twenty-nine of the seventy-five legislators returned questionnaires, a response rate of 39 percent. While this is not a particularly high rate of response, it is about average for a mailed survey of this type. The sample returned came proportionally from the two houses, with replies received from ten of twenty-four Senators (41 percent) and nineteen of fifty-one Representatives (37 percent).

The ethnic distribution of the respondents matches that of the legislature (Table 1). Persons who voted for repeal of the abortion law are somewhat overrepresented in the sample (76 percent) as compared to the whole legislature (61 percent).

Although the sample is small, it appears to be adequate for the informal analysis undertaken above.

TABLE 1. Ethnic Distribution of Questionnaire Sample and Legislature

Ethnicity	*Sample* N	*Sample* %	*Legislature* N	*Legislature* %
Japanese-American	15	54	37	49
Chinese-American	4	14	10	13
Filipino-American	2	7	6	8
Caucasian-American	6	21	19	25
Other	1	4	3	4
Total	28*	100%	75	99%

*Ethnicity of one respondent was unknown.

July 21, 1970

Dear Hawaii Legislator:

Under the auspices of The Population Council, we are undertaking a study of how Hawaii's new abortion legislation was passed.

Although we would like to talk with each of you personally concerning your participation and opinions on this issue, the pressures of time make this impossible. Instead, we would appreciate it very much if you could take five minutes to fill out the enclosed questionnaire, which when combined with the questionnaires of all other legislators will give us a general picture of what factors influenced the change.

The survey is anonymous, and your name cannot be connected with the information you provide. However, if you return the enclosed postcard at the time you return the completed questionnaire (separately) we will have an independent check of those who have returned the forms. If you forget to fill out and return the questionnaire and postcard, we will send you a friendly reminder in a week or two.

We sincerely appreciate your cooperation in this matter, and hope you will see the benefits of such research for legislators as well as scholars and the general public. If you have any further questions concerning the research, or if you would like to contribute further information, we would be happy to meet with you at your convenience.

Sincerely yours,

Patricia G. Steinhoff
Milton Diamond

1. When did you first become interested in the abortion issue?

2. What argument impressed you most?

3. What problems worried you most?

4. How much communication did you get from your constituents on the abortion issue?

   letters: number pro ______ phone calls: number pro ______
   number con ______ number con ______

   How does this compare with the amount of communication you have received on other issues?

5. At what point did you make up your mind about how you would vote on the abortion bill?

6. Was there some crucial turning point or factor in your decision?

7. To what extent did you participate in this particular issue?

	yes	no	comments
voted			
read news media regarding abortion			
conducted own poll or survey of constituency			
discussed with colleagues			
discussed with professionals or experts			
discussed with constituents or organization representatives			
read relevant educational material			
attended the public hearings			
attended other public meetings (panels, speeches)			
attended legislative caucuses			
was member of Public Health, Welfare and Housing			
was member of Conference Committee			
participated in legislative debate			
introduced amendment			

8. How did you respond to the following expressions of public opinion concerning the abortion issue?

	Influenced my thinking	Did not influence my thinking	Specific Comments
individual letters from constituents			
mimeographed or duplicated letters from constituents			
office visits from constituents			
phone calls from constituents			
letters to the editor in newspapers			
advertisements in newspapers			
editorials in newspapers			
regular articles in newspapers			
testimony at the public hearings: by clergymen			
by physicians			
by lawyers			
by scholars			
by private citizens giving personal views			
by persons offering personal experiences			
reading of organization positions			
statistics			

	Influenced my thinking	Did not influence my thinking	Specific Comments
moral arguments			
speakers' remarks at panels and speeches			
audience response at panels and speeches			
educational materials given legislators by organizations			
movies about abortion shown on television			
official positions taken by organizations			
demonstrations at the Capitol Building			
Bishop Scanlan's private audience with legislature			
public opinion polls			
sermons in your church			

9. Which way did you vote on the final roll call? pro____ con____

10. Did you have any reservations about your vote?

11. Do you have any suggestions for Hawaii constituents who want to affect the legislative process?

12. Do you have any suggestions for citizens in other states who wish to affect pro or con the legislative process concerning abortion?

13. Member of: · Senate______ House______

14. Number of terms in office______

15. Are you up for re-election this year? yes______ no______

16. Are you a Committee Chairman? yes______ no______

17. What is your religious preference? ______________________

18. What is your ethnic or racial background? ______________________

19. Have you ever had any personal experience with abortion through friends or relatives? yes______ no______

20. Was the coming election a consideration in your vote on the abortion bill?

21. Do you feel you voted on this issue for your constituents or for your personal conscience?

__________ constituents __________ conscience

September 10, 1970

Dear Hawaii Legislator:

We have not yet received your return postcard, indicating that you have returned the questionnaire on Hawaii's new abortion legislation which we sent to you recently. We know you are extremely busy, but we hope you will take a few minutes to fill out the questionnaire and return it to us. It is important that we find out your experience and your views in order to get a full picture of the legislature.

We sincerely appreciate your cooperation in this matter, and hope you will see the benefits of our research for legislators as well as scholars and the general public. If you have any further questions concerning the research, or if you would like to contribute further information, we would be happy to meet with you at your convenience.

Sincerely yours,

Patricia G. Steinhoff
Milton Diamond

Notes

CHAPTER 1

1. *The State of Hawaii Data Book 1972, A Statistical Abstract* (Honolulu: Dept. of Planning and Economic Development, 1972), p. 8.

2. Tom Coffman, *Catch a Wave: Hawaii's New Politics* (Honolulu: Honolulu Star-Bulletin, 1972), pp. 14–34.

3. *The State of Hawaii Data Book 1972,* pp. 99–100.

4. *The Penal Laws of the Hawaiian Islands, 1897* (Honolulu: Gazette Printers, 1897), p. 75.

5. *The Territory v. Hart,* 35 Haw. 582.

6. *Revised Laws of Hawaii, 1925: Comprising the Statutes of the Territory, Consolidated, Revised and Annotated,* ch. 280.

7. *Revised Laws of Hawaii 1955,* footnote to ch. 309, sec. 3–5. The clarification followed a Hawaii Supreme Court ruling in *The Territory v. Young,* 37 Haw. 150.

8. *The Territory v. Hart,* 35 Haw. 582; *The Territory v. Young,* 37 Haw. 150; *The Territory v. Young and Nozawa,* 37 Haw. 189; *The Territory v. Decorian,* 38 Haw. 121; *The Territory v. Shishido,* 39 Haw. 265.

9. *The Territory v. Young and Nozawa,* 37 Haw. 189; *The Territory v. Shishido,* 39 Haw. 265.

10. See *The Territory v. Young,* 37 Haw. 150; *The Territory v. Young and Nozawa,* 37 Haw. 189; *Young v. The Territory of Hawaii,* 163 F2d 490; *The Territory v. Hart,* 35 Haw. 582.

11. Information courtesy of Department of Regulatory Agencies, State of Hawaii.

12. R. G. Smith, B. Manner, and G. Goto, "Physicians' Attitudes on the Abortion Law," *Hawaii Medical Journal* 29, no. 3 (January-February, 1970):21.

13. P. G. Steinhoff, J. Palmore, R. G. Smith, and M. Diamond, "Ethnic Variations in the Use of Abortion which affect Live Birth Distributions in Hawaii" (Paper presented at Population Association of America meetings, April, 1973); P. G. Steinhoff, M. Diamond, J. Palmore and R. G. Smith, "Who are the New Abortion Patients?" (Paper presented at Abortion Workshop, Population Association of America meetings, April, 1973).

14. Personal interview with Dr. George Goto.

15. The law required that physicians and hospitals report all stillbirths until 1951 and all "fetal deaths" thereafter. The change was made to standardize reporting procedures and explicitly included abortions. Hawaii State Legislature, "Standing Committee Report 726 *re:* S.B. 100," *House Journal* (1951):579.

16. P. G. Steinhoff and R. G. Smith, "Abortion Law Ideology and Reality" (Unpublished paper, 1973), pp. 8–9.

17. *Ibid.*

18. Roy Lucas, "Laws of the United States," in *Abortion in a Changing World,* edited by Robert E. Hall, vol. 1 (New York: Columbia University Press, 1970), pp. 127–136.

19. In the Soviet Union, abortion was freely permitted from 1920 to 1935, and from 1955 on. Abortions were permitted for liberal social and medical indications in Poland and Hungary from 1956, in Czechoslovakia from 1957, and in Yugoslavia from 1960. Romania permitted abortion for any reason from 1960 to 1966, when conditions were restricted to medical and psychiatric grounds. See Henry P. David, *Family Planning and Abortion in the Socialist Countries of Central and Eastern Europe* (New York: The Population Council, 1970), pp. 18–19.

20. Madeleine Simms and Keith Hindell, *Abortion Law Reformed* (London: Peter Owen Limited, 1971), pp. 108–109; and Russell Shaw, *Abortion on Trial* (London: Robert Hale and Company, 1968), pp. 19–20.

21. Lawrence Lader, *Abortion II: Making the Revolution* (Boston: Beacon Press, 1973), pp. 68–69.

22. The most prominent of these were the Association for the Study of Abortion (New York), The Society for Humane Abortion (San Francisco), The California Committee on Therapeutic Abortion (Los Angeles), and The Illinois Committee for Medical Control of Abortion (Chicago).

23. Planned Parenthood Federation of America held a conference on Abortion in the United States in April, 1955. An interdisciplinary First International Conference on Abortion was held in Washington, D.C. in the fall of 1967, sponsored by the Harvard Divinity School and the Joseph P. Kennedy, Jr. Foundation. The Association for the Study of Abortion held an international conference in Hot Springs, Virginia in November, 1968. The National Institute of Child Health and Human Development and the National Institute of Mental Health jointly sponsored two workshops on abortion in the late 1960s. The first, "Abortion: A National Public and Mental Health Problem—Past, Present and Proposed Research," was held in October, 1968; the second, "Abortion Obtained and Denied: Research Approaches," was held in December, 1969.

24. In 1964, Representative Manuel Henriques introduced H.B. 115, the purpose of which was to stiffen the penalties for illegal abortion. The bill died in committee.

25. Hawaii State Legislature, Senate, Fourth Legislature "S.B. 619, A Bill for an Act Relating to Abortion and Amending Chapter 309, *Revised Laws of Hawaii 1955,*" March 7, 1967.

26. Cosigning were Representatives Akira Sakima, Manuel Henriques, Pedro de la Cruz, Thomas Tagawa, Jack Suwa, Ted Morioka, and Clarence Akizaki.

27. Hawaii State Legislature, House, Fourth Legislature, H.B. 76, "A Bill for An Act Relating to Abortion and Amending Chapter 309, *Revised Laws of Hawaii 1955,*" February 15, 1967.

28. Personal interview with George Loo.

29. George Goto, "Abortion—Hawaii's Experience, Private Physician's Role" (Unpublished paper, 1970), pp. 1–2.

30. Hawaii State Legislature, House, Fourth Legislature, "Standing Committee Report No. 373 *re:* H.B. 76," March 31, 1967.

31. Concurring were Representatives George Loo (chairman), Mitsuo Uechi (vice-chairman), Akira Sakima, Richard Wong, Dorothy Devereux, Howard Oda, Tony Kunimura, and Cliff Kreuger; signing with reservations were Representatives Ted Morioka and Clarence Akizaki, both of whom had cosigned the original bill; not concurring were Representatives Akoni Pule, Francis Wong, and Mamoru Yamasaki.

32. Personal interview with George Loo.

33. Cosigners of the bill were Representatives Jack Suwa, Tony Kunimura, and Peter Iha. Representative Suwa had cosigned H.B. 76 the previous year, and Representative Kunimura had approved it as a member of the Committee on Housing and Consumer Protection.

34. Lader, *Abortion II:* p. 69.

35. Abortion Act 1967, reprinted in Simms and Hindell, *Abortion Law Reformed,* pp. 249–253.

36. Edmund G. Overstreet, "California's Abortion Law—A Second Look," in The California Committee on Therapeutic Abortion, *Abortion and the Unwanted Child,* edited by Carl Reiterman (New York: Springer Publishing Co., 1971), pp. 15–25; Simms and Hindell, *Abortion Law Reformed,* p. 214.

37. Hawaii State Legislature, Senate, Fifth Legislature, "S.B. 168, A Bill for An Act Relating to Abortion and Defenses to the Offenses of Abortion," February 24, 1969.

38. Senators D. G. Anderson, Hebden Porteus, Eureka Forbes, Wadsworth Yee, Percy Mirikitani, Fred Rohlfing, and Toshio Ansai.

39. Hawaii State Legislature, Senate, Fifth Legislature, "S.B. 521, A Bill For An Act Relating To Abortion," March 4, 1969.

40. Personal interview with George Loo.

41. Reported by L. Kasaoka at meeting of abortion law campaign participants, May 27, 1970.

42. Chairman Loo's minutes of March 10, 1969 hearings on H.B. 61, 104, 107, 204, State of Hawaii Public Archives.

43. For a fuller exposition of the Drinan argument, see R. E. Cooke, A. E. Hellegers, R. G. Hoyt, and H. W. Richardson (eds.) *The Terrible Choice: The Abortion Dilemma,* based on proceedings of the International Conference on Abortion sponsored by the Harvard Divinity School and the Joseph P. Kennedy, Jr. Foundation (New York: Bantam Books, 1968), pp. 57, 102.

44. Hawaii State Legislature, House, Fifth Legislature, "House Standing Committee Report No. 80 *re:* H.B. 61," April 2, 1969, p. 6.

45. Personal interview with Dorothy Devereux.

46. Hawaii State Legislature, House, *Journal,* 5th Legislature, Regular Session, April 3, 1969, p. 235.

47. Hawaii State Legislature, House, *Journal,* 5th Legislature, Regular Session, April 7, 1969, pp. 250–251.

CHAPTER 2

1. Personal interview with Vincent Yano.

2. Joan Hayes, "Abortion Law: A Case History—or Helping a 'Hopeless Cause' become a Political Possibility" (Unpublished paper, 1970), pp. 1–3.

3. Reported by Joan Hayes at meeting of abortion law campaign participants, May 27, 1970.

4. Roy G. Smith, "Changing Hawaii's Abortion Laws," *Pacific Health* 3 (1970):3.

5. Harvey L. Zipf, "Recent Abortion Law Reforms (or Much Ado About Nothing)," *The Journal of Criminal Law, Criminology and Police Science* 60, no. 1 (1969):3–23.

6. Personal interview with George Loo.

7. Cooke *et al., The Terrible Choice.*

8. Robert F. Drinan, "The Right of the Foetus to be Born," *The Dublin Review* 514 (Winter):365–381.

9. Personal interview with Vincent Yano

10. Personal interview with Joan Hayes.

11. Personal interview with Joan Hayes.

12. "Burns Terms Legal Abortion Matter of One's Conscience," by Claude Burgett and Tom Coffman, *Honolulu Star-Bulletin,* October 22, 1969, p. A1.

13. Personal interview with George Loo.

14. Bishop John Scanlan, "Abortion Has Been Consistently Condemned by the Catholic Church," *Hawaii Catholic Herald,* October 31, 1969, p. 1.

15. "Bishop Says Abortion is an 'Unspeakable Crime,' " by Nadine Stuart, *Honolulu Star-Bulletin,* October 30, 1969, p. A1; "Scanlan Restates Church Position Abortion a Crime," *Honolulu Advertiser,* October 31, 1969, p. A4.

16. Bishop John Scanlan, "Legislators Have Duty to Hold Line in Preventing Erosion of Morality," *Hawaii Catholic Herald,* November 7, 1969, p. 1.

17. Memorandum to Bishop Scanlan from D. J. Dever *re:* Abortion, February 5, 1970.

18. Personal interview with Robert Pearson.

19. Pearson's offer had no takers until after the abortion law had been repealed, at which time women began to seek his help. Initially, he welcomed women into his own home. As more arrived, he added rooms to his house.

CHAPTER 3

1. "Abortion Foe Loses Half His Audience," *Honolulu Advertiser,* February 7, 1970, p. A8.

2. "Federation Calls for Repeal of 'Archaic' Abortion Law," by Eric Cavaliero, *Honolulu Advertiser,* September 22, 1969, p. A5.

3. Martha D. McDaniel, "Church Stand on Abortion" (letter to the editor), *Honolulu Advertiser,* October 17, 1969, p. A19.

4. "Episcopal Nuns Gain New Status," by Nadine Stuart, *Honolulu Star-Bulletin,* October 27, 1969, p. A19.

5. "ILWU Leaders Favor Repeal of Hawaii's Abortion Law," *Honolulu Star-Bulletin,* November 5, 1969, p. A1.

6. "Abortion Repeal Gets More Support," *Honolulu Star-Bulletin,* December 2, 1969, p. E4.

7. "New Support to Repeal Abortion Law," *Honolulu Star-Bulletin,* December 16, 1969, p. A20.

8. "Judicial Council Would Legalize Abortion, Gaming," by Tom Coffman, *Honolulu Star-Bulletin,* December 2, 1969, p. D1.

9. "Association Airs Views," *Honolulu Advertiser,* January 2, 1970, p. E3.

10. "Abortion Repeal Vote," *Honolulu Star-Bulletin,* January 15, 1970, p. C2.

11. "C of C Board Backs Repeal of Abortion Law," *Honolulu Advertiser,* January 22, 1970, p. C4.

12. "Child Service Opposes Law on Abortion," *Honolulu Star-Bulletin,* January 22, 1970, p. A7.

13. "Favor Abortion," *Honolulu Star-Bulletin,* January 26, 1970, p. A8.

14. "Abortion Law Repeal Gets Board Support," *Honolulu Advertiser,* January 28, 1970, p. A12.

15. "Church Council Backs Abortion Law Repeal," *Honolulu Star-Bulletin,* January 30, 1970, p. A13.

16. "Public Hearing Tonight on Abortion Law Repeal," by Douglas Boswell, *Honolulu Advertiser,* February 3, 1970, p. A6.

17. "Abortion Bill is Debated," *Honolulu Star-Bulletin,* February 13, 1970, p. A4.

18. "Chamber Backs Abortion Appeal," *Honolulu Advertiser,* February 14, 1970, p. B1.

19. "Support Repeal of Abortion Law" (paid advertisement), *Honolulu Star-Bulletin*, February 16, 1970, p. A10 and *Honolulu Advertiser*, February 17, 1970, p. B16.

20. "Lehua Jaycees Take No Stand," *Hawaii Tribune Herald*, February 13, 1970, p. 1.

21. "Abortion Veto Plea Fails in Civic Clubs," *Honolulu Star-Bulletin*, February 21, 1970, p. A12.

22. Personal interview with Joan Hayes.

23. Lawrence Lader, *Abortion II: Making the Revolution* (Boston: Beacon Press, 1973), p. 116.

24. "96% of Doctors Answering Abortion Poll Back Change," *Honolulu Star-Bulletin*, October 31, 1969, p. A12.

25. "Sampling of Buddhist Sentiment Favors Abortion," *Honolulu Star-Bulletin*, January 14, 1970, p. B7.

26. "Speak Up! On Abortion," *Honolulu Star-Bulletin*, October 25, 1969, p. A10.

27. "Repeal of Abortion Law Heavily Favored in Poll," *Honolulu Star-Bulletin*, October 29, 1969, p. A1; "Islanders Speak Up 20–1 for Abortion Repeal," by Claude Burgett, *Honolulu Star-Bulletin*, November 7, 1969, pp. A1, A6; "Speak Up," *Honolulu Star-Bulletin*, November 12, 1969, p. A20.

28. "Abortion Law Change Has Support in Poll," *Honolulu Star-Bulletin*, December 22, 1969, p. D15.

29. "Survey Indicates Abortion Repeal Favored by 55% of Voters," *Honolulu Star-Bulletin*, February 13, 1970, p. A1.

30. "New Poll Shows Voters Still OK Abortion Repeal," *Honolulu Star-Bulletin*, March 3, 1970, p. A1.

31. "The Abortion Debate," *Honolulu Star-Bulletin and Advertiser*, March 16, 1969, p. B2.

32. "Liberalizing Abortion," *Honolulu Star-Bulletin*, April 12, 1969, p. A14.

33. "Church and State," *Honolulu Star-Bulletin*, April 8, 1969, p. A18.

34. "A Matter of Conscience," *Honolulu Star-Bulletin*, September 13, 1969, p. A10.

35. "The Abortion Choice," *Honolulu Advertiser*, February 9, 1970, p. A14.

36. Catherine Dunn, "Dissent—Says Abortion Always Takes Human Life," *Honolulu Advertiser*, January 27, 1969, p. A9.

37. Claire Booth Luce, "Dissent—Decries Abortion Bid, Asks Veto," *Honolulu Advertiser*, March 4, 1970, p. A13.

38. *People v. Belous*, 71 Cal. 2d 954, 458 p.2d 194; 80 Cal. Repr. 354 (1969).

39. *United States v. Vuitch*, 350 F Supp. 1032 (D.D.C. 1969). The U.S. Supreme Court subsequently upheld the constitutionality of the District of Columbia statute, which allowed abortion "necessary for the preservation of the mother's life or health." (*United States v. Vuitch*, 402 U.S. 62 [1971]). The Court interpreted "health" to include mental health. It also changed the rule on burden of proof, so that in a criminal statute the burden would be on the prosecution to plead and prove that the abortion was not necessary to preserve the woman's life or health rather than, as formerly, on the physician to prove that the abortion was necessary for these reasons.

40. "Birth Control Pills 'Safe,' Drug Agency Report Says," by Richard D. Lyons, *The New York Times*, September 5, 1969, p. 1; "British Panel Links Some Birth Pills to a Risk of Blood Clots," by Gloria Emerson, *The New York Times*, December 12, 1969, p. 34; "Senate Panel to Open Hearing on Birth Pill," *The New York Times*, January 14, 1970, p. 13; "Poll Finds 18% Dip in Use of Birth Control Pills," *The New York Times*, February 2, 1970, p. 38.

41. "Support Repeal of Abortion Law" (paid advertisement), *Honolulu Star-Bulletin,* February 16, 1970, p. A10 and *Honolulu Advertiser,* February 17, 1970, p. B16.

42. "Right to Life . . . " (paid advertisement), *Honolulu Star-Bulletin,* January 31, 1970, p. A9 and *Honolulu Advertiser,* January 31, 1970, p. A7.

43. "So that You Can Better Understand the Drama of Life Before Birth" (paid advertisement), *Honolulu Star-Bulletin,* February 16, 1970, p. A14, and *Honolulu Advertiser,* February 16, 1970, p. A9.

44. "History Repeats Abortions" (paid advertisement), *Honolulu Advertiser,* February 19, 1970, p. C4 and *Honolulu Star-Bulletin,* February 19, 1970, p. C6.

45. Robert W. Gardner and Eleanor C. Nordyke, *The Demographic Situation in Hawaii,* Papers of the East-West Population Institute no. 31 (Honolulu: June 1974), p. 26.

46. "History Repeats Abortions," *Honolulu Advertiser,* C4.

47. Dr. George Goto, "A Clarification" (letter to the editor), *Honolulu Star-Bulletin,* February 23, 1970, p. A14 and "Dr. Goto on Dr. Doyle" (letter to the editor), *Honolulu Advertiser,* February 26, 1970, p. A15.

48. Dr. George H. Mills, "Dr. Goto on Dr. Doyle" (letter to the editor), *Honolulu Advertiser,* February 26, 1970, p. A15 and "Dr. Goto Defended" (letter to the editor), *Honolulu Star-Bulletin,* February 27, 1970, p. A17. See also David J. Harada, "Dedicated Service" (letter to the editor), *Honolulu Advertiser,* March 3, 1970, p. A9; Anonymous, "Dr. Goto Defended" (letter to the editor), *Honolulu Star-Bulletin,* February 27, 1970, p. A17; and David J. Harada, "Defends Dr. Goto" (letter to the editor), *Honolulu Advertiser,* February 28, 1970, p. A14.

49. Gerri Madden, letter to the editor, *Honolulu Advertiser,* March 3, 1970, p. A9.

50. "Fasi Attacks TV Stations' Film Refusal," by Bruce Benson, *Honolulu Advertiser,* March 4, 1970, p. A1.

51. "Fasi Ends TV Station Fight," by Ron Staton, *Honolulu Star-Bulletin,* March 6, 1970, p. A6.

52. "Fasi Blasts Newspaper Coverage of Abortion Law Controversy," by Bruce Benson, *Honolulu Star-Bulletin,* February 20, 1970, p. A12.

CHAPTER 4

1. "Pregnant Girl, 14, Marches to Protest Abortion Law," by Tomi Knaefler, *Honolulu Star-Bulletin,* January 13, 1970, p. A4.

2. "Handicapped Support Antiabortion Protest," by Phil Mayer, *Honolulu Star-Bulletin,* February 2, 1970, p. A14.

3. "Vote for Repeal Is Likely Today," by Gerry Kier, *Honolulu Advertiser,* February 10, 1970, p. A1; "Only a Few Lawmakers Hear Protest," by Beverly Creamer, *Honolulu Star-Bulletin,* February 10, 1970, p. A1.

4. Howard Wiig (Zero Population Growth), Hawaii State Legislature, Senate Committee on Public Health, Welfare and Housing, Public Hearing on H.B. 61, February 3 and 4, 1970, written testimony, p. 2.

5. Reprinted in *Honolulu Star-Bulletin,* February 12, 1970, p. A17.

6. "Letters Protest Repeal" (picture), *Honolulu Advertiser,* February 17, 1970, p. B2.

7. See appendix for details of the administration of the questionnaire.

8. Laurel Kasaoka, letter to legislators dated January 2, 1970.

9. Personal interview with Howard Wiig.

10. Personal interview with Joan Hayes.

11. One of the authors (PGS) attended the meeting as a representative of the University Abortion and Birth Control Committee.

12. "Complete Statement on Abortion by Bishop: Thoughts for Legislators," *Hawaii Catholic Herald,* February 13, 1970, p. 1.

13. "Professor Asks Equal Time," *Honolulu Star-Bulletin and Advertiser,* February 8, 1970, p. A6.

14. Bishop John J. Scanlan, "Bishop Explains Special Meeting" (letter to the editor), *Honolulu Advertiser,* February 13, 1970, p. A13 and "The Bishop Explains," *Honolulu Star-Bulletin,* February 13, 1970, p. A17.

15. "Fasi Sends Plea Against Repeal," *Honolulu Advertiser,* February 19, 1970, p. B1.

16. "Fasi Says He'll Ask Burns to Veto Abortion Measures," by Bruce Benson, *Honolulu Advertiser,* February 27, 1970, p. A8.

17. The University of Hawaii requires faculty members to state that they are acting as private citizens when testifying before the legislature and enjoins them from representing the university or any of its components without permission of the administration.

18. *Hawaii Legislative Manual, A Handbook for Legislators,* 4th ed., Report no. 1 (Honolulu: Legislative Reference Bureau, 1971), p. 47.

CHAPTER 5

1. See Appendix for details of the administration of the questionnaire.

2. The analysis is based on Senator Yano's personal copy of the written testimony submitted to the committee, plus a tape recording of the live radio broadcast of the full two nights of hearings. If material was presented in written form only, or in both the written and oral testimony, citation is to the written testimony, by page. If a comment occurred only in the oral testimony, citation is by date. In the citations that follow, a person's title or organization enclosed in parentheses indicates that the person represented the organization as an official spokesman. A listing without parentheses is for purposes of identification only; the person testified as a private citizen.

3. Paul Ehrlich, *The Population Bomb* (New York: Ballantine Books, 1968).

4. Norman St. John-Stevas, *The Right to Life* (New York: Holt, Rinehart and Winston, 1964).

5. Hawaii State Legislature, Fifth Legislature, Senate Committee on Public Health, Welfare and Housing, Public Hearing on H.B. 61, February 3 and 4, 1970, Dr. Roy G. Smith, pediatrician, written testimony, summary and p. 3.

6. *Ibid.,* Fumi Ige (AFL-CIO), written testimony, p. 1.

7. *Ibid.,* Dr. Roy G. Smith, pediatrician, written testimony, p. 3.

8. *Ibid.,* Fumi Ige (AFL-CIO), written testimony, p. 2.

9. *Ibid.,* Dr. Roy G. Smith, pediatrician, written testimony, summary and p. 5.

10. *Ibid.,* Dr. George Goto, obstetrician; written testimony, pp. 1–2.

11. *Ibid.,* Anonymous, written testimony, pp. 1–2.

12. *Ibid.,* Mickey Hummer, social worker (Committee for the Protection of Children), written testimony, p. 3.

13. This argument was advanced particularly by *Ibid.,* Peggy Hillman (American Civil Liberties Union), written testimony, p. 1; Louise MacDonald, editor of *Pacific Health,* University of Hawaii School of Public Health, written testimony, p. 1; Ah Quon McElrath (ILWU, Local 142), written testimony, p. 3; Mrs. Steven Levinski (Students for a Democratic Society), written testimony, p. 1; Curtis McLain (Committee to End Crimes Without Victims, Honolulu Young Democrats), written testimony, pp. 1–2; and Dr. John Blaylock, psychologist, (John Howard Association), written testimony, p. 1.

14. *Ibid.,* Dr. Roy G. Smith, pediatrician, written testimony, p. 4.

15. *Ibid.,* Dr. J. L. Erickson, physician, oral testimony, March 4, 1970.

16. *Ibid.*, Reverend Claude du Teil, Episcopal Minister (Clergy Counseling Service), written testimony, p. 2.

17. Patricia G. Steinhoff and Roy G. Smith, "Abortion Law Ideology and Reality" (Unpublished paper, 1973), p. 17.

18. Public Hearing on H.B. 61, Dr. Patricia Steinhoff, sociologist, written testimony, p. 1.

19. *Ibid.*, Dr. Robert Noyes, Chief, Section of Obstetrics and Gynecology, University of Hawaii School of Medicine, oral testimony, February 3, 1970; Antoinette Unis (Women's Rights Committee, Honolulu Young Democrats), written testimony, p. 2; Paul Brumage, graduate student, written testimony, p. 2.

20. *Ibid.*, Mrs. Colin Herrick (Hawaii Planned Parenthood), written testimony, p. 1; Betty Jean Soares, written testimony, p. 2; Antoinette Unis (Women's Rights Committee, Honolulu Young Democrats), written testimony, p. 2; Dr. Patricia Steinhoff, sociologist, written testimony, p. 1; Paul Brumage, graduate student, written testimony, p. 2.

21. *Ibid.*, Dr. Milton Diamond, sexologist, written testimony, p. 5.

22. *Ibid.*, Jean Avery, social worker (National Association of Social Workers), written testimony, p. 1; Rosemarie Emery, social worker (Child and Family Service), written testimony, p. 1; Dr. Ronald Pion, obstetrician, oral testimony, February 4, 1970.

23. *Ibid.*, Dr. William Hindle, obstetrician (Chairman of Public Affairs Committee, Child and Family Service), written testimony, pp. 1–2.

24. *Ibid.*, Dr. Patricia Steinhoff, sociologist, written testimony, p. 3.

25. *Ibid.*, William G. Among (Director, Department of Social Services and Housing), written testimony, p. 1.

26. *Ibid.*, Dr. Patricia Steinhoff, sociologist, written testimony, p. 3.

27. *Ibid.*, Laurel Kasaoka, graduate student (Democratic Action Group), written testimony, p. 1.

28. *Ibid.*, Dr. Roy G. Smith, pediatrician, written testimony, p. 2.

29. Hans Forssman and Inge Thuwe, "One Hundred and Twenty Children Born After Application for Therapeutic Abortion Refused," *Acta Psychiatrica Scandinavia,* 42 (1966):71–88.

30. Among those who referred to the social problems associated with unwanted children in their testimony were Dr. J. L. Erickson, physician, Public Hearing on H.B. 61, February 4, 1970; Earlene Chambers, social worker, written testimony, p. 1; Mickey Hummer, social worker (Committee for the Protection of Children), written testimony, p. 1; Peter Kaaialii (Chairman, Honolulu Community Action Program Board), written testimony, p. 1; George Felton (Public Health Committee, Chamber of Commerce of Hawaii), written testimony, p. 1.

31. Public Hearing on H.B. 61, Jean Avery (Hawaii Chapter, National Association of Social Workers), written testimony, p. 1.

32. *Ibid.*, Dr. John Blaylock, psychologist (John Howard Association), written testimony, p. 1.

33. *Ibid.*, Dr. Charles Stewart, psychiatrist (Hawaii Psychiatric Society), written testimony, p. 1.

34. *Ibid.*, Interchange between Senator Vincent Yano, Senator Percy Mirikitani and Edwin Tam (Department of Social Services), February 3, 1970.

35. *Ibid.*, Kay Foy, social worker, written testimony, p. 1.

36. *Ibid.*, Marie Stires, community worker, written testimony, p. 1.

37. *Ibid.*, Sarah Pegg (recent graduate section, American Association of University Women), written testimony, p. 1.

38. *Ibid.*, Earlene Chambers, social worker, written testimony, pp. 1–2.

39. *Ibid.*, Dr. Milton Diamond, sexologist and specialist in sexual behavior, written testimony, pp. 1–2.

40. *Ibid.*, Interchange between Senator Vincent Yano and Dr. Milton Diamond, February 4, 1970.

41. *Ibid.*, Dr. J. L. Erickson, physician, February 4, 1970.

42. *Ibid.*, Barbara Higbee (Sierra Club), written testimony, p. 1.

43. *Ibid.*, February 4, 1970.

44. *Ibid.*, Paul Brumage, zoology graduate student, written testimony, p. 3.

45. *Ibid.*, Howard Wiig (Zero Population Growth), February 4, 1970.

46. *Ibid.*, Interchange among Dr. James Dator, political scientist and futurist, Senator Percy Mirikitani, and Senator Wadsworth Yee, February 4, 1970.

47. *Ibid.*, George Felton (Public Health Committee, Chamber of Commerce), written testimony, p. 1; Laurel Kasaoka (Democratic Action Group), written testimony, p. 1; Peggy Hillman (American Civil Liberties Union), February 4, 1974; Ah Quon McElrath (ILWU Local 142), written testimony, pp. 1–2; Antoinette Unis (Honolulu Young Democrats), written testimony, p. 2; and Gwendolyn Kim (University of Hawaii Social Work Students), written testimony, p. 1.

48. *Ibid.*, Paul Brumage, graduate student, written testimony, pp. 1–2; Rosemarie Emery, social worker (Child and Family Service), written testimony, p. 1.

49. *Ibid.*, Interchange between Dr. Ronald Pion, obstetrician and Visiting Professor of Public Health, University of Hawaii, and Senator Wadsworth Yee, February 4, 1970.

50. *Ibid.*, Dr. Charles W. Stewart, psychiatrist (Hawaii Psychiatric Society), written testimony, p. 1.

51. Harvey L. Zipf, "Recent Abortion Law Reforms (or Much Ado About Nothing)," *The Journal of Criminal Law, Criminology and Police Science* 60, no. 1 (1969).

52. Public Hearing on H.B. 61, Ray Elizabeth Herkner (Episcopal Churchwomen of Hawaii), written testimony, p. 1; Beverly A. Wothke, written testimony, p. 1; Dr. Charles Stewart, psychiatrist (Hawaii Psychiatric Society), written testimony, p. 2; Marie Stires, community worker, written testimony, p. 1; Dr. George Goto, obstetrician (Hawaii Medical Association), written testimony, p. 3.

53. *Ibid.*, Judge Samuel P. King (Family Court), written testimony, p. 1.

54. *Ibid.*, Reverend Claude du Teil, Episcopal clergyman (Clergy Counseling Service), written testimony, p. 1; Reverend David Harada, Methodist clergyman, February 4, 1970; Reverend Yoshiaki Fujitani (Honpa Hongwanji Buddhist Temple), written testimony, p. 1; Donald Cundy, written testimony, pp. 1–2; Beverly A. Wothke, written testimony, p. 1; Ah Quon McElrath (ILWU Local 142), written testimony, p. 3; Marie Stires, community worker, written testimony, p. 2; Dr. Shigeaki Fujitani, psychologist, written testimony, p. 1.

55. *Ibid.*, Interchange between Senator Wadsworth Yee and Dr. George Goto, February 3, 1970.

56. *Ibid.*, Reverend Yoshiaki Fujitani, Buddhist priest (Honpa Hongwanji Temple), written testimony, p. 1.

57. *Ibid.*, Ray Elizabeth Herkner (Episcopal Churchwomen of Hawaii), written testimony, p. 2; Carole Freeman (Women's Society of Christian Service, Kilohana Methodist Church), written testimony, p. 1; Dr. John Blaylock, psychologist (John Howard Association), written testimony, p. 1; George Felton (Public Health Committee, Chamber of Commerce), written testimony, p. 2; Alan Yukitomo, student (Associated Students of University of Hawaii Senate), written testimony, p. 1; Dr. James Dator, political scientist and futurist, written testimony, p. 2; Audrey Fowler, written testimony, p. 1; Donald Cundy, February 4, 1970.

58. *Ibid.*, Sister Mary Heenan, Roman Catholic nun, Maryknoll Order, written testimony, pp. 1–2.

59. *Ibid.*, Sister Maureen, Roman Catholic nun (Chief Administrator, St. Francis Hospital), written testimony, p. 2.

60. *Ibid.*, Mrs. Donald Cundy, written testimony, p. 1.

61. *Ibid.*, Jean Avery, social worker (Hawaii Chapter, National Association of Social Workers), written testimony, p. 1; Dr. Shigeaki Fujitani, psychologist, written testimony, p. 1; Peggy Hillman (American Civil Liberties Union), written testimony, p. 1; Karen Lum, student (Hawaii Women's Liberation), written testimony, p. 1; Marie Stires, community worker, written testimony, p. 1; Laurel Kasaoka (Democratic Action Group), written testimony, p. 1; Howard Yuh, (Executive Secretary, Commission on Children and Youth), written testimony, p. 1.

62. *Ibid.*, Laurel K. Kasaoka (Democratic Action Group), written testimony, p. 1.

63. *Ibid.*, Marie Stires, volunteer community worker, written testimony, p. 1.

64. *Ibid.*, Karen Lum, graduate student (Hawaii Women's Liberation Front), written testimony, pp. 1–2.

65. *Ibid.*, Interchange between Karen Lum and Senator Wadsworth Yee, February 4, 1970.

66. *Ibid.*, Dr. Patricia Steinhoff, sociologist (University Abortion and Birth Control Committee), written testimony, pp. 4–5.

67. *Ibid.*, Dr. George Goto, obstetrician (Hawaii Medical Association), written testimony, p. 4.

68. *Ibid.*, Dr. Charles Stewart, psychiatrist (Hawaii Psychiatric Society), written testimony, p. 2.

69. *Ibid.*, Interchange between Senator Donald Ching and Dr. Roy G. Smith, pediatrician and Associate Professor of Maternal and Child Health, University of Hawaii, February 3, 1970.

70. *Ibid.*

71. *Ibid.*, Interchange between Senator Donald Ching, Senator Vincent Yano and Dr. Ronald Pion, obstetrician and Visiting Professor of Public Health, University of Hawaii, February 4, 1970.

72. *Ibid.*, Interchange between Senator Donald Ching and Dr. George Goto, obstetrician, February 3, 1970.

73. *Ibid.*, Interchange between Senator Donald Ching and Dr. Robert Noyes, Chief of Section on Obstetrics and Gynecology, University of Hawaii Medical School, February 3, 1970.

74. *Ibid.*, Dr. George Goto, obstetrician (Hawaii Medical Association), written testimony, p. 5.

CHAPTER 6

1. Hawaii State Legislature, Fifth Legislature, Senate Committee on Public Health, Welfare and Housing, Public Hearing on H.B. 61, February 3 and 4, 1970, Dr. Peter Rotar, agronomist (Knights of Columbus), written testimony, p. 2.

2. *Ibid.*, Gerri Madden, written testimony, p. 5.

3. *Ibid.*, Monsignor Francis A. Marzen, Editor, *Hawaii Catholic Herald* (Roman Catholic Diocese of Honolulu), written testimony, p. 1.

4. *Ibid.*, Dr. Frederick A. Dodge, physician, written testimony, p. 1; and Dr. Neil Bryson, dentist, oral testimony, February 4, 1970.

5. *Ibid.*, Robert Pearson, written testimony, p. 3.

6. *Ibid.*, Robert Pearson, February 3, 1970.

7. *Ibid.*, Mrs. Edward S. Ehlen (Catholic Women's Guild), written testimony, pp. 1–2.

8. *Ibid.*, Monsignor Francis A. Marzen (Roman Catholic Diocese of Honolulu), written testimony, pp. 1–2.

9. *Ibid.*, Mrs. Edward S. Ehlen (Catholic Women's Guild), written testimony, p. 1; Albert F. Laigle, written testimony, p. 1.

10. *Ibid.*, Dr. Frederick A. Dodge, physician, written testimony, p. 1.

11. *Ibid.*, Dr. Peter Rotar, agronomist (Knights of Columbus), written testimony, p. 2; Albert F. Laigle, written testimony, p. 1; Raymond E. Dorais, social worker (Catholic Social Services), written testimony, p. 1; Dr. William N. Bergin, physician, written testimony, p. 1.

12. *Ibid.*, Interchange between Senator Vincent Yano and Mary Nielson, February 4, 1970.

13. Dr. William Bergin, "Somebody's Going to Get Killed," *Hawaii Medical Journal* 26 (November-December, 1966):105.

14. Public Hearing on H.B. 61, Robert Pearson, oral testimony, February 3, 1970.

15. *Ibid.*, Interchange between Dr. Neil Bryson, dentist, and Senator Vincent Yano, February 4, 1970.

16. *Ibid.*, Interchange between Robert Pearson and Senator Percy Mirikitani, February 3, 1970.

17. *Ibid.*, Interchange between Monsignor Francis A. Marzen (Catholic Diocese of Honolulu) and Senator Percy Mirikitani, February 3, 1970.

18. *Acta Apostolicae Sedis* 43(1951):43, quoted in Daniel Callahan, *Abortion: Law, Choice and Morality* (New York: The MacMillan Company, 1970), p. 415.

19. Public Hearing on H.B. 61, Interchange between Senator Percy Mirikitani and Monsignor Francis A. Marzen, February 3, 1970.

20. *Ibid.*

21. Joseph Fuchs, S. J., *Natural Law,* trans. H. Neckter and J. A. Davling (New York: Sheed and Ward, 1965) p. 131, quoted in Callahan, *Abortion,* p. 425.

22. Public Hearing on H.B. 61, Father Daniel Dever, S. J. (Superintendent of Catholic Schools), written testimony, pp. 1–2.

23. See Callahan, *Abortion,* pp. 422–424.

24. Public Hearing on H.B. 61, Dr. Neil Bryson, dentist, oral testimony, February 4, 1970.

25. *Ibid.*, Dr. Peter Rotar, agronomist (Knights of Columbus), written testimony, p. 1.

26. *Ibid.*

27. *Ibid.*, Dr. Frederick A. Dodge, physician, written testimony, p. 1.

28. *Ibid.*, Catherin Dunn, social worker, written testimony, p. 2.

29. *Ibid.*, Dr. Peter Rotar, agronomist (Knights of Columbus), oral testimony, February 4, 1970.

30. *Ibid.*, Raymond E. Dorais, social worker (Catholic Social Services), written testimony, p. 2.

31. *Ibid.*, Dr. Frederick A. Dodge, written testimony, p. 1.

32. *Ibid.*, Dr. Peter Rotar, agronomist (Knights of Columbus), written testimony, pp. 1–2; Gerri Madden, written testimony, p. 1; Catherine Dunn, social worker, written testimony, p. 2.

33. *Ibid.*, Mary Nielson, February 4, 1970; Robert Pearson, February 3, 1970; Gerri Madden, February 3, 1970.

34. *Ibid.*, Monsignor Francis A. Marzen (Roman Catholic Diocese of Honolulu), written testimony, p. 2.

35. John T. Noonan, Jr., *Contraception* (Cambridge, Mass.: Harvard University Press, 1965), pp. 42, 284–285, 426–432.

36. Public Hearing on H.B. 61, Dr. Neil Bryson, dentist, oral testimony, February

4, 1970; Monsignor Daniel J. Dever (Superintendent of Catholic Schools), written testimony, p. 3; Dr. Frederick A. Dodge, written testimony, p. 1.

37. *Ibid.*, Dr. Neil Bryson, dentist, oral testimony, February 4, 1970.

38. *Ibid.*, Interchange between Senator Vincent Yano and Dr. Neil Bryson, February 4, 1970.

39. *Ibid.*, Arthur K. Trask, attorney, oral testimony, February 4, 1970.

40. *Ibid.*, Mrs. Edward S. Ehlen (Catholic Women's Guild), February 4, 1970.

41. *Ibid.*, Gerri Madden, written testimony, p. 4.

42. *Ibid.*, Dr. William Bergin, written testimony, p.2.

43. *Ibid.*, Sister Maureen (St. Francis Hospital), written testimony, p. 2; Dr. Neil Bryson, dentist, February 4, 1970; Robert Pearson, February 3, 1970; Monsignor Daniel Dever (Superintendent of Catholic Schools), written testimony, p. 3.

44. *Ibid.*, Robert Pearson, oral testimony, February 3, 1970, and written testimony, pp. 1–2.

45. *Ibid.*, Clarence Kamai, oral testimony, February 4, 1970.

46. *Ibid.*, Catherine Dunn, social worker, written testimony, p. 1.

47. *Ibid.*, Raymond E. Dorais (Exective Director, Catholic Social Services), written testimony, pp. 2–3.

48. *Ibid.*, Catherine Dunn, social worker, written testimony, p. 1.

49. *Ibid.*, Gerri Madden, written testimony, p. 3.

50. *Ibid.*, Mary Nielson, oral testimony, February 4, 1970.

51. *Ibid.*, Dr. Neil Bryson, dentist, oral testimony, February 4, 1970.

52. *Ibid.*, Mrs. Edward S. Ehlen (Catholic Women's Guild), oral testimony, February 3, 1970.

53. *Ibid.*, Gerri Madden, written testimony, p. 2.

54. *Ibid.*, Dr. Frederick Dodge, physician, written testimony, p. 1.

55. *Ibid.*, Raymond E. Dorais (Executive Director, Catholic Social Services), written testimony, p. 2.

56. *Ibid.*, Catherine Dunn, social worker, written testimony, pp. 1–2.

57. *Ibid.*, Dr. William Bergin, physician, written testimony, p. 1.

58. *Ibid.*, Dr. Keith Kuhlman, physician, oral testimony, February 4, 1970.

59. *Ibid.*, Dr. William Bergin, written testimony, pp. 4–5.

60. *Ibid.*, Robert Pearson, written testimony, p. 1; Gerri Madden, written testimony, p. 1.

61. *Ibid.*, Monsignor Francis A. Marzen (Roman Catholic Diocese of Honolulu), written testimony, p. 3.

62. *Ibid.*, Mary Nielson, oral testimony, February 4, 1970.

63. *Ibid.*, Sister Maureen (Chief Administrator, St. Francis Hospital), written testimony, pp. 1–2.

64. *Ibid.*, Father Daniel J. Dever, S. J. (Superintendent of Catholic Schools), written testimony, p. 4.

65. *Ibid.*, Father Daniel J. Dever, S. J. (Superintendent of Catholic Schools), oral testimony, February 3, 1970.

66. *Ibid.*, Dr. Frederick A. Dodge, physician, written testimony, p. 1.

67. *Ibid.*, Interchange between Senator Vincent Yano and Dr. Keith Kuhlman, physician, February 4, 1970.

68. *Ibid.*, Sister Mary Heenan, Roman Catholic nun, Maryknoll Order, written testimony, pp. 1–2.

CHAPTER 8

1. See Tom Coffman, *Catch A Wave* (Honolulu: *Honolulu Star-Bulletin*, 1972).
2. Determination of ethnicity and religion was based on information in Betty

Finley Buher, (ed.), *Men and Women of Hawaii 1972: A Biographical Directory of Noteworthy Men and Women of Hawaii* (Honolulu: Star-Bulletin Printing Co., Inc., 1972); and *Who's Who in Government: State of Hawaii 1969–1970* (Honolulu: Chamber of Commerce of Hawaii, 1969).

3. G. B. Sansom, *Japan: A Short Cultural History,* rev. ed. (New York: Appleton-Century-Crofts, 1962), p. 516.

4. Personal interview with Vincent Yano.

5. Hawaii State Legislature, Senate, Fifth Legislature, *Journal,* Regular Session, 1970, February 10, 1970, p. 123.

6. "Senate Invocation by Abortion Foe," *Honolulu Advertiser,* February 10, 1970, p. A8.

7. *Hawaii Legislative Manual, A Handbook for Legislators,* 4th ed. Report no. 1 (Honolulu: Legislative Reference Bureau, 1971), p. 50.

8. Coffman, *Catch A Wave,* p. 81.

9. Personal interview with Dr. George Goto.

10. "Burns Terms Legal Abortion Matter of One's Conscience" by Claude Burgett and Tom Coffman, *Honolulu Star-Bulletin,* October 22, 1969, p. A1.

11. Personal interview with Dr. George Goto.

12. Personal interview with Vincent Yano.

13. Hawaii State Legislature, Senate, Fifth Legislature, "Standing Committee Report No. 5-70, *Re:* H.B. No. 61, H.D. 1," January 29, 1970, p. 1. Amendments 1 and 3 were minor technical changes.

14. Hawaii State Legislature, House, Fifth Legislature, "H.B. No. 61, H.D. 1, S.D. 1, A Bill for an Act Relating to Abortion and Amending Chapter 768, *Hawaii Revised Statutes,*" January 29, 1970.

15. Hawaii State Legislature, "Senate, 5th Legislature, Regular Session, January 29, 1970," p. 73.

16. *Revised Laws of Hawaii, 1925, Comprising the Statutes of the Territory,* consolidated, revised and annotated, ch. 280.

17. Hawaii State Legislature, Senate, Fifth Legislature, "Standing Committee Report No. 15-70. *Re:* H.B. No. 61, H.D. 1, S.D. 1, February 9, 1970, p. 1.

18. *Ibid.,* p. 2.

19. *Ibid.,* p. 3.

20. Harvey L. Zipf, "Recent Abortion Law Reforms (or Much Ado About Nothing)," *The Journal of Criminal Law, Criminology, and Police Science* 60, no. 1 (1969).

21. "Senate Standing Committee Report No. 15-70." p. 3.

22. *Ibid.,* pp. 4–5.

23. *Ibid.,* p. 6.

24. *Ibid.,* pp. 6–7.

25. Hawaii State Legislature, Senate, 5th Legislature, *Journal,* Regular Session, February 10, 1970, p. 131.

26. *Ibid.,* p. 131.

27. *Ibid.,* pp. 131–132.

28. *Ibid.,* p. 132.

29. *Ibid.,* p. 132.

30. *Ibid.,* pp. 132–133.

31. *Ibid.,* p. 133.

32. *Ibid.,* p. 133.

33. *Ibid.,* p. 133.

34. *Ibid.,* p. 133.

35. *Ibid.,* p. 134.

36. *Ibid.*, p. 134.
37. *Ibid.*, p. 134.
38. *Ibid.*, p. 134.

CHAPTER 9

1. *Hawaii Legislative Manual, A Handbook for Legislators,* 4th ed., Report no. 1, (Honolulu: Legislative Reference Bureau, 1971), p. 49.
2. Hawaii, Attorney General Opinion No. 70-2, January 21, 1970.
3. Personal interview with George Loo.
4. *Ibid.*
5. Personal interview with Vincent Yano.
6. Personal interview with Dorothy Devereux.
7. Hawaii State Legislature, House, Fifth Legislature, "H.B. 61, H.D. 1, S.D. 2, C.D.1, A Bill For an Act Relating To Abortion and Amending Chapter 768, *Hawaii Revised Statutes,*" February 17, 1970.
8. Hawaii State Legislature, Fifth Legislature, "Conference Committee Report No. 1, *Re:* H.B. No. 61, H.D. 1, S.D. 2," February 17, 1970, p. 3.
9. Personal interview with Dorothy Devereux.
10. Hawaii State Legislature, Fifth Legislature, "Conference Committee Report No. 1, *Re:* H.B. No. 61, H.D. 1, S.D. 2," p. 6.
11. *Ibid.*
12. *Ibid.*, p. 7.
13. *Ibid.*, p. 8.
14. Personal interview with Vincent Yano.
15. *Ibid.*
16. Hawaii State Legislature, House, Fifth Legislature, "H.B. No. 61, H.D. 1, S.D. 1, C.D. 2, A Bill For An Act Relating to Abortion and Amending Chapter 768, *Hawaii Revised Statutes,*" p.2.
17. *Ibid.*
18. Hawaii State Legislature, Fifth Legislature, "Conference Committee Report No. 2, *Re:* H.B. No. 61, H.D. 1, S.D. 2, C.D. 1," February 18, 1970, p. 6.
19. *Ibid.*, pp. 6–7.
20. Hawaii State Legislature, Fifth Legislature, "Conference Committee Report No. 3, *Re:* H.B. No. 61, H.D. 1, S.D. 2, C.D. 2," February 19, 1970, p. 7.
21. Personal interview with Dorothy Devereux.
22. Personal interview with George Loo.
23. Personal interview with Dorothy Devereux.
24. Hawaii State Legislature, House, Fifth Legislature, *Journal,* Regular Session, February 20, 1970, pp. 168–169.
25. *Ibid.*, p. 174.
26. *Ibid.*, p. 179–180.
27. *Ibid.*, p. 177.
28. *Ibid.*, p. 179.
29. *Ibid.*, p. 181.
30. *Ibid.*, p. 174.
31. *Ibid.*, p. 179.
32. *Ibid.*, p. 181.
33. *Ibid.*, p. 170.
34. *Ibid.*, pp. 170–171.
35. *Ibid.*, p. 174.
36. *Ibid.*, pp. 180, 177.
37. Hawaii State Legislature, House, Fifth Legislature, "H.B. No. 61, H.D. 1,

S.D. 2, C.D. 3, A Bill for an Act Relating to Abortion and Amending Chapter 768, *Hawaii Revised Statutes,*" February 19, 1970, p. 2.

38. Hawaii State Legislature, House, Fifth Legislature, *Journal,* Regular Session, February 20, 1970, p. 182.

39. *Ibid.*, p. 185.

40. *Ibid.*, p. 184.

41. *Ibid.*, p. 173.

42. *Ibid.*, p. 180.

43. *Ibid.*, p. 188.

44. *Ibid.*, p. 189.

45. *Ibid.*, p. 178.

46. *Ibid.*, pp. 186–187.

47. *Ibid.*, p. 178.

48. *Ibid.*

49. *Ibid.*, p. 190.

50. *Ibid.*, p. 181.

51. Hawaii State Legislature, Senate, Fifth Legislature, *Journal,* Regular Session, February 24, 1970, p. 167.

52. *Ibid.*, pp. 166–167.

53. *Ibid.*, p. 167.

54. Personal interview with Dr. George Goto.

55. Personal interview with Vincent Yano.

56. Hawaii State Legislature, House, Fifth Legislature, *Journal,* Regular Session, February 25, 1970, p. 204.

57. Personal interview with George Loo.

58. Personal interview with Vincent Yano.

59. Hawaii Deputy Attorney General Thomas M. Pico, Jr., "Memorandum to Honorable John A. Burns, Governor; From Department of the Attorney General; Subject H.B. No. 61 Relating to Abortion and Amending Chapter 768, Hawaii Revised Statutes" (March 2, 1970), pp. 1–11.

60. "Abortion Bill Backers See Burns," by Tom Coffman, *Honolulu Star-Bulletin,* March 6, 1970, p. A2.

61. Dr. Steinhoff was present at the meeting as a representative of the University Abortion and Birth Control Committee.

62. Coffman, *Catch A Wave,* pp. 80–81.

63. Statement by Governor John A. Burns on enactment of House Bill 61, March 11, 1970, p. 1.

64. *Ibid.*, p. 2–3.

65. *Ibid.*, p. 5.

66. *Ibid.*, pp. 6–7.

67. *Ibid.*, p. 7.

CHAPTER 10

1. Milton Diamond, Roy G. Smith, Patricia G. Steinhoff, and James A. Palmore, Jr., "Abortion in Hawaii: The First Year," Report to the Legislature, State of Hawaii, January 24, 1972, pp. 11–12.

2. *Ibid.*, pp. 3–4.

3. "Final Report of the Ad Hoc Committee on Abortions at Kapiolani Maternity and Gynecological Hospital," March 13, 1970, p. 1.

4. Roy G. Smith, Patricia G. Steinhoff, Milton Diamond, and Norma Brown, "Abortion in Hawaii: The First 124 Days," *American Journal of Public Health* 61 (March, 1971):534.

5. John F. McDermott and Walter F. Char, "Abortion Repeal in Hawaii: An Unexpected Crisis in Patient Care," *American Journal of Orthopsychiatry* 41 (July, 1971):620–626.

6. Diamond, *et al.*, "Abortion in Hawaii: The First Year," p. 15.

7. *Doe et al.* v. *Bolton*, January 22, 1973, 410 US 179.

8. Hawaii, Attorney General Opinion 74–17 (October 10, 1974).

9. Douglas MacDougal and Wayne P. Nasser, "The Abortion Decision and Evolving Limits on State Intervention," *Hawaii Bar Journal* 11, no. 3 (1974):52–72.

10. Diamond *et al.*, "Abortion in Hawaii: The First Year," p. 11.

11. Smith *et al.*, "Abortion in Hawaii: The First 124 Days," p. 13.

12. Diamond *et al.*, "Abortion in Hawaii: The First Year," p. 13.

13. Roy G. Smith, Patricia G. Steinhoff, James A. Palmore, and Milton Diamond, "Abortion in Hawaii: 1970–1971," *Hawaii Medical Journal* 32 (July-August, 1973):217.

14. "State to Protest Medicaid Abortion Change," by Tomi Knaefler, *Honolulu Star-Bulletin*, December 9, 1974, p. A22.

15. "Final Report of the Ad Hoc Committee on Abortions," p. 3.

16. Smith *et al.*, "Abortion in Hawaii: 1970–1971," p. 217.

17. Unpublished finding. Hawaii Pregnancy, Birth Control and Abortion Study.

18. Joseph J. Leon and Patricia G. Steinhoff, "Catholics' Use of Abortion," *Sociological Analysis* 36 (July, 1975):134.

19. Unpublished figures were supplied courtesy of Hawaii Pregnancy, Birth Control and Abortion Study.

20. See Sharon Gedan, "Abortion Counseling with Adolescents," *American Journal of Nursing* 74 (October, 1974):1856–1868; and Sharon Gedan, "Pre-Abortion Emotional Counseling" (Unpublished paper, 1974).

21. Patricia G. Steinhoff, "Premarital Pregnancy and the First Birth," in *The First Child and Family Formation*, edited by W. B. Miller and L. Newman (Carolina Population Center, in press).

22. "Study on Adoptions" (Paper prepared by the Health and Community Services Council for Aloha United Fund, October, 1971), 31 pp.

23. Personal interview with Paulina Lee, director of Booth Services for Young Women, The Salvation Army.

24. "Archbishop Sheen will Speak At Benefit for Mary Jane Home," *Hawaii Catholic Herald*, January 11, 1974, p.1.

25. Roy G. Smith, "Changing Hawaii's Abortion Laws," *Pacific Health* 3 (1970):3.

26. Personal interview with Dr. Roy G. Smith.

27. Fumi Ige, Hawaii State Legislature, Fifth Legislature, Senate Committee on Public Health, Welfare and Housing, Public Hearing on H.B. 61, February 3 and 4, 1970, written testimony, p. 1.

28. Diamond *et al.*, "Abortion in Hawaii: The First Year," p. 1.

29. Unpublished figures were supplied courtesy of Hawaii Pregnancy, Birth Control and Abortion Study. These figures are slightly higher than the official reports of the Hawaii Department of Health for the same years because the study's data were collected directly from hospital records, while the state figures were based on fetal death certificates filed with the Department of Health.

30. Patricia G. Steinhoff and Roy G. Smith, "Abortion Law Ideology and Reality" (Unpublished paper, 1973), p. 6.

31. *Ibid.*, p. 12.

32. Roy G. Smith, Patricia G. Steinhoff, and James A. Palmore, "The Potential

Reduction in Medical Complications Associated with Induced Abortion," *Population Reports* (in press).

33. Patricia G. Steinhoff, "Background Characteristics of Abortion Patients," in *The Abortion Experience,* edited by H. Osofsky and J. Osofsky (New York: Harper and Row, 1973), pp. 206–231.

34. Diamond *et al.,* "Abortion in Hawaii: The First Year," pp. 13–14.

35. Patricia G. Steinhoff, "Ethnic Group Differences in the Use of Abortion" (Paper presented at Population Studies Seminar, East-West Center, University of Hawaii, November, 1971).

36. Joseph J. Leon and Patricia G. Steinhoff, "Catholics' Use of Abortion."

37. Patricia G. Steinhoff, Milton Diamond, James A. Palmore, and Roy G. Smith, "Who are the New Abortion Patients?" Paper presented at the Abortion Research Workshop. Report No. 7 of the Hawaii Pregnancy, Birth Control and Abortion Study, April, 1973, p. 10.

38. Robert W. Gardner and Eleanor C. Nordyke, *The Demographic Situation in Hawaii,* Papers of the East-West Population Institute, no. 31 (Honolulu: East-West Center, June, 1974), pp. 39–40.

39. *The State of Hawaii Data Book 1974, A Statistical Abstract* (Honolulu: Department of Planning and Economic Development, 1974), p. 41.

40. Unpublished figures were supplied courtesy of Hawaii Pregnancy, Birth Control and Abortion Study.

41. Diamond *et al.,* "Abortion in Hawaii: The First Year," p. 18.

42. *Ibid.*

43. Milton Diamond, Patricia G. Steinhoff, James A. Palmore, and Roy G. Smith, "Sexuality, Birth Control and Abortion: A Decision-making Sequence," *Journal of Biosocial Science* 5 (July, 1973):355.

44. Roy G. Smith, Beverly Manner, and George Goto, "Physicians' Attitudes on the Abortion Law," p. 21.

45. Alice Beechert and Roy G. Smith, "Physicians' Attitudes Toward Legal Induced Abortion" (Unpublished paper, 1973), p. 6.

46. *Roe et al.* v. *Wade* and *Doe et al.* v. *Bolton,* January 22, 1973, 410 US 179.

47. "Bishop Urges All to Participate in March," *Hawaii Catholic Herald,* January 17, 1975; also quoted in "Isle Bishop Renews Attack on Abortion," by Janice Wolf, *Honolulu Advertiser,* January 17, 1975, p. C3.

48. "Antiabortion Pamphlet Assailed," *Honolulu Advertiser,* January 21, 1975, p. A3.

49. "500 Foes of Abortion Rally at State Capitol," by Leslie Wilcox, *Honolulu Star-Bulletin,* January 22, 1975, p. A3.

50. *Ibid.*

51. "A New Abortion Law is Proposed," by Lois Taylor, *Honolulu Star-Bulletin,* February 9, 1974, p. B2.

52. Letter of March 11, 1974.

53. Hawaii, Attorney-General Opinion No. 74-17, October 10, 1974, p. 4.

54. *Doe et al.* v. *Bolton,* January 22, 1973, 410 US 179.

55. Hawaii, Attorney-General Opinion No. 74-17, fn. 3, p. 4.

56. Beechert and Smith, "Physicians' Attitudes," pp. 7–8.

57. MacDougal and Nasser, "The Abortion Decision," pp. 52–72.

Index

PEOPLE

GENERAL

About the Authors

Patricia G. Steinhoff holds a doctorate from Harvard University and is a professor of sociology at the University of Hawaii. She was co-principal investigator for the Hawaii Pregnancy, Birth Control, and Abortion Study, 1970–1975, and has contributed to such periodicals as *Family Planning Perspectives,* and *Sociological Analysis.* She is also a specialist in Japanese society.

Milton Diamond holds a combined doctorate in anatomy and psychology from the University of Kansas. He is a sexologist with a joint appointment as professor of reproductive biology at the University of Hawaii School of Medicine and research professor of psychiatry and behavioral science at the SUNY-Stony Brook School of Medicine. His research efforts over the past decade have resulted in more than fifty publications in psychological, sociological, and biological journals on subjects related to reproduction and sexual behavior. He was co-principal investigator of the Hawaii Pregnancy, Birth Control, and Abortion Study, 1970–1975.

Production Notes

The text of this book has been designed by Roger J. Eggers and typeset on the Unified Composing System by the design & production staff of The University Press of Hawaii.

The text typeface is Garamond No. 49. The display face is Avant Garde.

Offset presswork and binding is the work of Vail-Ballou Press. Text paper is Glatfelter P & S Offset, basis 55.

work on speech
study for math test